The Essenti

Cirrhosis Diet

Cookbook

800 EASY AND DELICIOUS RECIPES TO REVERSE LIVER CIRRHOSIS AND TO IMPROVE OVERALL HEALTH

NEDRA BOUTIN

CONTENTS

CHAPTER 4 : LUNCH...................................40

CHAPTER 5 : SNACK..72

CHAPTER 7 : DRINKS RECIPES AND SMOOTHIE RECIPES..........134

RECIPE INDEX.................................140

CHAPTER ONE : UNDERSTANDING THE ROLE OF CIRRHOSIS DIET IN LIVER HEALTH

The liver is the largest internal organ in the human body. It is also one of the most important, considering its function in digestion and detoxification. In fact, the liver has numerous vital functions. It filters the blood by removing oestrogen and aldosterone. Apart from detoxification, it also plays a very important role in the metabolization of fats, carbohydrates, and proteins. The bile produced by the liver helps in the breakdown and absorption of fats and certain vitamins. Other vitamins, minerals, and glycogen reserves are stored in the liver. The importance of a healthy liver cannot be stressed enough. So it is imperative that we keep our liver in good health for it to perform its functions properly.

1. Understanding Liver Damage

The liver's function as the body's main detoxifier also makes it vulnerable to damage. All toxins that are consumed by us pass through the liver first. It is important to keep in mind that the liver is a self-regenerating organ. This means that it heals itself unless severely impaired. While toxins are filtered out, sustained intake of these could cause permanent and irreversible damage to the liver.

The most common cause for liver Diseases is the prolonged and excess consumption of alcohol. Occasional to moderate alcohol consumption may not cause lasting damage to the liver, but any excesses certainly will. Regular and excess consumption of alcohol leads to a build-up of fatty deposits in the liver, impairing its ability to function normally. Similarly, steroid supplements taken by body builders and trainers also lead to serious liver damage. Protein supplements, on the other hand, promote liver health. Apart from alcohol and steroid intake, excess consumption of sugars can also lead to the condition called fatty liver. Obesity is another cause for the occurrence of fatty liver. If not handled timely, fatty liver could ultimately lead to liver cirrhosis.

2. The Significance of Cirrhosis Diet in Liver Health

It remains established without any doubt that diet is central to maintaining the well-being of the human body. A healthy and nutritious diet is one that has the right proportion of carbohydrates, proteins and fats (the macronutrients), and vitamins and minerals (the micronutrients). Just as unhealthy and imbalanced diet can lead to the development of a fatty liver, giving up on unhealthy dietary habits can help reverse the condition, experts believe.

3. A Closer Look at the Dietary Changes for A Healthy Liver

Let us now take a closer look at the major components of our Cirrhosis diet and the role each plays in the maintenance of liver health. To function optimally, the cells in our body require energy and this energy is supplied from the glucose in our food. This metabolic fuel, the glucose, is primarily supplied by the carbohydrates in our diet. A diet rich in carbohydrate leads to its conversion into glycogen which is eventually deposited as visceral fat.

Proteins are the building blocks of our bones and muscles. A sedentary lifestyle leads to the conversion of proteins into glucose instead of being utilized in muscle building. What this means is that even in the absence of carbohydrates in the diet, glucose is formed in the body. Apart from this, when a person's diet is deficient in carbohydrate, the body starts utilizing the stored glycogen deposits, thus naturally reversing obesity and melting away visceral fat. Since the diet cannot be deficient in protein (or it will lead to muscle breakdown), it is important to cut down on the carbohydrates and avoid all sugars to reverse a fatty liver condition.

High protein foods such as meat, eggs, pulses, soybean and cottage cheese have the go ahead from dieticians and nutritionists. Vitamins and minerals in the diet come from raw vegetables and fruits. This means lots of salads, fruits, and juices make up an essential part of a healthy diet. However, it is fibre that must provide the bulk to the food. Lack of fibre damages the intestinal lining and in turn damages the liver.

Ultimately, a balanced and healthy diet that sustains liver health must be low in carbohydrate, moderate in fats, and high on protein with generous portions of fruits and vegetables. Not only will it keep up a healthy liver but also keep a person in great health.

CHAPTER TWO: CIRRHOSIS DIET RECOMMENDATIONS FOR LIVER CIRRHOSIS PEOPLE

Malnutrition can be common in patients with liver cirrhosis and may be associated with poorer outcomes. Approximately 20% of people with early cirrhosis and close to 100% of people with severe cirrhosis have malnutrition. Due to liver dysfunction that can be associated with cirrhosis, the liver is not able to produce some nutritional proteins, store energy appropriately, or produce types of fat that are used for energy stores. As a result, metabolic compensatory changes can occur that mimic what occurs in non-cirrhotic people who are suffering from starvation. Therefore, people who have cirrhosis may need extra calories and protein. Other side effects of cirrhosis may include loss of appetite, nausea, vomiting, and unintentional weight loss. Due to all these changes it can help to eat small, frequent meals (4 to 7 times a day), including an evening snack.

A good place to start is with a healthful diet. Foods like fruits, vegetables, whole grains, and lean proteins are good choices. Try to eat plant based proteins or very lean cuts of meat such as chicken breast or turkey breast. Some studies show that patients with cirrhosis do better when they obtain protein from vegetables (such as beans, lentils, and tofu) and dairy products (eggs, milk, yogurt) instead of meats. It is better to eat a low fat diet versus high fat, as high fat diets have been implicated in worsening cirrhosis.

In addition to dietary changes, it is a good idea to take a daily multivitamin. Depending on the degree of cirrhosis, patients may lack the key minerals and fat-soluble vitamins (which are Vitamins A, D, E, and K) that the body requires. However, a balanced diet should easily provide these and in the rare case when it doesn't, supplements can be prescribed. Too much sodium (or salt) in the diet can also be harmful, because sodium encourages the body to retain water. This may cause and/or worsen ascites and swelling in your legs/feet. Oftentimes patients are asked to limit sodium intake to about 2,000mg a day or less.

In summary, if you have cirrhosis be careful to limit additional liver damage:

● Don't drink alcohol. Drinking alcohol may cause further liver damage.

● Eat a low-sodium diet. Excess salt can cause your body to retain fluids, worsening swelling in your abdomen and legs. Use herbs for seasoning your food, rather than salt. Choose prepared foods that are low in sodium.

● Eat a healthy diet. People with cirrhosis can experience malnutrition. Combat this with a healthy plant-based diet that includes a variety of fruits and vegetables. Choose lean protein, such as legumes, poultry or fish. Avoid raw seafood.

Bacon Veggies Combo

Servings:4

Cooking Time:35 Minutes

Ingredients:

- ½ green bell pepper, seeded and chopped
- 2 bacon slices
- ¼ cup Parmesan Cheese
- ½ tablespoon mayonnaise
- 1 scallion, chopped

Directions:

1. Preheat the oven to 375 degrees F and grease a baking dish.
2. Place bacon slices on the baking dish and top with mayonnaise, bell peppers, scallions and Parmesan Cheese.
3. Transfer in the oven and bake for about 25 minutes.
4. Dish out to serve immediately or refrigerate for about 2 days wrapped in a plastic sheet for meal preparation ping.

Nutrition:

- Calories: 197 Fat: 13.8g Carbohydrates: 4.7g Protein: 14.3g Sugar: 1.9g Sodium: 662mg

Citrus Chicken With Delicious Cold Soup

Servings:3

Cooking Time:30 Minutes

Ingredients:

- 2 tablespoons extra-virgin olive oil
- 500g ounces chicken breast
- 1 teaspoon fresh rosemary
- 1 lemon, sliced
- 1 orange, sliced
- For the Cold Soup:
- 2 tablespoons apple cider vinegar
- 1/4 cup green pepper, chopped
- 1/4 cup cucumber, chopped
- 1/2 cup onion, chopped
- 3 cloves garlic, minced
- 1 cup stewed tomatoes

Directions:

1. Generously coat chicken with extra virgin olive oil and cover with rosemary, lemon and orange slices. Bake in the oven at 350°F for about 30 minutes.
2. In a blender, blend together all the soup ingredients until very smooth and then serve with chicken and cooked brown rice.

Nutrition:

- 3g carbs 10g fat 12g protein 165 Calories

Turkey And Spinach Scramble On Melba Toast

Servings:2

Cooking Time:15 Minutes

Ingredients:

- Extra virgin olive oil – 1 teaspoon
- Raw spinach – 1 cup
- Garlic – ½ clove, minced
- Nutmeg – 1 teaspoon grated
- Cooked and diced turkey breast – 1 cup
- Melba toast – 4 slices
- Balsamic vinegar – 1 teaspoon

Directions:

1. Heat a pot over a source of heat and add oil.
2. Add turkey and heat through for 6 to 8 minutes.
3. Add spinach, garlic, and nutmeg and stir-fry for 6 minutes more.
4. Plate up the Melba toast and top with spinach and turkey scramble.
5. Drizzle with balsamic vinegar and serve.

Nutrition:

- Calories: 301 ,Fat: 19g ,Carb: 12g ,Phosphorus: 215mg ,Potassium: 269mg ,Sodium: 360mg ,Protein: 19g

Cauliflower Couscous Salad

Servings:4

Cooking Time:25 Minutes

Ingredients:

- 1 large head cauliflower, cut into florets
- 3-4 green onions, thinly sliced
- 2 garlic cloves, finely minced
- 1 jalapeño, seeds and ribs removed, minced
- 1 cup shredded carrots

- 1 cup diced celery
- 1 cup diced cucumber
- 1 green apple, diced
- Juice of 1 lemon
- 1 tablespoon extra-virgin olive oil
- Sea salt
- Freshly ground black peppe

Directions:

1. Using two batches, set your cauliflower to pulse in a food processor until finely chopped.
2. Transfer to a mixing bowl with the remaining ingredients then gently toss until combined.
3. Serve and enjoy.

Nutrition:

- 3g carbs 10g fat 12g protein 165 Calories

Tahini Pine Nuts Toast

Servings:4
Cooking Time:10 Minutes

Ingredients:

- 2 whole wheat bread slices, toasted
- 1 teaspoon water
- 1 tablespoon tahini paste
- 2 teaspoons feta cheese, crumbled
- Juice of ½ lemon
- 2 teaspoons pine nuts
- A pinch of black pepper

Directions:

1. In a bowl, mix the tahini with the water and the lemon juice, whisk really well and spread over the toasted bread slices.
2. Top each serving with the remaining ingredients and serve for breakfast.

Nutrition:

- calories 142, fat 7.6, fiber 2.7, carbs 13.7, protein 5.8

Spiced French Toast

Servings:4
Cooking Time:12 Minutes

Ingredients:

- 4 eggs
- ½ cup Homemade Rice Milk (here, or use unsweetened store-bought) or almond milk
- ¼ cup freshly squeezed orange juice
- 1 teaspoon ground cinnamon

- ½ teaspoon ground ginger
- Pinch ground cloves
- 1 tablespoon unsalted butter, divided
- 8 slices white bread

Directions:

1. Whisk eggs, rice milk, orange juice, cinnamon, ginger, and cloves until well blended in a large bowl.
2. Melt half the butter in a large skillet. It should be in medium-high heat only.
3. Dredge four of the bread slices in the egg mixture until well soaked, and place them in the skillet.
4. Cook the toast until golden brown on both sides, turning once, about 6 minutes total.
5. Repeat with the remaining butter and bread.
6. Serve 2 pieces of hot French toast to each person.

Nutrition:

- Calories: 236; Total fat: 11g; Saturated fat: 4g; Cholesterol: 220mg; Sodium: 84mg; Carbohydrates: 27g; Fiber: 1g; Phosphorus: 119mg; Potassium: 158mg; Protein: 11g

Orzo And Veggie Bowls

Servings:4
Cooking Time:10 Minutes

Ingredients:

- 2 and ½ cups whole-wheat orzo, cooked
- 14 ounces canned cannellini beans, drained and rinsed
- 1 yellow bell pepper, cubed
- 1 green bell pepper, cubed
- A pinch of salt and black pepper
- 3 tomatoes, cubed
- 1 red onion, chopped
- 1 cup mint, chopped
- 2 cups feta cheese, crumbled
- 2 tablespoons olive oil
- ¼ cup lemon juice
- 1 tablespoon lemon zest, grated
- 1 cucumber, cubed
- 1 and ¼ cup kalamata olives, pitted and sliced
- 3 garlic cloves, minced

Directions:

1. In a salad bowl, combine the orzo with the beans, bell peppers and the rest of the ingredients, toss, divide the mix between plates and serve for breakfas

Nutrition:

- calories 411, fat 17, fiber 13, carbs 51, protein 14

Red Pepper And Artichoke Frittata

Servings:2

Cooking Time:15 Minutes

Ingredients:

- 4 large eggs
- 1 can (14-ounce) artichoke hearts, rinsed, coarsely chopped
- 1 medium red bell pepper, diced
- 1 teaspoon dried oregano
- 1/4 cup Parmesan cheese, freshly grated
- 1/4 teaspoon red pepper, crushed
- 1/4 teaspoon salt, or to taste
- 2 garlic cloves, minced
- 2 teaspoons extra-virgin olive oil, divided
- Freshly ground pepper, to taste

Directions:

1. In a 10-inch non-stick skillet, heat 1 teaspoon of the olive oil over medium heat. Add the bell pepper; cook for about 2 minutes or until tender. Add the garlic and the red pepper; cook for about 30 seconds, stirring. Transfer the mixture to a plate and wipe the skillet clean.

2. In a medium mixing bowl, whisk the eggs. Stir in the artichokes, cheese, the bell pepper mixture, and season with salt and pepper.

3. Place an over rack 4 inches from the source of heat; preheat broiler.

4. Brush the skillet with the remaining 1 teaspoon olive oil and heat over medium heat. Pour the egg mixture into the skillet and tilt to evenly distribute. Reduce the heat to medium low; cook for about 3-4 minutes, lifting the edges to allow the uncooked egg to flow underneath, until the bottom of the frittata is light golden.

5. Transfer the pan into the broiler, cook for about 1 1/2-2 1/2 minutes, or until the top is set.

6. Slide into a platter; cut into wedges and serve

Nutrition:

- 305 Cal, 18 g total fat (6 g sat. fat, 8 g mono), 432 mg chol., 734 mg sodium, 1639 mg pot., 18 g carb.,8 g fiber, 21 g protein.

Mexican Style Burritos

Servings:2

Cooking Time:15 Minutes

Ingredients:

- Olive oil – 1 Tablespoon
- Corn tortillas – 2
- Red onion – ¼ cup, chopped
- Red bell peppers – ¼ cup, chopped
- Red chili – ½, deseeded and chopped
- Eggs – 2
- Juice of 1 lime
- Cilantro – 1 Tablespoon chopped

Directions:

1. Turn the broiler to medium heat and place the tortillas underneath for 1 to 2 minutes on each side or until lightly toasted.

2. Remove and keep the broiler on.

3. Sauté onion, chili and bell peppers for 5 to 6 minutes or until soft.

4. Place the eggs on top of the onions and peppers and place skillet under the broiler for 5-6 minutes or until the eggs are cooked.

5. Serve half the eggs and vegetables on top of each tortilla and sprinkle with cilantro and lime juice to serve

Nutrition:

- Calories: 202 ,Fat: 13g ,Carb: 19g ,Phosphorus: 184mg ,Potassium: 233mg ,Sodium: 77mg ,Protein: 9g

Deviled Eggs

Servings:8

Cooking Time:20 Minutes

Ingredients:

- 8 eggs
- ½ cup Greek Yogurt
- 1 tablespoon mustard
- 1 tsp smoked paprika
- 1 tablespoon green onions

Directions:

1. In a saucepan add the eggs and bring to a boil

2. Cover and boil for 10-15 minutes

3. When ready slice the eggs in half and remove the yolks

4. In a bowl combine remaining ingredients and mix well

5. Spoon 1 tablespoon of the mixture into each egg

6. Garnish with green onions and serve

Nutrition:

- 35g carbs 30g fat 20g protein 460 Calories

Crunchy Peach, Cranberry And Flax Meal Super Bowl

Servings:3

Cooking Time:10 Minutes

Ingredients:

- 10 ounces frozen cranberries
- 10 ounces frozen peaches (or mangoes)
- 1 cup almond milk
- 1 cup water
- 1/4 cup flax meal
- 1/3 cup chia seeds
- 1/4 cup raw honey
- Toasted walnuts and toasted coconut for serving

Directions:

1. In a blender, combine water and peaches and blend until very smooth; transfer to a bowl.

2. Blend almond milk and cranberries until very smooth.

3. In a serving bowl, mix together the fruit purees and then stir in flax meal, chia seeds, and raw honey until well combined.

4. Let sit for at least 10 minutes before serving. Serve topped with toasted walnuts and toasted coconut

Nutrition:

- 242 Calories 7g Carbs 19g Fat 12g Protein

Eggs And Veggies

Servings:4

Cooking Time:10 Minutes

Ingredients:

- 2 tomatoes, chopped
- 2 eggs, beaten
- 1 bell pepper, chopped
- 1 teaspoon tomato paste
- ¼ cup of water
- 1 teaspoon butter
- ½ white onion, diced
- ½ teaspoon chili flakes
- 1/3 teaspoon sea salt

Directions:

1. Put butter in the pan and melt it.

2. Add bell pepper and cook it for 3 minutes over the medium heat. Stir it from time to time.

3. After this, add diced onion and cook it for 2 minutes more.

4. Stir the vegetables and add tomatoes.

5. Cook them for 5 minutes over the medium-low heat.

6. Then add water and tomato paste. Stir well.

7. Add beaten eggs, chili flakes, and sea salt.

8. Stir well and cook menemen for 4 minutes over the medium-low heat.

9. The cooked meal should be half runny.

Nutrition:

- calories 67, fat 3.4, fiber 1.5, carbs 6.4, protein 3.8

Beets Omelette

Servings:1

Cooking Time:10 Minutes

Ingredients:

- 2 eggs
- ¼ tsp salt
- ¼ tsp black pepper
- 1 tablespoon olive oil
- ¼ cup cheese
- ¼ tsp basil
- 1 cup beets

Directions:

1. In a bowl combine all ingredients together and mix well

2. In a skillet heat olive oil and pour the egg mixture

3. Cook for 1-2 minutes per side

4. When ready remove omelette from the skillet and serve

Nutrition:

- 50g carbs 11g fat 10g protein 320 Calories

Seeds And Lentils Oats

Servings:4

Cooking Time:50 Minutes

Ingredients:

- ½ cup red lentils
- ¼ cup pumpkin seeds, toasted
- 2 teaspoons olive oil
- ¼ cup rolled oats
- ¼ cup coconut flesh, shredded
- 1 tablespoon honey
- 1 tablespoon orange zest, grated
- 1 cup Greek yogurt
- 1 cup blackberries

Directions:

1. Spread the lentils on a baking sheet lined with parchment paper, introduce in the oven and roast at 370 degrees F for 30 minutes.

2. Add the rest of the ingredients except the yogurt and the berries, toss and bake at 370 degrees F for 20 minutes more.

3. Transfer this to a bowl, add the rest of the ingredients, toss, divide into smaller bowls and serve for breakfast.

Nutrition:
- calories 204, fat 7.1, fiber 10.4, carbs 27.6, protein 9.5

Detox Soup

Servings:3
Cooking Time:40 Minutes

Ingredients:
- 4 cloves garlic, crushed
- 2 medium leeks, chopped
- 1 serrano pepper, thinly sliced
- 4 celery stalks, chopped
- 4 carrots, diced
- 3 rutabagas, peeled and diced
- 8 cups water
- 2 cups pinto beans, cooked with cooking liquids
- 3 tomatoes, diced
- 3 zucchini, diced
- 2 bunches kale, thinly sliced
- 3 tablespoons lemon juice
- Sea salt
- Freshly cracked black pepper

Directions:
1. Heat a pot over medium heat; add garlic, leeks, and serranoes. Cook for about 5 minutes, stirring.

2. Add celery, carrots, and rutabagas; cook for about 3 minutes more and stir in water, pinto beans, and tomatoes; simmer for about 30 minutes or until the beans are cooked through.

3. Stir in zucchini and kale, 15 minutes before serving. Remove from heat and stir in lemon juice; season with sea salt and black pepper and serve.

Nutrition:
- 283.6 Calories 11.5g fat 31g carbs 10.9g protein

Ham Spinach Ballet

Servings:4

Cooking Time:40 Minute

Ingredients:
- 4 teaspoons cream
- ¾ pound fresh baby spinach
- 7-ounce ham, sliced
- Salt and black pepper, to taste
- 1 tablespoon unsalted butter, melted
- Preheat the oven to 360 degrees F. and grease 2 ramekins with butter.
- Put butter and spinach in a skillet and cook for about 3 minutes.
- Add cooked spinach in the ramekins and top with ham slices, cream, salt and black pepper.
- Bake for about 25 minutes and dish out to serve hot.
- For meal preparation ping, you can refrigerate this ham spinach ballet for about 3 days wrapped in a foil.

Nutrition:
- Calories: 188 Fat: 12.5g Carbohydrates: 4.9g Protein: 14.6g Sugar: 0.3g Sodium: 1098mg

Cinnamon Roll Oats

Servings:4
Cooking Time:10 Minutes

Ingredients:
- ½ cup rolled oats
- 1 cup milk
- 1 teaspoon vanilla extract
- 1 teaspoon ground cinnamon
- 2 teaspoon honey
- 2 tablespoons Plain yogurt
- 1 teaspoon butter

Directions:
1. Pour milk in the saucepan and bring it to boil.

2. Add rolled oats and stir well.

3. Close the lid and simmer the oats for 5 minutes over the medium heat. The cooked oats will absorb all milk.

4. Then add butter and stir the oats well.

5. In the separated bowl, whisk together Plain yogurt with honey, cinnamon, and vanilla extract.

6. Transfer the cooked oats in the serving bowls.

7. Top the oats with the yogurt mixture in the shape of the wheel.

Nutrition:
- Calories 243, fat 20.2, fiber 1, carbs 2.8, protein 13.3

Almond Cream Cheese Bake

Servings:4

Cooking Time:60 Minutes

Ingredients:

- 1 cup cream cheese
- 4 tablespoons honey
- 1 oz almonds, chopped
- ½ teaspoon vanilla extract
- 3 eggs, beaten
- 1 tablespoon semolina

Directions:

1. Put beaten eggs in the mixing bowl.
2. Add cream cheese, semolina, and vanilla extract.
3. Blend the mixture with the help of the hand mixer until it is fluffy.
4. After this, add chopped almonds and mix up the mass well.
5. Transfer the cream cheese mash in the non-sticky baking mold.
6. Flatten the surface of the cream cheese mash well.
7. Preheat the oven to 325F.
8. Cook the breakfast for 2 hours.
9. The meal is cooked when the surface of the mash is light brown.
10. Chill the cream cheese mash little and sprinkle with honey

Nutrition:

- calories 352, fat 27.1, fiber 1, carbs 22.6, protein 10.4

Muffins

Servings:4

Cooking Time:20 Minutes

Ingredients:

- 2 eggs
- 1 tablespoon olive oil
- 1 cup milk
- 2 cups whole wheat flour
- 1 tsp baking soda
- ¼ tsp baking soda
- 1 tsp cinnamon

Directions:

1. In a bowl combine all wet ingredients
2. In another bowl combine all dry ingredients
3. Combine wet and dry ingredients together

4. Pour mixture into 8-12 preparation ared muffin cups, fill 2/3 of the cups
5. Bake for 18-20 minutes at 375 F
6. When ready remove from the oven and serve

Nutrition:

- 2g carbs 6g fat 10g protein 100 Calories

Keto Egg Fast Snickerdoodle Crepes

Servings:2

Cooking Time:15 Minutes

Ingredients:

- 5 oz cream cheese, softened
- 6 eggs
- 1 teaspoon cinnamon
- Butter, for frying
- 1 tablespoon Swerve
- 2 tablespoons granulated Swerve
- 8 tablespoons butter, softened
- 1 tablespoon cinnamon

Directions:

1. For the crepes: Put all the ingredients together in a blender except the butter and process until smooth.
2. Heat butter on medium heat in a non-stick pan and pour some batter in the pan.
3. Cook for about 2 minutes, then flip and cook for 2 more minutes.
4. Repeat with the remaining mixture.
5. Mix Swerve, butter and cinnamon in a small bowl until combined.
6. Spread this mixture onto the centre of the crepe and serve rolled up.

Nutrition:

- Calories: 543 Carbs: 8g Fats: 51.6g Proteins: 15.7g Sodium: 455mg Sugar: 0.9g

Chicken Stir Fry With Red Onions & Cabbage

Servings:3

Cooking Time:10 Minutes

Ingredients:

- 550g chicken, thinly sliced strips
- 1 tablespoon apple cider wine
- 2 teaspoons balsamic vinegar
- Pinch of sea salt
- pinch of pepper

- 4 tablespoons extra-virgin olive oil
- 1 large yellow onion, thinly chopped
- 1/2 red bell pepper, sliced
- 1/2 green bell pepper, sliced
- 1 tablespoon toasted sesame seeds
- 1 teaspoon crushed red pepper flakes
- 4 cups cabbage
- 1 ½ avocados, diced

Directions:

1. Place meat in a bowl; stir in rice wine and vinegar, sea salt and pepper. Toss to coat well.

2. Heat a tablespoon of olive oil in a pan set over medium high heat; add meat and cook for about 2 minutes or until meat is browned; stir for another 2 minutes and then remove from heat.

3. Heat the remaining oil to the pan and sauté onions for about 2 minutes or until caramelized; stir in pepper and cook for 2 minutes more.

4. Stir in cabbage and cook for 2 minutes; return meat to pan and stir in sesame seeds and red pepper flakes. Serve hot topped with diced avocado

Nutrition:

- 283.6 Calories 11.5g fat 31g carbs 10.9g protein

Buckwheat Pancakes

Servings:3

Cooking Time:15 Minutes

Ingredients:

- 1/2 cup buckwheat flour
- 2 ripe bananas
- 2 tablespoons olive
- 2 tablespoons water
- 1 teaspoon ground cinnamon
- 1 teaspoon vanilla extract
- 1/2 teaspoon baking soda
- 2 teaspoons apple cider vinegar
- 1/4 cup fresh blueberries for serving

Directions:

1. Preheat your oven to 350 degrees.

2. Add the ripe banana to a large bowl and mash until smooth; whisk in ground buckwheat flour, water, oil, vanilla, vinegar, cinnamon and baking powder until well combined.

3. Heat a skillet over medium heat; add in oil and heat until hot but not smoky; add in about a quarter cup of batter and spread to cover the bottom of the pan.

4. Cook for about 2 minutes and then flip to cook the other side for about 1 minute or until browned.

5. Serve right away topped with fresh blueberries.

Nutrition:

- 242 Calories 25g carbs 12g fat 13g protein

Pancakes

Servings:4

Cooking Time:30 Minute

Ingredients:

- 1 cup whole wheat flour
- ¼ tsp baking soda
- ¼ tsp baking powder
- 2 eggs
- 1 cup milk

Directions:

1. In a bowl combine all ingredients together and mix well

2. In a skillet heat olive oil

3. Pour ¼ of the batter and cook each pancake for 1-2 minutes per side

4. When ready remove from heat and serve

Nutrition:

- 2g carbs 6g fat 10g protein 100 Calories

Avocado Crab Omelet

Servings:2

Cooking Time:10 Minutes

Ingredients:

- 1/4 pound crab meat
- 4 large free-range eggs, beaten
- 1/2 medium avocado, diced
- 1 medium tomato, diced
- 1 teaspoon olive oil
- 1/8 teaspoon freshly ground black pepper
- A pinch of salt
- 1 tablespoon freshly chopped cilantro

Directions:

1. Cook crab in a skillet following the instructions on the packet; chop the cooked crab and set aside.

2. In a small bowl, toss together avocado, tomato, and cilantro; season with sea salt and pepper and set aside.

3. In a separate bowl, beat the eggs and set aside.

4. Set a skillet over medium heat; add olive oil and heat until hot.

5. Add half of the egg to the skillet and tilt the skillet to cover the bottom. When almost cooked, add crab onto one side of the egg and fold in half. Cook for 1 minute more and top with the avocado-tomato mixture.

6. Repeat with the remaining ingredients for the second omelet.

Nutrition:

- 242 Calories 7g Carbs 19g Fat 12g Protein

Apple Oatmeal

Servings:3

Cooking Time:8 Minutes

Ingredients:

- 1/2 tsp ground cinnamon
- 4 tbsp. fat free vanilla yogurt
- 1 1/2 cups quick oats
- 1/4 cup maple syrup
- 3 cups apple juice
- 1/4 cup raisins
- 1/2 cup chopped apple
- 1/4 cup chopped walnuts

Directions:

1. Combine your cinnamon and apple juice in a saucepan and allow to boil.

2. Stir in your raisins, maple syrup, apples and oats.

3. Switch the heat to low and cook while stirring until most of juice is absorbed. Fold in walnuts, serve and top with yogurt.

Nutrition:

- 242 Calories 25g carbs 12g fat 13g protein

Olive Frittata

Servings:5

Cooking Time:15 Minutes

Ingredients:

- 9 large eggs, lightly beaten
- 8 kalamata olives, pitted, chopped
- 1/4 cup olive oil
- 1/3 cup parmesan cheese, freshly grated
- 1/3 cup fresh basil, thinly sliced
- 1/2 teaspoon salt
- 1/2 teaspoon pepper
- 1/2 cup onion, chopped
- 1 sweet red pepper, diced
- 1 medium zucchini, cut to 1/2-inch cubes
- 1 package (4 ounce) feta cheese, crumbled

Directions:

1. In a 10-inch oven-proof skillet, heat the olive oil until hot. Add the olives, zucchini, red pepper, and the onions, constantly stirring, until the vegetables are tender.

2. Ina bowl, mix the eggs, feta cheese, basil, salt, and pepper; pour in the skillet with vegetables. Adjust heat to medium-low, cover, and cook for about 10-12 minutes, or until the egg mixture is almost set.

3. Remove from the heat and sprinkle with the parmesan cheese. Transfer to the broiler.

4. With oven door partially open, broil 5 1/2 from the source of heat for about 2-3 minutes or until the top is golden. Cut into wedges.

Nutrition:

- 288.5 Cal, 22.8 g total fat (7.8 g sat. fat), 301 mg chol., 656 mg sodium, 5.6 g carb.,1.2 g fiber,3.3g sugar, 15.2 g protein.

Blueberry Muffins

Servings:4

Cooking Time:30 Minutes

Ingredients:

- 2 eggs
- 1 tablespoon olive oil
- 1 cup milk
- 2 cups whole wheat flour
- 1 tsp baking soda
- ¼ tsp baking soda
- 1 tsp cinnamon
- 1 cup blueberries

Directions:

1. In a bowl combine all wet ingredients

2. In another bowl combine all dry ingredients

3. Combine wet and dry ingredients together

4. Fold in blueberries and mix well

5. Pour mixture into 8-12 preparation ared muffin cups, fill 2/3 of the cups

6. Bake for 18-20 minutes at 375 F, when ready remove and serve

Nutrition:

- 2g carbs 6g fat 10g protein 100 Calories

Detox Porridge

Servings:2
Cooking Time:2 Minutes

Ingredients:

- 1 cup unsweetened almond milk
- 2 tablespoons ground golden flax
- 1/2 cup coconut flour
- 1 tablespoon coconut oil
- 1 teaspoon cinnamon
- 1 cup water
- 1 tablespoon raw honey
- Toasted coconut to serve
- Toasted almonds to serve

Directions:

1. In a microwave safe bowl, stir together all the ingredients until well combined; place in the microwave and heat for 1 minute.

2. Stir again to mix well and microwave for another 1 minute. Serve right away topped with toasted almonds and toasted coconut.

Nutrition:

- 242 Calories 7g Carbs 19g Fat 12g Protein

Toxin Flush & Detox Salad

Servings:3
Cooking Time:10 Minutes

Ingredients:

- For the salad:
- 2 cups broccoli florets
- 2 cups red cabbage, thinly sliced
- 2 cups chopped kale
- 1 cup grated carrot
- 1 red bell pepper, sliced into strips
- 2 avocados, diced
- 1/2 cup chopped parsley
- 1 cup walnuts
- 1 tablespoon sesame seeds
- For the dressing:
- 2 teaspoons gluten-free mustard
- 1 tablespoon freshly grated ginger
- 1/2 cup fresh lemon juice
- 1/3 cup grapeseed oil
- 1 teaspoon raw honey
- 1/4 teaspoon salt

Directions:

1. In a blender, blend all the dressing ingredients until well blended; set aside.

2. In a salad bowl, mix broccoli, cabbage, kale, carrots and bell pepper; pour the dressing over the salad and toss until well coated.

3. Add diced avocado, parsley, walnuts and sesame seed; toss again to coat and serve.

Nutrition:

- 283.6 Calories 11.5g fat 31g carbs 10.9g protein

Bacon, Vegetable And Parmesan Combo

Servings:2
Cooking Time:30 Minutes

Ingredients:

- 2 slices of bacon, thick-cut
- ½ tbsp mayonnaise
- ½ of medium green bell pepper, deseeded, chopped
- 1 scallion, chopped
- ¼ cup grated Parmesan cheese
- 1 tbsp olive oil
- Switch on the oven, then set its temperature to 375°F and let it preheat.
- Meanwhile, take a baking dish, grease it with oil, and add slices of bacon in it.
- Spread mayonnaise on top of the bacon, then top with bell peppers and scallions, sprinkle with Parmesan cheese and bake for about 25 minutes until cooked thoroughly.
- When done, take out the baking dish and serve immediately.
- For meal preparation ping, wrap bacon in a plastic sheet and refrigerate for up to 2 days.
- When ready to eat, reheat bacon in the microwave and then serve

Nutrition:

- Calories 197, Total Fat 13.8g, Total Carbs 4.7g, Protein 14.3g, Sugar 1.9g, Sodium 662mg

Omelette

Servings:4

Cooking Time:15 Minutes

Ingredients:

- 2 eggs
- ¼ tsp salt
- ¼ tsp black pepper
- 1 tablespoon olive oil
- ¼ cup cheese
- ¼ tsp basil

Directions:

1. In a bowl combine all ingredients together and mix well
2. In a skillet heat olive oil and pour the egg mixture
3. Cook for 1-2 minutes per side
4. When ready remove omelette from the skillet and serve

Nutrition:

- 2g carbs 6g fat 10g protein 100 Calories

Vegetable Omelet

Servings:3

Cooking Time:10 Minutes

Ingredients:

- Egg whites – 4
- Egg – 1
- Chopped fresh parsley – 2 Tablespoons.
- Water – 2 Tablespoons.
- Olive oil spray
- Chopped and boiled red bell pepper – ½ cup
- Chopped scallion – ¼ cup, both green and white parts
- Ground black pepper

Directions:

1. Whisk together the egg, egg whites, parsley, and water until well blended. Set aside.
2. Spray a skillet with olive oil spray and place over medium heat.
3. Sauté the peppers and scallion for 3 minutes or until softened.
4. Over the vegetables, you can now pour the egg and cook, swirling the skillet, for 2 minutes or until the edges start to set. Cook until set.
5. Season with black pepper and serve.

Nutrition:

- Calories: 77 ,Fat: 3g ,Carb: 2g ,Phosphorus: 67mg ,Potassium: 194mg ,Sodium: 229mg ,Protein: 12g

Chilled Green Goddess Soup

Servings:3

Cooking Time:10 Minutes

Ingredients:

- 6 cups cucumber
- 2 stalks celery chopped
- 1-2 cups water (depending how thin you want it)
- 2 tablespoons fresh lime juice
- 1 cup watercress leaves
- 1 cup rocket leaves
- ½ cup mashed avocado (roughly 1 avocado)
- 1 teaspoon wheatgrass power or a mixed green powder, optional
- Sea salt to tast

Directions:

1. Blend all ingredients except the avocado in a blender until a broth forms. Strain the liquid through a cheesecloth or fine sieve. Then return to blender and add the avocado and blend until smooth.
2. Garnish with a few watercress leaves and cracked black pepper.

Nutrition:

- 283.6 Calories 11.5g fat 31g carbs 10.9g protein

Nectarine Pancakes

Servings:4

Cooking Time:30 Minutes

Ingredients:

- 1 cup whole wheat flour
- ¼ tsp baking soda
- ¼ tsp baking powder
- 1 cup nectarines
- 2 eggs
- 1 cup milk

Directions:

1. In a bowl combine all ingredients together and mix well
2. In a skillet heat olive oil
3. Pour ¼ of the batter and cook each pancake for 1-2 minutes per side
4. When ready remove from heat and serve

Nutrition:

- 7g carbs 14g fat 15g protein 210 Calories

Asparagus With Egg

Servings:4
Cooking Time:20 Minutes
Ingredients:
- 1 lb. asparagus
- 4-5 pieces prosciutto
- ¼ tsp salt
- 2 eggs

Directions:
1. Trim the asparagus and season with salt
2. Wrap each asparagus pieces with prosciutto
3. Place the wrapped asparagus in a baking dish
4. Bake at 375 F for 22-25 minutes
5. When ready remove from the oven and serve

Nutrition:
- 35g carbs 30g fat 20g protein 460 Calories

Peanut Butter And Cacao Breakfast Quinoa

Servings:1
Cooking Time:10 Minutes
Ingredients:
- 1/3 cup quinoa flakes
- 1/2 cup unsweetened nondairy milk,
- 1/2 cup of water
- 1/8 cup raw cacao powder
- One tablespoon natural creamy peanut butter
- 1/8 teaspoon ground cinnamon
- One banana, mashed
- Fresh berries of choice, for serving
- Chopped nuts of choice, for servin

Directions:
1. Using an 8-quart pot over medium-high heat, stir together the quinoa flakes, milk, water, cacao powder, peanut butter, and cinnamon. Cook and stir it until the mixture begins to simmer. Turn the heat to medium-low and cook for 3 to 5 minutes, stirring frequently.
2. Stir in the bananas and cook until hot.
3. Serve topped with fresh berries, nuts, and a splash of milk

Nutrition:
- Calories: 471 ,Fat: 16g ,Protein: 18g ,Carbohydrates: 69g ,Fiber: 16g

Avocado Spread

Servings:8
Cooking Time:10 Minutes
Ingredients:
- 2 avocados, peeled, pitted and roughly chopped
- 1 tablespoon sun-dried tomatoes, chopped
- 2 tablespoons lemon juice
- 3 tablespoons cherry tomatoes, chopped
- ¼ cup red onion, chopped
- 1 teaspoon oregano, dried
- 2 tablespoons parsley, chopped
- 4 kalamata olives, pitted and chopped
- A pinch of salt and black pepper

Directions:
1. Put the avocados in a bowl and mash with a fork.
2. Add the rest of the ingredients, stir to combine and serve as a morning spread.

Nutrition:
- calories 110, fat 10, fiber 3.8, carbs 5.7, protein 1.2

Peaches Muffins

Servings:4
Cooking Time:30 Minutes
Ingredients:
- 2 eggs
- 1 tablespoon olive oil
- 1 cup milk
- 2 cups whole wheat flour
- 1 tsp baking soda
- ¼ tsp baking soda
- 1 cup peaches
- 1 tsp cinnamon
- ¼ cup molasses

Directions:
1. In a bowl combine all wet ingredients
2. In another bowl combine all dry ingredients
3. Combine wet and dry ingredients together
4. Pour mixture into 8-12 preparation ared muffin cups, fill 2/3 of the cups
5. Bake for 18-20 minutes at 375 F, when ready remove and serve

Nutrition:
- 2g carbs 6g fat 10g protein 100 Calories

Eggplant Rollatini

Servings:4

Cooking Time:25 Minutes

Ingredients:

- 1 eggplant
- 12 oz. ricotta cheese
- 2 oz. mozzarella cheese
- 1 can tomatoes
- ¼ tsp salt
- 2 tablespoons seasoning

Directions:

1. Lay the eggplant on a baking sheet
2. Roast at 350 F for 12-15 minutes
3. In a bowl combine mozzarella, seasoning, tomatoes, ricotta cheese and salt
4. Add cheese mixture to the eggplant and roll
5. Place the rolls into a baking dish and bake for another 10-12 minutes
6. When ready remove from the oven and serve

Nutrition:

- 35g carbs 30g fat 20g protein 460 Calories

Toasted Crostini

Servings:4

Cooking Time:15 Minutes

Ingredients:

- 12 slices (1/3-inch thick) whole-wheat baguette, toasted
- Coarse salt and freshly ground pepper
- For the spread:
- 1 can chickpeas (15 1/2 ounces), drained, rinsed
- 1/4 cup olive oil, extra-virgin
- 1 tablespoon lemon juice, freshly squeezed
- 1 small clove garlic, minced
- 2 tablespoons olive oil, extra-virgin, divided
- 2 tablespoons celery, finely diced, plus celery leaves for garnish
- 8 large green olives, pitted, cut into 1/8-inch slivers

Directions:

1. In a food processor, combine the spread ingredients and season with salt and pepper; set aside.
2. In a small mixing bowl, combine 1 tablespoon of olive oil and the remaining ingredients. Season with salt and pepper. Set aside.

3. Divide the spread between the toasted baguette slices, top with the relish. Drizzle the remaining1 tablespoon of olive oil over each and season with pepper. If desired, garnish with the celery leaves. Serve immediately.

Nutrition:

- 603 Cal, 3.7 g total fat (3.7 g sat. fat), 0 mg chol., 781 mg sodium, 483 mg pot, 79.2 g carb.,9.6 g fiber,6.8 g sugar, 19.1 g protein.

Chili Scramble

Servings:4

Cooking Time:13 Minutes

Ingredients:

- 3 tomatoes
- 4 eggs
- ¼ teaspoon of sea salt
- ½ chili pepper, chopped
- 1 tablespoon butter
- 1 cup water, for cooking

Directions:

1. Pour water in the saucepan and bring it to boil.
2. Then remove water from the heat and add tomatoes.
3. Let the tomatoes stay in the hot water for 2-3 minutes.
4. After this, remove the tomatoes from water and peel them.
5. Place butter in the pan and melt it.
6. Add chopped chili pepper and fry it for 3 minutes over the medium heat.
7. Then chop the peeled tomatoes and add into the chili peppers.
8. Cook the vegetables for 5 minutes over the medium heat. Stir them from time to time.
9. After this, add sea salt and crack then eggs.
10. Stir (scramble) the eggs well with the help of the fork and cook them for 3 minutes over the medium heat.

Nutrition:

- calories 105, fat 7.4, fiber 1.1, carbs 4, protein 6.4

Herbed Eggs And Mushroom Mix

Servings:4

Cooking Time:20 Minutes

Ingredients:

- 1 red onion, chopped
- 1 bell pepper, chopped
- 1 tablespoon tomato paste
- 1/3 cup water

- ½ teaspoon of sea salt
- 1 tablespoon butter
- 1 cup cremini mushrooms, chopped
- 1 tablespoon fresh parsley
- 1 tablespoon fresh dill
- 1 teaspoon dried thyme
- ½ teaspoon dried oregano
- ½ teaspoon paprika
- ½ teaspoon chili flakes
- ½ teaspoon garlic powder
- 4 eggs

Directions:
1. Toss butter in the pan and melt it.
2. Then add chopped mushrooms and bell pepper.
3. Roast the vegetables for 5 minutes over the medium heat.
4. After this, add red onion and stir well.
5. Sprinkle the ingredients with garlic powder, chili flakes, dried oregano, and dried thyme. Mix up well
6. After this, add tomato paste and water.
7. Mix up the mixture until it is homogenous.
8. Then add fresh parsley and dill.
9. Cook the mixture for 5 minutes over the medium-high heat with the closed lid.
10. After this, stir the mixture with the help of the spatula well.
11. Crack the eggs over the mixture and close the lid.
12. Cook shakshuka for 10 minutes over the low heat.

Nutrition:
- calories 123, fat 7.5, fiber 1.7, carbs 7.8, protein 7.

Kumquat Muffins

Servings:4
Cooking Time:30 Minutes
Ingredients:
- 2 eggs
- 1 tablespoon olive oil
- 1 cup milk
- 2 cups whole wheat flour
- 1 tsp baking soda
- ¼ tsp baking soda
- 1 tsp cinnamon
- 1 cup kumquat
- In a bowl combine all wet ingredients
- In another bowl combine all dry ingredients

- Combine wet and dry ingredients together
- Pour mixture into 8-12 preparation ared muffin cups, fill 2/3 of the cups
- Bake for 18-20 minutes at 375 F
- When ready remove from the oven and serve

Nutrition:
- 2g carbs 6g fat 10g protein 100 Calorie

Carrot Omelette

Servings:4
Cooking Time:20 Minutes
Ingredients:
- 2 eggs
- ¼ tsp salt
- ¼ tsp black pepper
- 1 tablespoon olive oil
- ¼ cup cheese
- ¼ tsp basil
- 1 cup carrot

Directions:
1. In a bowl combine all ingredients together and mix well
2. In a skillet heat olive oil and pour the egg mixture
3. Cook for 1-2 minutes per side
4. When ready remove omelette from the skillet and serv

Nutrition:
- 50g carbs 11g fat 10g protein 320 Calories

Passionfruit, Cranberry & Coconut Yoghurt Chia Parfait

Servings:3
Cooking Time:10 Minutes
Ingredients:
- 4 tablespoons organic chia seeds
- 2 cups almond milk
- ½ teaspoon raw honey
- ½ teaspoon natural vanilla extract
- 1 cup organic frozen cranberries
- 1/2 fresh banana
- 1/3 cup almond milk
- 1 tablespoon Lucuma powder
- 1 tablespoon raw honey
- 1 cup fresh passionfruit pulp

- 1 cup coconut yogurt

Directions:

1. Kvocados mit TomMake the chia base by mixing milk, chia seeds, raw honey and vanilla extract until well combined; let rest for a few minutes.

2. In a blender, blend together the frozen cranberries, almond milk, banana, lucuma powder and raw honey until very smooth.

3. To assemble, divide the chia seeds base among the bottom of tall serving glasses; layer with coconut yogurt, passion fruit pulp, and top with cranberry smooth. Serve garnished with fresh fruit and toasted walnuts.

Nutrition:

- 283.6 Calories 11.5g fat 31g carbs 10.9g protein

Stuffed Figs

Servings:2
Cooking Time:15 Minutes

Ingredients:

- 7 oz fresh figs
- 1 tablespoon cream cheese
- ½ teaspoon walnuts, chopped
- 4 bacon slices
- ¼ teaspoon paprika
- ¼ teaspoon salt
- ½ teaspoon canola oil
- ½ teaspoon honey

Directions:

1. Make the crosswise cuts in every fig.

2. In the shallow bowl mix up together cream cheese, walnuts, paprika, and salt.

3. Fill the figs with cream cheese mixture and wrap in the bacon.

4. Secure the fruits with toothpicks and sprinkle with honey.

5. Line the baking tray with baking paper.

6. Place the preparation ared figs in the tray and sprinkle them with olive oil gently.

7. Bake the figs for 15 minutes at 350F.

Nutrition:

- Calories 299, fat 19.4, fiber 2.3, carbs 16.7, protein 15.2

Raspberry Overnight Porridge

Servings:12
Cooking Time:20 Minute

Ingredients:

- ⅓ cup of rolled oats
- ½ cup almond milk
- 1 tablespoon of honey
- 5-6 raspberries, fresh or canned and unsweetened
- ⅓ cup of rolled oats
- ½ cup almond milk
- 1 tablespoon of honey
- 5-6 raspberries, fresh or canned and unsweetened

Directions:

1. Combine the oats, almond milk, and honey in a mason jar and place into the fridge for overnight.

2. Serve the next morning with the raspberries on top.

Nutrition:

- Calories: 143.6 kcal ,Carbohydrate: 34.62 g ,Protein: 3.44 g ,Sodium: 77.88 mg ,Potassium: 153.25 mg ,Phosphorus: 99.3 mg ,Dietary Fiber: 7.56 g ,Fat: 3.91 g

Olive And Milk Bread

Servings:6
Cooking Time:50 Minutes

Ingredients:

- 1 cup black olives, pitted, chopped
- 1 tablespoon olive oil
- ½ teaspoon fresh yeast
- ½ cup milk, preheated
- ½ teaspoon salt
- 1 teaspoon baking powder
- 2 cup wheat flour, whole grain
- 2 eggs, beaten
- 1 teaspoon butter, melted
- 1 teaspoon sugar

Directions:

1. In the big bowl combine together fresh yeast, sugar, and milk. Stir it until yeast is dissolved.

2. Then add salt, baking powder, butter, and eggs. Stir the dough mixture until homogenous and add 1 cup of wheat flour. Mix it up until smooth.

3. Add olives and remaining flour. Knead the non-sticky dough.

4. Transfer the dough into the non-sticky dough mold.

5. Bake the bread for 50 minutes at 350 F.

6. Check if the bread is cooked with the help of the toothpick. Is it is dry, the bread is cooked.

7. Remove the bread from the oven and let it chill for 10-15 minutes.

8. Remove it from the loaf mold and slice.

Nutrition:

- calories 238, fat 7.7, fiber 1.9, carbs 35.5, protein 7.2

Raspberry Pudding

Servings:2

Cooking Time:30 Minutes

Ingredients:

- ½ cup raspberries
- 2 teaspoons maple syrup
- 1 ½ cup Plain yogurt
- ¼ teaspoon ground cardamom
- 1/3 cup Chia seeds, dried

Directions:

1. Mix up together Plain yogurt with maple syrup and ground cardamom.

2. Add Chia seeds. Stir it gently.

3. Put the yogurt in the serving glasses and top with the raspberries.

4. Refrigerate the breakfast for at least 30 minutes or overnight.

Nutrition:

- calories 303, fat 11.2, fiber 11.8, carbs 33.2, protein 15.5

Chocolate Muffins

Servings:7

Cooking Time:30 Minutes

Ingredients:

- 2 eggs
- 1 tablespoon olive oil
- 1 cup milk
- 2 cups whole wheat flour
- 1 tsp baking soda
- ¼ tsp baking soda
- 1 tsp cinnamon
- 1 cup chocolate chip

Directions:

1. In a bowl combine all dry ingredients

2. In another bowl combine all dry ingredients

3. Combine wet and dry ingredients together

4. Fold in chocolate chips and mix well

5. Pour mixture into 8-12 preparation ared muffin cups, fill 2/3 of the cups

6. Bake for 18-20 minutes at 375 F, when ready remove and serve

Nutrition:

- 2g carbs 6g fat 10g protein 100 Calories

Brown Rice Salad

Servings:4

Cooking Time:10 Minutes

Ingredients:

- 9 ounces brown rice, cooked
- 7 cups baby arugula
- 15 ounces canned garbanzo beans, drained and rinsed
- 4 ounces feta cheese, crumbled
- ¾ cup basil, chopped
- A pinch of salt and black pepper
- 2 tablespoons lemon juice
- ¼ teaspoon lemon zest, grated
- ¼ cup olive oil

Directions:

1. In a salad bowl, combine the brown rice with the arugula, the beans and the rest of the ingredients, toss and serve cold for breakfast.

Nutrition:

- calories 473, fat 22, fiber 7, carbs 53, protein 13

Breakfast Tostadas

Servings:6

Cooking Time:30 Minutes

Ingredients:

- ½ white onion, diced
- 1 tomato, chopped
- 1 cucumber, chopped
- 1 tablespoon fresh cilantro, chopped
- ½ jalapeno pepper, chopped
- 1 tablespoon lime juice
- 6 corn tortillas
- 1 tablespoon canola oil
- 2 oz Cheddar cheese, shredded
- ½ cup white beans, canned, drained
- 6 eggs
- ½ teaspoon butter
- ½ teaspoon Sea salt

Directions:

1. Make Pico de Galo: in the salad bowl combine together diced white onion, tomato, cucumber, fresh cilantro, and jalapeno pepper.
2. Then add lime juice and a ½ tablespoon of canola oil. Mix up the mixture well. Pico de Galo is cooked.
3. After this, preheat the oven to 390F.
4. Line the tray with baking paper.
5. Arrange the corn tortillas on the baking paper and brush with remaining canola oil from both sides.
6. Bake the tortillas for 10 minutes or until they start to be crunchy.
7. Chill the cooked crunchy tortillas well.
8. Meanwhile, toss the butter in the skillet.
9. Crack the eggs in the melted butter and sprinkle them with sea salt.
10. Fry the eggs until the egg whites become white (cooked). Approximately for 3-5 minutes over the medium heat.
11. After this, mash the beans until you get puree texture.
12. Spread the bean puree on the corn tortillas.
13. Add fried eggs.
14. Then top the eggs with Pico de Galo and shredded Cheddar cheese

Nutrition:
- Calories 246, fat 11.1, fiber 4.7, carbs 24.5, protein 13.7

Vanilla Oats

Servings:4
Cooking Time:10 Minutes
Ingredients:
- ½ cup rolled oats
- 1 cup milk
- 1 teaspoon vanilla extract
- 1 teaspoon ground cinnamon
- 2 teaspoon honey
- 2 tablespoons Plain yogurt
- 1 teaspoon butter

Directions:
1. Pour milk in the saucepan and bring it to boil.
2. Add rolled oats and stir well.
3. Close the lid and simmer the oats for 5 minutes over the medium heat. The cooked oats will absorb all milk.
4. Then add butter and stir the oats well.
5. In the separated bowl, whisk together Plain yogurt with honey, cinnamon, and vanilla extract.

6. Transfer the cooked oats in the serving bowls.
7. Top the oats with the yogurt mixture in the shape of the whe

Nutrition:
- calories 243, fat 20.2, fiber 1, carbs 2.8, protein 13.3

Baked Curried Apple Oatmeal Cups

Servings:6
Cooking Time:20 Minutes
Ingredients:
- 3½ cups old-fashioned oats
- 3 tablespoons brown sugar
- 2 teaspoons of your preferred curry powder
- ⅛ teaspoon salt
- 1 cup unsweetened almond milk
- 1 cup unsweetened applesauce
- 1 teaspoon vanilla
- ½ cup chopped walnuts

Directions:
1. Preheat the oven to 375°F. Then spray a 12-cup muffin tin with baking spray then set aside.
2. Combine the oats, brown sugar, curry powder, and salt, and mix in a medium bowl.
3. Mix together the milk, applesauce, and vanilla in a small bowl,
4. Stir the liquid ingredients into the dry ingredients and mix until just combined. Stir in the walnuts.
5. Using a scant ⅓ cup for each divide the mixture among the muffin cups.
6. Bake this for 18 to 20 minutes until the oatmeal is firm. Serve.

Nutrition:
- calories 243, fat 20.2, fiber 1, carbs 2.8, protein 13.3

Lemon Muffins

Servings:4
Cooking Time:30 Minutes
Ingredients:
- 2 eggs
- 1 tablespoon olive oil
- 1 cup milk
- 2 cups whole wheat flour
- 1 tsp baking soda
- ¼ tsp baking soda
- 1 tsp cinnamon

- 1 cup lemon slices

Directions:
1. In a bowl combine all wet ingredients
2. In another bowl combine all dry ingredients
3. Combine wet and dry ingredients together
4. Pour mixture into 8-12 preparation ared muffin cups, fill 2/3 of the cups
5. Bake for 18-20 minutes at 375 F
6. When ready remove from the oven and serve

Nutrition:
- 2g carbs 6g fat 10g protein 100 Calories

Walnuts Yogurt Mix

Servings:6
Cooking Time:10 Minutes

Ingredients:
- 2 and ½ cups Greek yogurt
- 1 and ½ cups walnuts, chopped
- 1 teaspoon vanilla extract
- ¾ cup honey
- 2 teaspoons cinnamon powder

Directions:
1. In a bowl, combine the yogurt with the walnuts and the rest of the ingredients, toss, divide into smaller bowls and keep in the fridge for 10 minutes before serving for breakfast.

Nutrition:
- calories 388, fat 24.6, fiber 2.9, carbs 39.1, protein 10.2

Brown Rice And Grilled Chicken Salad

Servings:3
Cooking Time:10 Minutes

Ingredients:
- 300g grilled chicken breasts
- 3/4 cup brown rice
- 1 1/4 cup coconut water
- 1 teaspoon minced garlic
- 2 tablespoons teriyaki sauce
- 1 tablespoon extra-virgin olive oil
- 2 tablespoons cider vinegar
- 1 small red onion, chopped
- 5 radishes, sliced
- 1 cup broccoli, chopped

- Dash of pepper

Directions:
1. Cook rice in coconut water following package instructions. Remove from heat and let cool completely, and then fluff with a fork.
2. Whisk together garlic, teriyaki sauce, extra virgin olive oil, and vinegar. Stir in red onion, radishes, broccoli and rice. Season with pepper and stir until well blended. Serve with grilled chicken breasts.

Nutrition:
- 283.6 Calories 11.5g fat 31g carbs 10.9g protein

Mediterranean Egg Casserole

Servings:4
Cooking Time:50 Minutes

Ingredients:
- 1 1/2 cups (6 ounces) feta cheese, crumbled
- 1 jar (6 ounces) marinated artichoke hearts, drained well, coarsely chopped
- 10 eggs
- 2 cups milk, low-fat
- 2 cups fresh baby spinach, packed, coarsely chopped
- 6 cups whole-wheat baguette, cut into 1-inch cubes
- 1 tablespoon garlic (about 4 cloves), finely chopped
- 1 tablespoon olive oil, extra-virgin
- 1/2 cup red bell pepper, chopped
- 1/2 cup Parmesan cheese, shredded
- 1/2 teaspoon pepper
- 1/2 teaspoon red pepper flakes
- 1/2 teaspoon salt
- 1/3 cup kalamata olives, pitted, halved
- 1/4 cup red onion, chopped
- 1/4 cup tomatoes (sun-dried) in oil, drained, chopped

Directions:
1. Preheat oven to 350F.
2. Grease a 9x13-inch baking dish with olive oil cooking spray.
3. In an 8-inch non-stick pan over medium heat, heat the olive oil. Add the onions, garlic, and bell pepper; cook for about 3 minutes, frequently stirring, until slightly softened. Add the spinach; cook for about 1 minute or until starting to wilt.
4. Layer half of the baguette cubes in the preparation ared baking dish, then 1 cup of the eta, 1/4 cup Parmesan, the bell pepper mix, artichokes, the olives, and the

tomatoes. Top with the remaining baguette cubes and then with the remaining 1/2 cup of feta.

5. In a large mixing bowl, whisk the eggs and the low-fat milk together. Beat in the pepper, salt and the pepper. Pour the mix over the bread layer in the baking dish, slightly pressing down. Sprinkle with the remaining 1/4 cup Parmesan.

6. Bake for about 40-45 minutes, or until the center is set and the top is golden brown. Before serving, let stand for 15 minutes

Nutrition:

- 360 Cal, 21 g total fat (9 g sat. fat), 270 mg chol., 880 mg sodium, 24 g carb.,3 g fiber,7 g sugar, 20 g protein.

Breakfast Beans (ful Mudammas)

Servings:1
Cooking Time:10 Minutes
Ingredients:

- 1 (15-oz.) can chickpeas, rinsed and drained
- 1 (15-oz.) can fava beans, rinsed and drained
- 1 cup water
- 1 TB. minced garlic
- 1 tsp. salt
- 1/2 cup fresh lemon juice
- 1/2 tsp. cayenne
- 1/2 cup fresh parsley, chopped
- 1 large tomato, diced
- 3 medium radishes, sliced
- 1/4 cup extra-virgin olive oil

Directions:

1. In a 2-quart pot over medium-low heat, combine chickpeas, fava beans, and water. Simmer for 10 minutes.

2. Pour bean mixture into a large bowl, and add garlic, salt, and lemon juice. Stir and smash half of beans with the back of a wooden spoon.

3. Sprinkle cayenne over beans, and evenly distribute parsley, tomatoes, and radishes over top. Drizzle with extra-virgin olive oil, and serve warm or at room temperature

Nutrition:

- 35g carbs 30g fat 20g protein 460 Calories

Veggie Omelet

Servings:3
Cooking Time:20 Minutes
Ingredients:

- 3 egg whites
- 1 egg
- 1/2 teaspoon extra-virgin olive oil
- 1/8 teaspoon red pepper flakes
- 1/8 teaspoon ground nutmeg
- 1/8 teaspoon garlic powder
- A Pinch of salt
- 1/8 teaspoon ground black pepper
- 1/2 cup sliced fresh mushrooms
- 2 tablespoons chopped red bell pepper
- 1/4 cup chopped green onion
- 1/2 cup chopped tomato
- 1 cup chopped fresh spinach

Directions:

1. In a large bowl, whisk together egg whites, egg, garlic powder, red pepper flakes, nutmeg, salt and pepper until well blended.

2. Heat olive oil in a skillet over medium heat; add green onion, mushrooms and belle pepper and cook for about 5 minutes or until tender; stir in tomato and egg mixture and cook for about 5 minutes per side or until egg is set. Slice and serve hot.

Nutrition:

- 283.6 Calories 11.5g fat 31g carbs 10.9g protein

Herbed Spinach Frittata

Servings:4
Cooking Time:20 Minutes
Ingredients:

- 5 eggs, beaten
- 1 cup fresh spinach
- 2 oz Parmesan, grated
- 1/3 cup cherry tomatoes
- ½ teaspoon dried oregano
- 1 teaspoon dried thyme
- 1 teaspoon olive oi

Directions:

1. Chop the spinach into the tiny pieces and or use a blender.

2. Then combine together chopped spinach with eggs, dried oregano and thyme.

3. Add Parmesan and stir frittata mixture with the help of the fork.

4. Brush the springform pan with olive oil and pour the egg mixture inside.

5. Cut the cherry tomatoes into the halves and place them over the egg mixture.

6. Preheat the oven to 360F.

7. Bake the frittata for 20 minutes or until it is solid.

8. Chill the cooked breakfast till the room temperature and slice into the servings

Nutrition:

- calories 140, fat 9.8, fiber 0.5, carbs 2.1, protein 11.9

Pear Oatmeal

Servings:4

Cooking Time:20 Minutes

Ingredients:

- 1 cup oatmeal
- 1/3 cup milk
- 1 pear, chopped
- 1 teaspoon vanilla extract
- 1 tablespoon Splenda
- 1 teaspoon butter
- ½ teaspoon ground cinnamon
- 1 egg, beaten

Directions:

1. In the big bowl mix up together oatmeal, milk, egg, vanilla extract, Splenda, and ground cinnamon.

2. Melt butter and add it in the oatmeal mixture.

3. Then add chopped pear and stir it well.

4. Transfer the oatmeal mixture in the casserole mold and flatten gently. Cover it with the foil and secure edges.

5. Bake the oatmeal for 25 minutes at 350F.

Nutrition:

- calories 151, fat 3.9, fiber 3.3, carbs 23.6, protein 4.9

Feta And Eggs Mix

Servings:4

Cooking Time:5 Minutes

Directions:

1. Melt butter in the skillet and add beaten eggs.

2. Then add parsley, salt, and scrambled eggs. Cook the eggs for 1 minute over the high heat.

3. Add ground black pepper and scramble eggs with the help of the fork.

4. Cook the eggs for 3 minutes over the medium-high heat

Nutrition:

- calories 110, fat 8.4, fiber 0.1, carbs 1.1, protein 7.6

Spicy Cucumbers

Servings:7

Cooking Time:20 Minutes

Ingredients:

- 2 cucumbers
- 1 cup Greek yogurt
- 1 garlic clove
- 1 tsp paprika
- 1 tsp dill
- 1 tsp chili powder

Directions:

1. In a bowl combine all ingredients together except cucumbers

2. Cut the cucumbers into rounds and scoot out the inside

3. Fill each cucumber with the spicy mixture

4. When ready sprinkle paprika and serve

Nutrition:

- 3g carbs 10g fat 12g protein 165 Calories

Ultimate Liver Detox Soup

Servings:5

Cooking Time:20 Minutes

Ingredients:

- 2 tablespoons extra-virgin olive oil
- 1 cup chopped shallot
- 1 tablespoon grated ginger
- 2 cloves garlic, minced
- 4 cups homemade chicken broth
- 1 medium golden beet, diced
- 1 large carrot, sliced
- 1 cup shredded red cabbage
- 1 cup sliced mushrooms
- a handful of pea pods, halved
- 1 hot chili pepper, sliced
- 1 cup chopped cauliflower
- 1 cup chopped broccoli
- 1 bell pepper, diced
- A pinch of cayenne pepper
- A pinch of sea salt
- 1 cup baby spinach
- 1 cup chopped kale
- 1 cup grape tomatoes, halved

Directions:

1. In a large skillet, heat olive oil until hot but not smoky; sauté in shallots, ginger and garlic for about 2 minutes or until tender; stir in broth and bring the mixture to a gentle simmer.

2. Add in beets and carrots and simmer for about 5 minutes. Stir in hot pepper, cauliflower and broccoli and cook for about 3 minutes. stir in bell pepper, red cabbage, mushrooms, and peas and cook for 1 minute.

3. Remove from heat and stir in salt and pepper. Stir in leafy greens and tomatoes and cover the pot for about 5 minutes. Serve.

Nutrition:

- 3g carbs 10g fat 12g protein 165 Calories

Banana Quinoa

Servings:4

Cooking Time:12 Minutes

Ingredients:

- 1 cup quinoa
- 2 cup milk
- 1 teaspoon vanilla extract
- 1 teaspoon honey
- 2 bananas, sliced
- ¼ teaspoon ground cinnamon

Directions:

1. Pour milk in the saucepan and add quinoa.

2. Close the lid and cook it over the medium heat for 12 minutes or until quinoa will absorb all liquid.

3. Then chill the quinoa for 10-15 minutes and place in the serving mason jars.

4. Add honey, vanilla extract, and ground cinnamon.

5. Stir well.

6. Top quinoa with banana and stir it before serving.

Nutrition:

- Calories 279, fat 5.3, fiber 4.6, carbs 48.4, protein 10.7

Cauliflower Hash Brown Breakfast Bowl

Servings:2

Cooking Time:30 Minutes

Ingredients:

- 1 tablespoon lemon juice
- 1 egg
- 1 avocado

- 1 teaspoon garlic powder
- 2 tablespoons extra virgin olive oil
- 2 oz mushrooms, sliced
- ½ green onion, chopped
- ¼ cup salsa
- ¾ cup cauliflower rice
- ½ small handful baby spinach
- Salt and black pepper, to taste

Directions:

1. Mash together avocado, lemon juice, garlic powder, salt and black pepper in a small bowl.

2. Whisk eggs, salt and black pepper in a bowl and keep aside.

3. Heat half of olive oil over medium heat in a skillet and add mushrooms.

4. Sauté for about 3 minutes and season with garlic powder, salt, and pepper.

5. Sauté for about 2 minutes and dish out in a bowl.

6. Add rest of the olive oil and add cauliflower, garlic powder, salt and pepper.

7. Sauté for about 5 minutes and dish out.

8. Return the mushrooms to the skillet and add green onions and baby spinach.

9. Sauté for about 30 seconds and add whisked eggs.

10. Sauté for about 1 minute and scoop on the sautéed cauliflower hash browns.

11. Top with salsa and mashed avocado and serve

Nutrition:

- Calories: 400 Carbs: 15.8g Fats: 36.7g Proteins: 8g Sodium: 288mg Sugar: 4.2g

Farro Salad

Servings:2

Cooking Time:4 Minutes

Ingredients:

- 1 tablespoon olive oil
- A pinch of salt and black pepper
- 1 bunch baby spinach, chopped
- 1 avocado, pitted, peeled and chopped
- 1 garlic clove, minced
- 2 cups farro, already cooked
- ½ cup cherry tomatoes, cubed

Directions:

1. Heat up a pan with the oil over medium heat, add the spinach, and the rest of the ingredients, toss, cook for 4 minutes, divide into bowls and serve.

Nutrition:
- calories 157, fat 13.7, fiber 5.5, carbs 8.6, protein 3.6

Heavenly Egg Bake With Blackberry

Servings:4
Cooking Time:15 Minutes
Ingredients:
- Chopped rosemary
- 1 tsp lime zest
- ½ tsp salt
- ¼ tsp vanilla extract, unsweetened
- 1 tsp grated ginger
- 3 tbsp coconut flour
- 1 tbsp unsalted butter
- 5 organic eggs
- 1 tbsp olive oil
- ½ cup fresh blackberries
- Black pepper to taste

Directions:
1. Switch on the oven, then set its temperature to 350°F and let it preheat.
2. Meanwhile, place all the ingredients in a blender, reserving the berries and pulse for 2 to 3 minutes until well blended and smooth.
3. Take four silicon muffin cups, grease them with oil, evenly distribute the blended batter in the cups, top with black pepper and bake for 15 minutes until cooked through and the top has golden brown.
4. When done, let blueberry egg bake cool in the muffin cups for 5 minutes, then take them out, cool them on a wire rack and then serve.
5. For meal preparation ping, wrap each egg bake with aluminum foil and freeze for up to 3 days.
6. When ready to eat, reheat blueberry egg bake in the microwave and then serve.

Nutrition:
- Calories 144, Total Fat 10g, Total Carbs 2g, Protein 8.5g

Chicken Souvlaki

Servings:4
Cooking Time:2 Minutes
Ingredients:

- 4 pieces (6-inch) pitas, cut into halves
- 2 cups roasted chicken breast skinless, boneless, and sliced
- 1/4 cup red onion, thinly sliced
- 1/2 teaspoon dried oregano
- 1/2 cup Greek yogurt, plain
- 1/2 cup plum tomato, chopped
- 1/2 cup cucumber, peeled, chopped
- 1/2 cup (2 ounces) feta cheese, crumbled
- 1 tablespoon olive oil, extra-virgin, divided
- 1 tablespoon fresh dill, chopped
- 1 cup iceberg lettuce, shredded
- 1 1/4 teaspoons minced garlic, bottled, divided

Directions:
1. In a small mixing bowl, combine the yogurt, cheese, 1 teaspoon of the olive oil, and 1/4 teaspoon of the garlic until well mixed.
2. In a large skillet, heat the remaining olive oil over medium-high heat. Add the remaining 1 teaspoon garlic and the oregano; sauté for 20 seconds.
3. Add the chicken; cook for about 2 minutes or until the chicken are heated through.
4. Put 1/4 cup chicken into each pita halves. Top with 2 tablespoons yogurt mix, 2 tablespoons lettuce,1 tablespoon tomato, and 1 tablespoon cucumber. Divide the onion between the pita halves.

Nutrition:
- 414 Cal, 13.7 g total fat (6.4 g sat. fat, 1.4 g poly. Fat, 4.7 g mono), 81 mg chol., 595 mg sodium, 38 g carb.,2 g fiber, 32.3 g protein.

Quinoa And Potato Bowl

Servings:4
Cooking Time:20 Minutes
Ingredients:
- 1 sweet potato, peeled, chopped
- 1 tablespoon olive oil
- ½ teaspoon chili flakes
- ½ teaspoon salt
- 1 cup quinoa
- 2 cups of water
- 1 teaspoon butter
- 1 tablespoon fresh cilantro, chopped

Directions:
1. Line the baking tray with parchment.

2. Arrange the chopped sweet potato in the tray and sprinkle it with chili flakes, salt, and olive oil.

3. Bake the sweet potato for 20 minutes at 355F.

4. Meanwhile, pour water in the saucepan.

5. Add quinoa and cook it over the medium heat for 7 minutes or until quinoa will absorb all liquid.

6. Add butter in the cooked quinoa and stir well.

7. Transfer it in the bowls, add baked sweet potato and chopped cilantro

Nutrition:

- calories 221, fat 7.1, fiber 3.9, carbs 33.2, protein 6.6

Banana Pancakes

Servings:4

Cooking Time:20 Minutes

Ingredients:

- 1 cup whole wheat flour
- ¼ tsp baking soda
- ¼ tsp baking powder
- 1 cup mashed banana
- 2 eggs
- 1 cup milk

Directions:

1. In a bowl combine all ingredients together and mix well

2. In a skillet heat olive oil

3. Pour ¼ of the batter and cook each pancake for 1-2 minutes per side

4. When ready remove from heat and serve

Nutrition:

- 7g carbs 14g fat 15g protein 210 Calories

Pumpkin Muffins

Servings:12

Cooking Time:20 Minutes

Ingredients:

- 1 cup all-purpose flour
- 1 cup wheat bran
- 2 teaspoons Phosphorus Powder
- 1 cup pumpkin purée
- ¼ cup honey
- ¼ cup olive oil
- 1 egg
- 1 teaspoon vanilla extract
- ½ cup cored diced apple

Directions:

1. Preheat the oven to 400°F.

2. Line 12 muffin cups with paper liners.

3. Stir together the flour, wheat bran, and baking powder, mix this in a medium bowl.

4. In a small bowl, whisk together the pumpkin, honey, olive oil, egg, and vanilla.

5. Stir the pumpkin mixture into the flour mixture until just combined.

6. Stir in the diced apple.

7. Spoon the batter in the muffin cups.

8. Bake for about 20 minutes, or until a toothpick inserted in the center of a muffin comes out clean.

Nutrition:

- Calories: 125; Total Fat: 5g; Saturated Fat: 1g; Cholesterol: 18mg; Sodium: 8mg; Carbohydrates: 20g; Fiber: 3g; Phosphorus: 120mg; Potassium: 177mg; Protein: 2g

Pasta With Indian Lentils

Servings:6

Cooking Time:5 Minutes

Ingredients:

- ¼-½ cup fresh cilantro (chopped)
- 3 cups water
- 2 small dry red peppers (whole)
- 1 teaspoon turmeric
- 1 teaspoon ground cumin
- 2-3 cloves garlic (minced)
- 1 can diced tomatoes (w/juice)
- 1 large onion (chopped)
- ½ cup dry lentils (rinsed)
- ½ cup orzo or tiny pasta

Directions:

1. Combine all ingredients in the skillet except for the cilantro then boil on medium-high heat.

2. Ensure to cover and slightly reduce heat to medium-low and simmer until pasta is tender for about 35 minutes.

3. Afterwards, take out the chili peppers then add cilantro and top it with low-fat sour cream.

Nutrition:

- Calories: 175; Carbs: 40g; Protein: 3g; Fats: 2g; Phosphorus: 139mg; Potassium: 513mg; Sodium: 61mg

Cheesy Scrambled Eggs With Fresh Herbs

Servings:4

Cooking Time:10 Minutes

Ingredients:

- Eggs – 3
- Egg whites – 2
- Cream cheese – ½ cup
- Unsweetened rice milk – ¼ cup
- Chopped scallion – 1 Tablespoon green part only
- Chopped fresh tarragon – 1 Tablespoon
- Unsalted butter – 2 Tablespoons.
- Ground black pepper to taste

Directions:

1. In a container, mix the eggs, egg whites, cream cheese, rice milk, scallions, and tarragon until mixed and smooth.
2. Melt the butter in a skillet.
3. Pour in the egg mix and cook, stirring, for 5 minutes or until the eggs are thick and curds creamy.
4. Season with pepper and serve.

Nutrition:

- Calories: 221 ,Fat: 19g ,Carb: 3g ,Phosphorus: 119mg ,Potassium: 140mg ,Sodium: 193mg ,Protein: 8g

Coconut & Strawberry Smoothie Bowl

Servings:4

Cooking Time:10 Minutes

Ingredients:

- 2 cups fresh strawberries
- 2 cups fresh spinach
- 1 cup coconut water
- 1 ripe banana
- 2 tablespoons raw pumpkin seeds
- 2 tablespoons chia seeds
- ½ cup coconut flakes, toasted

Directions:

1. In a blender, blend together almond milk, banana, and spinach until very smooth and creamy; add in strawberries and pulse to combine well.
2. Divide the smooth among serving bowls and top each serving with fresh strawberries, pumpkin seeds, chia seeds and toasted coconut flakes.

3. Enjoy!

Pan-fried Chicken With Oregano-orange Chimichurri & Arugula Salad

Servings:3

Cooking Time:5 Minutes

Ingredients:

- 1 tablespoon orange juice
- 1 teaspoon orange zest
- 1 teaspoon dried oregano
- 1 small garlic clove, grated
- 2 teaspoon apple cider vinegar
- 1/2 cup chopped parsley
- 1 1/2 pound chicken, cut into 4 pieces
- 1 tablespoon lemon juice
- A pinch of pepper
- 1/4 cup olive oil
- 4 cups arugula
- 2 bulbs fennel, shaved
- 2 tablespoons whole-grain mustard

Directions:

1. Make chimichurri: In a medium bowl, combine orange zest, oregano and garlic. Mix in vinegar, orange juice and parsley and then slowly whisk in ¼ cup of olive oil until emulsified. Season with black pepper.
2. Sprinkle the chicken with lemon juice and pepper; heat the remaining olive oil in a large skillet and cook the chicken over medium high heat for about 6 minutes per side or until browned.
3. Remove from heat and let rest for at least 10 minutes. Toss chicken, greens, and fennel with mustard in a medium bowl; season with salt and pepper.
4. Serve steak with chimichurri and salad. Enjoy!

Nutrition:

- 3g carbs 10g fat 12g protein 165 Calories

Mediterranean Egg-feta Scramble

Servings:4

Cooking Time:20 Minutes

Ingredients:

- 3/4 cup crumbled feta cheese
- 2 tablespoons green onions, minced
- 2 tablespoons red peppers, roasted, diced
- 1/4 teaspoon kosher salt
- 1/4 teaspoon garlic powder
- 1/4 cup Greek yogurt
- 1/2 teaspoon dry oregano
- 1/2 teaspoon dry basil
- 1 teaspoon olive oil
- A few cracks freshly ground black pepper
- Warm whole-wheat tortillas, optional

Directions:

1. Preheat a skillet over medium heat.

2. In a bowl, whisk the eggs, the sour cream, basil, oregano, garlic powder, salt, and pepper. Gently add the feta.

3. When the skillet is hot, add the olive oil and then the egg mixture; allow the egg mix to set then scrape the bottom of the pan to let the uncooked egg to cook. Stir in the red peppers and the green onions. Continue cooking until the eggs mixture is cooked to your preferred doneness. Serve immediately.

4. If desired, sprinkle with extra feta and then wrap the scrambled eggs in tortillas

Nutrition:

- 260 Cal, 16 g total fat (8 g sat. fat), 350 mg chol., 750 mg sodium, 190 mg pot., 12 g carb.,>1 g fiber, 2 g sugar, 16 g protein.

Quick Cream Of Wheat

Servings:1

Cooking Time:12 Minutes

Ingredients:

- 4 cups whole milk
- 1/2 cup farina
- 1/2 tsp. salt
- 3 TB. sugar
- 3 TB. butter
- 3 TB. pine nuts

Directions:

1. In a large saucepan over medium heat, bring whole milk to a simmer, and cook for about 4 minutes. Do not allow milk to scorch.

2. Whisk in farina, salt, and sugar, and bring to a slight boil. Cook for 2 minutes, reduce heat to low, and cook for 3 more minutes. Stay close to the pan to ensure it doesn't boil over.

3. Pour mixture into 4 bowls, and let cool for 5 minutes.

4. Meanwhile, in a small pan over low heat, cook butter and pine nuts for about 3 minutes or until pine nuts are lightly toasted.

5. Evenly spoon butter and pine nuts over each bowl, and serve war

Nutrition:

- 3g carbs 10g fat 12g protein 165 Calories

Broccoli Omelette

Servings:1

Cooking Time:10 Minutes

Ingredients:

- 2 eggs
- ¼ tsp salt
- ¼ tsp black pepper
- 1 tablespoon olive oil
- ¼ cup cheese
- ¼ tsp basil
- 1 cup broccoli

Directions:

1. In a bowl combine all ingredients together and mix well

2. In a skillet heat olive oil and pour the egg mixture

3. Cook for 1-2 minutes per side

4. When ready remove omelette from the skillet and serve

Nutrition:

- 50g carbs 11g fat 10g protein 320 Calories

Pineapple, Macha & Beet Chia Pudding

Servings:4

Cooking Time:10 Minutes

Ingredients:

- 1 cup chia seeds
- 1 teaspoon raw honey
- 2 cups almond milk
- 1 teaspoon matcha green tea powder
- 2 tablespoons fresh beetroot juice
- 1 whole pineapple
- 1 cup freshly squeezed lemon juice
- 1 knob of fresh ginger
- Toasted almonds and figs to serve

Directions:

1. Green Chia pudding layer:

2. Add another half each of chia seeds, raw honey, almond milk, and matcha green tea powder to the blender and until very smooth; transfer to a bowl.

3. Beetroot layer: blend together beetroot and ginger with the remaining chia seeds, raw honey, vanilla, and coconut milk until very smooth; transfer to a separate bowl. In a food processor, puree the fresh pineapple until fine.

4. To assemble, layer the chia pudding in the bottom of serving glasses, followed by the pureed pineapple and then the beetroot layer. Top with figs and toasted almonds for a crunchy finish.

Chicken Liver

Servings:4

Cooking Time:10 Minutes

Ingredients:

- 2 lb. chicken liver
- 3 TB. extra-virgin olive oil
- 3 TB. minced garlic
- 1 tsp. salt
- 1/2 tsp. ground black pepper
- 1 cup fresh cilantro, finely chopped
- 1/4 cup fresh lemon juice

Directions:

1. Cut chicken livers in half, rinse well, and pat dry with paper towels.

2. Preheat a large skillet over medium heat. Add extra-virgin olive oil and garlic, and cook for 2 minutes.

3. Add chicken liver and salt, and cook, tossing gently, for 5 minutes. Remove the skillet from heat, and spoon liver onto a plate.

4. Add black pepper, cilantro, and lemon juice. Lightly toss, and serve warm

Nutrition:

- 35g carbs 30g fat 20g protein 460 Calories

Tapioca Pudding

Servings:3

Cooking Time:15 Minutes

Ingredients:

- ¼ cup pearl tapioca
- ¼ cup maple syrup
- 2 cups almond milk
- ½ cup coconut flesh, shredded
- 1 and ½ teaspoon lemon juice

Directions:

1. In a pan, combine the milk with the tapioca and the rest of the ingredients, bring to a simmer over medium heat, and cook for 15 minutes.

2. Divide the mix into bowls, cool it down and serve for breakfast.

Nutrition:

- calories 361, fat 28.5, fiber 2.7, carbs 28.3, protein 2.8

Milk Scones

Servings:4

Cooking Time:10 Minutes

Ingredients:

- ½ cup wheat flour, whole grain
- 1 teaspoon baking powder
- 1 tablespoon butter, melted
- 1 teaspoon vanilla extract
- 1 egg, beaten
- ¾ teaspoon salt
- 3 tablespoons milk
- 1 teaspoon vanilla sugar

Directions:

1. In the mixing bowl combine together wheat flour, baking powder, butter, vanilla extract, and egg. Add salt and knead the soft and non-sticky dough. Add more flour if needed.

2. Then make the log from the dough and cut it into the triangles.

3. Line the tray with baking paper.

4. Arrange the dough triangles on the baking paper and transfer in the preheat to the 360F oven.

5. Cook the scones for 10 minutes or until they are light brown.

6. After this, chill the scones and brush with milk and sprinkle with vanilla sugar.

Nutrition:

- calories 112, fat 4.4, fiber 0.5, carbs 14.3, protein 3.4

Mushroom-egg Casserole

Servings:3

Cooking Time:30 Minutes

Ingredients:

- ½ cup mushrooms, chopped
- ½ yellow onion, diced
- 4 eggs, beaten
- 1 tablespoon coconut flakes
- ½ teaspoon chili pepper
- 1 oz Cheddar cheese, shredded
- 1 teaspoon canola oil

Directions:

1. Pour canola oil in the skillet and preheat well.

2. Add mushrooms and onion and roast for 5-8 minutes or until the vegetables are light brown.

3. Transfer the cooked vegetables in the casserole mold.

4. Add coconut flakes, chili pepper, and Cheddar cheese.

5. Then add eggs and stir well.

6. Bake the casserole for 15 minutes at 360F

Nutrition:

- Calories 152, fat 11.1, fiber 0.7, carbs 3, protein 10.4

Gluten Free Pancakes

Servings:3

Cooking Time:

Ingredients:

- 1 cup almond flour
- 1/4 cup coconut flour
- 1/3 cup unsweetened almond milk
- 3 large eggs
- 1/4 cup olive oil
- 1 teaspoon baking powder
- 1 1/2 teaspoons vanilla extract

- 1 tablespoon raw honey
- 1 cup fresh blueberries for serving

Directions:

1. In a large bowl, whisk together all the ingredients until very smooth. Heat a pan and then add in oil; drop about three tablespoons of batter into the pan and cook for about 2 minutes. flip over and cook for 2 minutes more or until lightly browned on both sides. Repeat with the remaining batter.

2. Serve topped with fresh blueberries

Nutrition:

- 242 Calories 7g Carbs 19g Fat 12g Protein

Couscous With Artichokes, Sun-dried Tomatoes And Feta

Servings:4

Cooking Time:

Ingredients:

- 3 cups chicken breast, cooked, chopped
- 2 1/3 cups water, divided
- 2 jars (6-ounces each) marinated artichoke hearts, undrained
- 1/4 teaspoon black pepper, freshly ground
- 1/2 cup tomatoes, sun-dried
- 1/2 cup (2 ounces) feta cheese, crumbled
- 1 cup flat-leaf parsley, fresh, chopped
- 1 3/4 cups whole-wheat Israeli couscous, uncooked
- 1 can (14 1/2 ounces) vegetable broth

Directions:

1. In a microwavable bowl, combine 2 cups of the water and the tomatoes. Microwave on HIGH for about 3 minutes or until the water boils. When water is boiling, remove from the microwave, cover, and let stand for about 3 minutes or until the tomatoes are soft; drain, chop, and set aside.

2. In a large saucepan, place the vegetable broth and the remaining 1/3 cup of water; bring to boil. Stir in the couscous, cover, reduce heat, and simmer for about 8 minutes or until tender. Remove the pan from the heat; add the tomatoes and the remaining ingredients. Stir to combine.

Nutrition:

- 419 Cal, 14.1 g total fat (3.9 g sat. fat, 0.8 g poly. Fat, 1.4 g mono), 64 mg chol.,677 mg sodium, 42.5 g carb.,2.6 g fiber, 30.2 g protein.

Grilled Chicken Salad

Servings:2
Cooking Time:20 Minutes
Ingredients:
- 4 cups chopped broccoli
- 1/4 cup extra virgin olive oil
- 1/2 small red onion, thinly sliced
- 1 carrot, coarsely grated
- 4 chicken thighs, skinless
- 1 1/2 tablespoons Cajun seasoning
- 1/4 cup lemon juice
- 1 tablespoon drained baby capers
- 1 lemon, cut into wedges, to serve

Directions:
1. Drizzle chicken with oil and sprinkle with seasoning; rub to coat well.
2. Heat your grill to medium heat and grill the chicken for about 8 minutes per side or until cooked through and golden browned on the outside.
3. In the meantime, place the grated broccoli in a bowl and add in red onion, carrots, capers, lime juice and the remaining oil, salt and pepper; toss to combine well and serve with grilled chicken garnished with lemon wedges.

Nutrition:
- 283.6 Calories 11.5g fat 31g carbs 10.9g protein

Spinach Wrap

Servings:4
Cooking Time:10 Minutes
Ingredients:
- 4 pieces (10-inch) spinach wraps (or whole wheat tortilla or sun-dried tomato wraps)
- 1 pound chicken tenders
- 1 cup cucumber, chopped
- 3 tablespoons extra-virgin olive oil
- 1 medium tomato, chopped
- 1/3 cup couscous, whole-wheat
- 2 teaspoons garlic, minced
- 1/4 teaspoon salt, divided
- 1/4 teaspoon freshly ground pepper
- 1/4 cup lemon juice
- 1/2 cup water
- 1/2 cup fresh mint, chopped
- 1 cup fresh parsley, chopped

Directions:
1. In a small saucepan, pour the water and bring to a boil. Stir in the couscous, remove pan from heat, cover, and allow to stand for 5 minutes, then fluff using a fork; set aside.

2. Meanwhile, in a small mixing bowl, combine the mint, parsley, oil, lemon juice, garlic, 1/8 teaspoon of the salt, and the pepper.
3. In a medium mixing bowl, toss the chicken with the 1 tablespoon of the mint mixture and the remaining 1/8 teaspoon of salt.
4. Place the chicken mixture into a large non-stick skillet; cook for about 3-5 minutes each side, or until heated through. Remove from the skillet, allow to cool enough to handle, and cut into bite-sized pieces.
5. Stir the remaining mint mixture, the cucumber, and the tomato into the couscous.
6. Spread about 3/4 cup of the couscous mix onto each wrap and divide the chicken between the wraps, roll like a burrito, tucking the sides in to hold to secure the ingredients in. Cut in halves and serv

Nutrition:
- 479 Cal, 17 g total fat (3 g sat. fat, 11 g mono), 67 mg chol., 653 mg sodium, 382 pot., 49 g carb.,5 g fiber, 15 g protein

Chili Avocado Scramble

Servings:4
Cooking Time:0 Minutes
Ingredients:
- 4 eggs, beaten
- 1 white onion, diced
- 1 tablespoon avocado oil
- 1 avocado, finely chopped
- ½ teaspoon chili flakes
- 1 oz Cheddar cheese, shredded
- ½ teaspoon salt
- 1 tablespoon fresh parsley

Directions:
1. Pour avocado oil in the skillet and bring it to boil.
2. Then add diced onion and roast it until it is light brown.
3. Meanwhile, mix up together chili flakes, beaten eggs, and salt.
4. Pour the egg mixture over the cooked onion and cook the mixture for 1 minute over the medium heat.
5. After this, scramble the eggs well with the help of the fork or spatula. Cook the eggs until they are solid but soft.
6. After this, add chopped avocado and shredded cheese.
7. Stir the scramble well and transfer in the serving plates.
8. Sprinkle the meal with fresh parsley

Nutrition:
- calories 236, fat 20.1, fiber 4, carbs 7.4, protein 8.6

Chickpeas, Spinach And Arugula Bowl

Servings:5

Cooking Time:25 Minutes

Ingredients:

- 1 cup chickpeas, canned, drained
- ½ teaspoon butter
- ½ teaspoon salt
- ½ teaspoon ground paprika
- ¾ teaspoon onion powder
- 6 oz quinoa, dried
- 12 oz chicken stock
- 2 tomatoes, chopped
- 1 cucumber, chopped
- ½ cup fresh spinach, chopped
- ½ cup arugula, chopped
- ½ cup lettuce chopped
- 1 tablespoon olive oil
- 4 teaspoons hummus

Directions:

1. Place chickpeas in the skillet. Add butter and salt.
2. Roast the chickpeas for 5 minutes over the high heat. Stir them from time to time.
3. After this, place quinoa and chicken stock in the pan.
4. Cook the quinoa for 15 minutes over the medium heat.
5. Then make the salad: mix up together tomatoes, cucumber, spinach, arugula, lettuce, and olive oil. Shake the salad gently.
6. Arrange roasted chickpeas in every serving bowl.
7. Add salad and hummus.

Nutrition:

- calories 330, fat 8.4, fiber 10.9, carbs 51.6, protein 14.1

Sicilian-style Zoodle Spaghetti

Servings:2

Cooking Time:10 Minutes

Ingredients:

- 4 cups zoodles (spiraled zucchini)
- 2 ounces cubed bacon
- 4 ounces canned sardines, chopped
- ½ cup canned chopped tomatoes
- 1 tbsp capers
- 1 tbsp parsley
- 1 tsp minced garlic

Directions:

1. Pour some of the sardine oil in a pan. Add garlic and cook for 1 minute. Add the bacon and cook for 2 more minutes. Stir in the tomatoes and let simmer for 5 minutes. Add zoodles and sardines and cook for 3 minutes.

Nutrition:

- Calories 172, ,Fat 4g ,Fiber 0.6g ,Carbs 3g, ,Protein 34g

Citrus Quinoa & Chickpea Salad

Servings:4

Cooking Time:10 Minute

Ingredients:

- 2 cups cooked quinoa
- 1 can chickpeas, drained & rinsed
- 1 ripe avocado, diced
- 1 red bell pepper, diced
- 1/2 red onion, diced
- 1/4 cup lime juice
- 1/2 tbsp garlic powder
- 1/2 tbsp paprika
- 1/4-1/2 cup chopped cilantro
- 1 tbsp chopped jalapenos
- Sea salt to taste

Directions:

1. Add all ingredients in a large bowl and mix well.
2. Enjoy right away or refrigerate for later.

Nutrition:

- Calories per serving: 300; Carbs: 43.5g; Protein: 10.3g; Fat: 10.9g

Chicken And White Bean

Servings:3
Cooking Time:60 Minutes
Ingredients:
- 2 tbsp fresh cilantro, chopped
- 2 cups grated Monterey Jack cheese
- 3 cups water
- 1/8 tsp cayenne pepper
- 2 tsp pure chile powder
- 2 tsp ground cumin
- 1 4-oz can chopped green chiles
- 1 cup corn kernels
- 2 15-oz cans shite beans, drained and rinsed
- 2 garlic cloves
- 1 medium onion, diced
- 2 tbsp extra virgin olive oil
- 1 lb. chicken breasts, boneless and skinless

Directions:
1. Slice chicken breasts into ½-inch cubes and with pepper and salt, season it.
2. On high fire, place a large nonstick fry pan and heat oil.
3. Sauté chicken pieces for three to four minutes or until lightly browned.
4. Reduce fire to medium and add garlic and onion.
5. Cook for 5 to 6 minutes or until onions are translucent.
6. Add water, spices, chilies, corn and beans. Bring to a boil.
7. Once boiling, slow fire to a simmer and continue simmering for an hour, uncovered.
8. To serve, garnish with a sprinkling of cilantro and a tablespoon of cheese.

Nutrition:
- Calories per serving: 433; Protein: 30.6g; Carbs: 29.5g; Fat: 21.8g

Kidney Beans And Beet Salad

Servings:4
Cooking Time:15 Minutes
Ingredients:
- 1 14.5-ounce can kidney beans, drained and rinsed
- 1 tablespoon pomegranate syrup or juice
- 2 tablespoons olive oil
- 4 beets, scrubbed and stems removed
- 4 green onions, chopped
- Juice of 1 lemon
- Salt and pepper to taste

Directions:
1. Bring a pot of water to boil and add beets. Simmer for 10 minutes or until tender. Drain beets and place in ice bath for 5 minutes.
2. Peel bets and slice in halves.
3. Toss to mix the pomegranate syrup, olive oil, lemon juice, green onions, and kidney beans in a salad bowl.
4. Stir in beets. Season with pepper and salt to taste.
5. Serve and enjoy.

Nutrition:
- Calories per serving: 175; Protein: 6.0g; Carbs: 22.0g; Fat: 7.0g

Sour Cream Salmon With Parmesan

Servings:4
Cooking Time:25 Minutes
Ingredients:
- 1 cup sour cream
- ½ tbsp minced dill
- ½ lemon, zested and juiced
- Pink salt and black pepper to season
- 4 salmon steaks
- ½ cup grated Parmesan cheese

Directions:
1. Preheat oven to 400°F and line a baking sheet with parchment paper; set aside. In a bowl, mix the sour cream, dill, lemon zest, juice, salt and black pepper, and set aside.
2. Season the fish with salt and black pepper, drizzle lemon juice on both sides of the fish and arrange them in the baking sheet. Spread the sour cream mixture on each fish and sprinkle with Parmesan.
3. Bake the fish for 15 minutes and after broil the top for 2 minutes with a close watch for a nice a brown color. Plate the fish and serve with buttery green beans.

Nutrition:
- Calories 355, ,Fat: 31g ,Net Carbs: 6g ,Protein: 20g

Carrot And Potato Soup

Servings:6

Cooking Time:35 Minutes

Ingredients:

- 5 cups beef broth
- 4 carrots, peeled
- 1 teaspoon dried thyme
- ½ teaspoon ground cumin
- 1 teaspoon salt
- 1 ½ cup potatoes, chopped
- 1 tablespoon olive oil
- ½ teaspoon ground black pepper
- 1 tablespoon lemon juice
- 1/3 cup fresh parsley, chopped
- 1 chili pepper, chopped
- 1 tablespoon tomato paste
- 1 tablespoon sour cream

Directions:

1. Line the baking tray with baking paper.

2. Put sweet potatoes and carrot on the tray and sprinkle with olive oil and salt.

3. Bake the vegetables for 25 minutes at 365F.

4. Meanwhile, pour the beef broth in the pan and bring it to boil.

5. Add dried thyme, ground cumin, chopped chili pepper, and tomato paste.

6. When the vegetables are cooked, add them in the pan.

7. Boil the vegetables until they are soft.

8. Then blend the mixture with the help of the blender until smooth.

9. Simmer it for 2 minutes and add lemon juice. Stir well.

10. Then add sour cream and chopped parsley. Stir well.

11. Simmer the soup for 3 minutes more.

Nutrition:

- calories 123, fat 4.1, fiber 2.9, carbs 16.4, protein 5.3

Macedonian Greens And Cheese Pie

Servings:3

Cooking Time:50 Minutes

Ingredients:

- 1 bunch chicory
- 1 bunch rocket or arugula
- 1 bunch mint
- 1 bunch dill
- 10 sheets whole-wheat filo pastry
- 150 g halloumi, finely diced
- 150 g ricotta
- 200 g baby spinach
- 250 g Greek feta, crumbled
- 4 eggs
- 50 g dried whole-wheat breadcrumbs
- 6 green onions, trimmed
- Olive oil, to brush

Directions:

1. Trim the rocket stalks and the chicory. Finely chop the green onions and the dill (include the dill stems). Strip the mint leaves.

2. Pour water into a large-sized pan; bring to boil. Ready a bowl with iced water beside the stove. Add the chicory into the boiling water; blanch for 3 minutes and using a slotted spoon, transfer to the bowl with iced water. Repeat the process with the spinach and the rocket, blanching each for 1 minute; drain well.

3. A handful at a time, tightly wring the greens to squeeze out the excess liquid, then pat dry with paper towel. Finely chop the blanched greens. Combine them with the eggs, herbs, feta, 30 g of the breadcrumbs, ricotta, and 3/4 of the halloumi; season.

4. Preheat the oven to 180C.

5. Grease a 5-cm deep 25cmx pie tin.

6. Brush a filo sheet with the olive oil, place it in the pie tin, extending the edge of the filo outside the edge of the tin. Brush the remaining sheets of filo and add them to the pie tin, arranging them like wheel spokes.

7. Sprinkle the remaining breadcrumbs over the base of the layered filo sheets. Top with the filling mixture. Loosely fold the filo sheets over to cover the filling, brush with oil, sprinkle with water, and scatter the halloumi over.

8. Bake for 45 minutes. After 45 minutes, cover, and bake for additional 15 minutes, or until heated through.

Nutrition:

- 374.8 Cal, 20 g total fat (12 g sat. fat), 22 g carb., 2 g fiber, 3 g sugar, 25g protein, and 1506.7 mg sodium.

White Bean Soup

Servings:6

Cooking Time:8 Hours 30 Minutes

Ingredients:

- 1 cup celery, chopped
- 1 cup carrots, chopped
- 1 yellow onion, chopped
- 6 cups veggie stock
- 4 garlic cloves, minced
- 2 cup navy beans, dried
- ½ teaspoon basil, dried
- ½ teaspoon sage, dried
- 1 teaspoon thyme, dried
- A pinch of salt and black pepper

Directions:

1. In your slow cooker, combine the beans with the stock and the rest of the ingredients, put the lid on and cook on Low for 8 hours.
2. Divide the soup into bowls and serve right away.

Nutrition:

- calories 264, fat 17.5, fiber 4.5, carbs 23.7, protein 11.5

Grilled Chicken

Servings:4

Cooking Time:15 Minutes

Ingredients:

- 4 chicken breasts, skinless and boneless
- 1 ½ tsp dried oregano
- 1 tsp paprika
- 5 garlic cloves, minced
- ½ cup fresh parsley, minced
- ½ cup olive oil
- ½ cup fresh lemon juice
- Pepper
- Salt

Directions:

1. Add lemon juice, oregano, paprika, garlic, parsley, and olive oil to a large zip-lock bag. Season chicken with pepper and salt and add to bag. Seal bag and shake well to coat chicken with marinade. Let sit chicken in the marinade for 20 minutes.
2. Remove chicken from marinade and grill over medium-high heat for 5-6 minutes on each side. Serve and enjoy

Nutrition:

- Calories: 512 ,Fat: 36.5g ,Protein: 43.1g ,Carbs: 3g ,Sodium 110mg

Falafel

Servings:3

Cooking Time:40 Minutes

Ingredients:

- 1 pound (about 2 cups) dry chickpeas or garbanzo beans (use dry, DO NOT use canned)
- 1 1/2 tablespoons flour
- 1 3/4 teaspoons salt
- 1 small onion, roughly chopped
- 1 teaspoon ground coriander
- 1/4 cup fresh parsley, chopped
- 1/4 teaspoon black pepper
- 1/4 teaspoon cayenne pepper
- 2 teaspoons cumin
- 3-5 cloves garlic, roasted, if desired
- Pinch ground cardamom
- Canola, grapeseed, peanut oil, or oil with high smoking point, for frying

Directions:

1. Pour the chickpeas into a large-sized bowl, cover with about 3-inch cold water, and soak overnight. The chickpeas will double to about 4-5 cups after soaking.
2. Drain and then rinse well, pour into a food processor. Except for the oil for frying, add the remaining of the ingredients into the processor; pulse until the texture resembles a coarse meal. Periodically scrape the sides of the processor, pushing the mixture down the sides, process until the mixture resembles a texture that is between couscous and paste, making sure not to over process or they will turn into hummus.
3. Transfer into a bowl. With a fork, stir the mixture, removing any large chickpeas that remained unprocessed. Cover the bowl with a plastic wrap; refrigerate for about 1 to 2 hours.
4. Fill a skillet with 1 1/2-inch worth of oil. Slowly heat the oil over medium flame or heat.
5. Meanwhile, scoop out 2 tablespoons worth of the falafel mixture; with wet hands form it into round ball or slider-shaped. You can make them smaller or larger if you want. They may stick together loosely, but when they start to fry, they will bind nicely. If the balls won't hold,

add flour by the 1 tablespoon-worth until they hold. If they still don't hold, add 1-2 eggs.

6. Test the hotness of your oil with 1 piece falafel in the center of the pan. If the oil is at the right temperature the falafel will brown 5-6 minutes total or 2-3 minutes each side. If it browns faster, the oil is too hot. Slightly cool the oil down and then test again. When you reach the right temperature, cook the falafel in 5-6 pieces batches until both sides are golden brown. With a slotted spoon, remove from the skillet, and drain on paper towels.

7. Serve fresh and hot with hummus and then topped with tahini sauce.

Nutrition:

- 60 cal., 1.5 g total fat (0 g sat fat), 0 mg chol., 135 mg sodium, 140 mg potassium, 10 g carb., 3 g fiber, 2 g sugar, and 3 g protein.

Leek, Bacon And Pea Risotto

Servings:4

Cooking Time:60 Minutes

Ingredients:

- Salt and pepper to taste
- 2 tbsp fresh lemon juice
- ½ cup grated parmesan cheese
- ¾ cup frozen peas
- 1 cup dry white wine
- 2 ½ cups Arborio rice
- 4 slices bacon (cut into strips)
- 12 cups low sodium chicken broth
- 2 leeks cut lengthwise

Directions:

1. In a saucepan, bring the broth to a simmer over medium flame.

2. On another skillet, cook bacon and stir continuously to avoid the bacon from burning. Cook more for five minutes and add the leeks and cook for two more minutes.

3. Increase the heat to medium high and add the rice until the grains become translucent.

4. Add the wine and stir until it evaporates.

5. Add 1 cup of broth to the mixture and reduce the heat to medium low. Stir constantly for two minutes.

6. Gradually add the remaining broth until the rice becomes al dente and it becomes creamy.

7. Add the peas and the rest of the broth.

8. Remove the skillet or turn off the heat and add the Parmesan cheese.

9. Cover the skillet and let the cheese melt. Season the risotto with lemon juice, salt and pepper.

10. Serve the risotto with more parmesan cheese.

Nutrition:

- Calories per Serving: 742; Carbs: 57.6g; Protein: 38.67g; Fat: 39.6g

Salmon Bowls

Servings:3

Cooking Time:40 Minutes

Ingredients:

- 2 cups farro
- Juice of 2 lemons
- 1/3 cup olive oil+ 2 tablespoons
- Salt and black pepper
- 1 cucumber, chopped
- ¼ cup balsamic vinegar
- 1 garlic cloves, minced
- ¼ cup parsley, chopped
- ¼ cup mint, chopped
- 2 tablespoons mustard
- 4 salmon fillets, boneless

Directions:

1. Put water in a large pot, bring to a boil over medium-high heat, add salt and the farro, stir, simmer for 30 minutes, drain, transfer to a bowl, add the lemon juice, mustard, garlic, salt, pepper and 1/3 cup oil, toss and leave aside for now.

2. In another bowl, mash the cucumber with a fork, add the vinegar, salt, pepper, the parsley, dill and mint and whisk well.

3. Heat up a pan with the rest of the oil over medium heat, add the salmon fillets skin side down, cook for 5 minutes on each side, cool them down and break into pieces.

4. Add over the farro, add the cucumber dressing, toss and serve for lunch.

Nutrition:

- calories 281, fat 12.7, fiber 1.7, carbs 5.8, protein 36.5

44

Roasted Tomato And Chicken Pasta

Servings:4

Cooking Time:30 Minutes

Ingredients:

- 1 pound boneless, skinless chicken thighs, cut into bite-size pieces
- ⅛ Teaspoon kosher salt (optional)
- ¼ teaspoon freshly ground black pepper (optional)
- 4 cups cherry tomatoes, halved4garlic cloves, minced
- 1 tablespoon canola or sunflower oil
- 1 teaspoon dried basil
- 8 ounces uncooked whole-wheat rotini
- 10 kalamata olives, pitted and sliced
- ¼ teaspoon red pepper flakes (optional)
- ¼ cup grated Parmesan cheese (optional)

Directions:

1. Preheat the oven to 450°F.
2. Season the chicken with salt and pepper, if desired. Toss the chicken in a large bowl with the tomatoes, garlic, oil, and basil. Transfer to a rimmed baking sheet, and spread out evenly.
3. Roast until the chicken is cooked through, 15 to 20 minutes, tossing halfway though. A meat thermometer should read 165°F.
4. Meanwhile, cook the pasta to al dente according to the package directions. Drain.
5. In a large serving bowl, toss the chicken and tomatoes with the pasta, olives, and pepper flakes (if using). Top with Parmesan, if desired.

Nutrition:

- Calories: 458 ,Total Fat: 14g ,Saturated Fat: 3g ,Cholesterol: 110mg ,Sodium: 441mg ,Carbohydrates: 52g ,Fiber: 8g ,Protein: 34g

Salmon Panatela

Servings:4

Cooking Time:22 Minutes

Ingredients:

- 1 lb skinned salmon, cut into 4 steaks each
- 1 cucumber, peeled, seeded, cubed
- Salt and black pepper to taste
- 8 black olives, pitted and chopped
- 1 tbsp capers, rinsed
- 2 large tomatoes, diced
- 3 tbsp red wine vinegar

- ¼ cup thinly sliced red onion
- 3 tbsp olive oil
- 2 slices zero carb bread, cubed
- ¼ cup thinly sliced basil leaves

Directions:

1. Preheat a grill to 350ºF and preparation are the salad. In a bowl, mix the cucumbers, olives, pepper, capers, tomatoes, wine vinegar, onion, olive oil, bread, and basil leaves. Let sit for the flavors to incorporate.
2. Season the salmon steaks with salt and pepper; grill them on both sides for 8 minutes in total. Serve the salmon steaks warm on a bed of the veggies' salad.

Nutrition:

- Calories 338, ,Fat 27g ,Net Carbs 1g ,Protein 25g

Chickpea Salad Moroccan Style

Servings:6

Cooking Time:10 Minutes

Ingredients:

- 1/3 cup crumbled low-fat feta cheese
- ¼ cup fresh mint, chopped
- ¼ cup fresh cilantro, chopped
- 1 red bell pepper, diced
- 2 plum tomatoes, diced
- 3 green onions, sliced thinly
- 1 large carrot, peeled and julienned
- 3 cups BPA free canned chickpeas or garbanzo beans
- Pinch of cayenne pepper
- ¼ tsp salt
- ¼ tsp pepper
- 2 tsp ground cumin
- 3 tbsp fresh lemon juice
- 3 tbsp olive oil

Directions:

1. Make the dressing by whisking cayenne, black pepper, salt, cumin, lemon juice and oil in a small bowl and set aside.
2. Mix together feta, mint, cilantro, red pepper, tomatoes, onions, carrots and chickpeas in a large salad bowl.
3. Pour dressing over salad and toss to coat well.
4. Serve and enjoy.

Nutrition:

- Calories per serving: 300; Protein: 13.2g; Carbs: 35.4g; Fat: 12.8g

Tilapia With Avocado & Red Onion

Servings:4

Cooking Time:15 Minutes

Ingredients:

- Olive oil (1 tbsp.)
- Sea salt (.25 tsp.)
- Fresh orange juice (1 tbsp.)
- Tilapia fillets (four 4 oz. - more rectangular than square)
- Red onion (.25 cup)
- Sliced avocado (1)
- Also Needed: 9-inch pie plate

Directions:

1. Combine the salt, juice, and oil to add into the pie dish. Work with one fillet at a time. Place it in the dish and turn to coat all sides.

2. Arrange the fillets in a wagon wheel-shaped formation. (Each of the fillets should be in the center of the dish with the other end draped over the edge.)

3. Place a tablespoon of the onion on top of each of the fillets and fold the end into the center. Cover the dish with plastic wrap, leaving one corner open to vent the steam.

4. Place in the microwave using the high heat setting for three minutes. It's done when the center can be easily flaked.

5. Top the fillets off with avocado and serve.

Nutrition:

- Calories: 200 ,Protein: 22 grams ,Fat: 11 grams

Cherry Tomato Caper Chicken

Servings:4

Cooking Time:30 Minutes

Ingredients:

- 4 chicken breasts
- 3 tablespoons olive oil
- 4 garlic cloves, chopped
- 2 cups cherry tomatoes, halved
- 1 teaspoon capers, chopped
- ½ cup black olives, pitted and sliced
- 1 thyme sprig

Directions:

1. Heat the oil in a skillet and add the chicken. Cook on high heat for 5 minutes on each side.

2. Add the rest of the ingredients and season with salt and pepper.

3. Cook in the preheated oven at 350F for 35 minutes.

4. Serve the chicken and the sauce warm and fresh

Nutrition:

- Per Serving:Calories:320 Fat:19.9g Protein:30.1g Carbohydrates:5.6g

Spanish Rice Casserole With Cheesy Beef

Servings:2

Cooking Time:32 Minutes

Ingredients:

- 2 tablespoons chopped green bell pepper
- 1/4 teaspoon Worcestershire sauce
- 1/4 teaspoon ground cumin
- 1/4 cup shredded Cheddar cheese
- 1/4 cup finely chopped onion
- 1/4 cup chile sauce
- 1/3 cup uncooked long grain rice
- 1/2-pound lean ground beef
- 1/2 teaspoon salt
- 1/2 teaspoon brown sugar
- 1/2 pinch ground black pepper
- 1/2 cup water
- 1/2 (14.5 ounce) can canned tomatoes
- 1 tablespoon chopped fresh cilantro

Directions:

1. Kvocados mit TomPlace a nonstick saucepan on medium fire and brown beef for 10 minutes while crumbling beef. Discard fat.

2. Stir in pepper, Worcestershire sauce, cumin, brown sugar, salt, chile sauce, rice, water, tomatoes, green bell pepper, and onion. Mix well and cook for 10 minutes until blended and a bit tender.

3. Transfer to an ovenproof casserole and press down firmly. Sprinkle cheese on top and cook for 7 minutes at 400oF preheated oven. Broil for 3 minutes until top is lightly browned.

4. Serve and enjoy with chopped cilantro

Nutrition:

- Calories per serving: 460; Carbohydrates: 35.8g; Protein: 37.8g; Fat: 17.9g

Artichoke Feta Penne

Servings:4
Cooking Time:30 Minutes

Ingredients:

- 8 oz. penne pasta
- 2 tablespoons olive oil
- 1 shallot, chopped
- 4 garlic cloves, chopped
- 1 jar artichoke hearts, drained and chopped
- 1 cup diced tomatoes
- ¼ cup white wine
- ½ cup vegetable stock
- Salt and pepper to taste
- 4 oz. feta cheese, crumbled

Directions:

1. Heat the oil in a skillet and stir in the shallot and garlic. Cook for 2 minutes until softened.
2. Add the artichoke hearts, tomatoes, wine and stock, as well as salt and pepper to taste.
3. Cook on low heat for 15 minutes.
4. In the meantime, cook the penne in a large pot of water until al dente, not more than 8 minutes.
5. Drain the pasta well and mix it with the artichoke sauce.
6. Serve the penne with crumbled feta cheese.

Nutrition:

- Per Serving:Calories:325 Fat:14.4g Protein:11.1g Carbohydrates:35.8g

Stuffed Eggplants

Servings:3
Cooking Time:35 Minutes

Ingredients:

- 2 eggplants, halved lengthwise and 2/3 of the flesh scooped out
- 3 tablespoons olive oil
- 1 red onion, chopped
- 2 garlic cloves, minced
- 1 pint white mushrooms, sliced
- 2 cups kale, torn
- 2 cups quinoa, cooked
- 1 tablespoon thyme, chopped
- Zest and juice of 1 lemon
- Salt and black pepper to the taste
- ½ cup Greek yogurt
- 3 tablespoons parsley, chopped

Directions:

1. Rub the inside of each eggplant half with half of the oil and arrange them on a baking sheet lined with parchment paper.
2. Heat up a pan with the rest of the oil over medium heat, add the onion and the garlic and sauté for 5 minutes.
3. Add the mushrooms and cook for 5 minutes more.
4. Add the kale, salt, pepper, thyme, lemon zest and juice, stir, cook for 5 minutes more and take off the heat.
5. Stuff the eggplant halves with the mushroom mix, introduce them in the oven and bake 400 degrees F for 20 minutes.
6. Divide the eggplants between plates, sprinkle the parsley and the yogurt on top and serve for lunch.

Nutrition:

- calories 512, fat 16.4, fiber 17.5, carbs 78, protein 17.2

Cream Cheese Artichoke Mix

Servings:6
Cooking Time:45 Minutes

Ingredients:

- 4 sheets matzo
- ½ cup artichoke hearts, canned
- 1 cup cream cheese
- 1 cup spinach, chopped
- ½ teaspoon salt
- 1 teaspoon ground black pepper
- 3 tablespoons fresh dill, chopped
- 3 eggs, beaten
- 1 teaspoon canola oil
- ½ cup cottage cheese

Directions:

1. In the bowl combine together cream cheese, spinach, salt, ground black pepper, dill, and cottage cheese.
2. Pour canola oil in the skillet, add artichoke hearts and roast them for 2-3 minutes over the medium heat. Stir them from time to time.
3. Then add roasted artichoke hearts in the cheese mixture.
4. Add eggs and stir until homogenous.
5. Place one sheet of matzo in the casserole mold.
6. Then spread it with cheese mixture generously.

7. Cover the cheese layer with the second sheet of matzo.

8. Repeat the steps till you use all ingredients.

9. Then preheat oven to 360F.

10. Bake matzo mina for 40 minutes.

11. Cut the cooked meal into the servings.

Nutrition:

- calories 272, fat 17.3, fiber 4.3, carbs 20.2, protein 11.8

Smoked Salmon And Watercress Salad

Servings:4
Cooking Time:10 Minutes

Ingredients:

- 2 bunches watercress
- 1 pound smoked salmon, skinless, boneless and flaked
- 2 teaspoons mustard
- ¼ cup lemon juice
- ½ cup Greek yogurt
- Salt and black pepper to the taste
- 1 big cucumber, sliced
- 2 tablespoons chives, chopped

Directions:

1. In a salad bowl, combine the salmon with the watercress and the rest of the ingredients toss and serve right away.

Nutrition:

- Calories 244 , Fat 16.7 g , Fiber 4.5 g , Carbs 22.5 g , Protein 15.6 g

Chicken Avocado Wrap

Servings:3
Cooking Time:2 Minutes

Ingredients:

- 3-4 cups chopped cooked chicken (boiled or grilled with minimal oil)
- 1 large tomato, chopped
- 2 avocados, chopped
- 1 cup green onions, chopped, or purple onion
- juice of 2-3 fresh limes
- 1/3 cup fresh cilantro, chopped
- 3 jalapenos, minced (more or less)

- 1 tablespoon fajita seasoning
- 10 whole wheat tortillas
- minimal monterey jack cheese, shredded

Directions:

1. Combine all ingredients except for the tortillas and cheese, mixing well.

2. Place tortillas on a baking sheet, very lightly coated with oil. Top each tortilla with a light sprinkle of cheese and bake at 400 degrees for about a minute or until cheese melts.

3. Spoon chicken mixture evenly on tortillas. Roll up and place on plate or serving platter seam side down.

Nutrition:

- Calories: 384, Fat: 19.8g, Total Carbs: 42.9g, Sugars: 3.6g, Protein: 11.7g

Turkey And Quinoa Stuffed Peppers

Servings:6
Cooking Time:55 Minutes

Ingredients:

- 3 large red bell peppers
- 2 tsp chopped fresh rosemary
- 2 tbsp chopped fresh parsley
- 3 tbsp chopped pecans, toasted
- ¼ cup extra virgin olive oil
- ½ cup chicken stock
- ½ lb. fully cooked smoked turkey sausage, diced
- ½ tsp salt
- 2 cups water
- 1 cup uncooked quinoa

Directions:

1. On high fire, place a large saucepan and add salt, water and quinoa. Bring to a boil.

2. Once boiling, reduce fire to a simmer, cover and cook until all water is absorbed around 15 minutes.

3. Uncover quinoa, turn off fire and let it stand for another 5 minutes.

4. Add rosemary, parsley, pecans, olive oil, chicken stock and turkey sausage into pan of quinoa. Mix well.

5. Slice peppers lengthwise in half and discard membranes and seeds. In another boiling pot of water, add peppers, boil for 5 minutes, drain and discard water.

6. Grease a 13 x 9 baking dish and preheat oven to 350oF.

7. Place boiled bell pepper onto preparation ared baking dish, evenly fill with the quinoa mixture and pop into oven.

8. Bake for 15 minutes.

Nutrition:

- Calories per Serving: 255.6; Carbs: 21.6g; Protein: 14.4g; Fat: 12.4g

Shrimp Soup

Servings:3
Cooking Time:5 Minutes

Ingredients:

- 1 cucumber, chopped
- 3 cups tomato juice
- 3 roasted red peppers, chopped
- 3 tablespoons olive oil
- 2 tablespoons balsamic vinegar
- 1 garlic clove, minced
- Salt and black pepper to the taste
- ½ teaspoon cumin, ground
- 1 pounds shrimp, peeled and deveined
- 1 teaspoon thyme, chopped

Directions:

1. In your blender, mix cucumber with tomato juice, red peppers, 2 tablespoons oil, the vinegar, cumin, salt, pepper and the garlic, pulse well, transfer to a bowl and keep in the fridge for 10 minutes.

2. Heat up a pot with the rest of the oil over medium heat, add the shrimp, salt, pepper and the thyme and cook for 2 minutes on each side.

3. Divide cold soup into bowls, top with the shrimp and serve.

Nutrition:

- calories 263, fat 11.1, fiber 2.4, carbs 12.5, protein 6.32

Cranberry And Roasted Squash Delight

Servings:8
Cooking Time:60 Minutes

Ingredients:

- ¼ cup chopped walnuts
- ¼ tsp thyme
- ½ tbsp chopped Italian parsley
- 1 cup diced onion

- 1 cup fresh cranberries
- 1 small orange, peeled and segmented
- 2 tsp canola oil, divided
- 4 cups cooked wild rice
- 4 cups diced winter squash, peeled and cut into ½-inch cubes
- Pepper to taste
- Grease roasting pan with cooking spray and preheat oven to 400oF.
- In preparation ped roasting pan place squash cubes, add a teaspoon of oil and toss to coat. Place in oven and roast until lightly browned, around 40 minutes.
- On medium high fire, place a nonstick fry pan and heat remaining oil. Once hot, add onions and sauté until lightly browned and tender, around 5 minutes.
- Add cranberries and continue stir frying for a minute.
- Add remaining ingredients into pan and cook until heated through around four to five minutes.
- Best served warm.

Nutrition:

- Calories per Serving: 166.2; Protein: 4.8g; Carbs: 29.1g; Fat: 3.4g

Sweet Cream Cheese Breakfast

Servings:3
Cooking Time:30 Minutes

Ingredients:

- 400 g of grainy cream cheese
- 120 g strawberries
- 100 g blueberries
- 1 tbsp lemon juice
- Fresh mint

Directions:

1. Wash and clean the strawberries and cut into small pieces. Wash blueberries.

2. Pour the cream cheese into a bowl and mix with the berries and lemon juice.

3. Wash the mint, shake dry and pluck some leaves.

4. Fill the cream cheese into two bowls, garnish with a few mint leaves and serve.

5. Note: Grainy cream cheese is recommendedparticularly for fatty liver because the fat content is low and the protein content is high. An ideal alternative is not only for breakfast, but also as a spread or instead of high-fat cheeses for warm meals.

49

Nutrition:

- Calories: 300 Total Fat: 17g Saturated Fat: 4g Cholesterol: 16mg Sodium: 59mg Total Carbohydrates: 34g Fiber: 2g Protein: 7g

Oven Vegetables With Salmon Fillet

Servings:2

Cooking Time:30 Minutes

Ingredients:

- 250 g salmon fillet
- 1 medium zucchini
- 1 red pepper
- 300 g cherry tomatoes
- 150 g mushrooms
- 100 g of low-fat feta
- 1 tbsp olive oil
- Salt and pepper

Directions:

1. Preheat the oven to 180 degrees top and bottom heat.
2. Rub the salmon fillet with salt and pepper.
3. Wash the zucchini and cut into large pieces. Wash the peppers, remove the core and cut into strips. Wash the cherry tomatoes and cut in half. Clean the mushrooms then cut off the hard stem ends and quarter. Put the vegetables and mushrooms in a bowl, drizzle with the olive oil, season with salt and pepper and mix well.
4. Drain the feta and cut into cubes.
5. Spread the vegetables in a baking dish, sprinkle with the feta cubes and serve the salmon fillet on top.
6. Cook on the middle rack for 30-35 minutes.
7. Take out of the oven, let cool down a little and serve.

Nutrition:

- Calories: 300 Total Fat: 17g Saturated Fat: 4g Cholesterol: 16mg Sodium: 59mg Total Carbohydrates: 34g Fiber: 2g Protein: 7g

Creamy Salmon Soup

Servings:6

Cooking Time:30 Minutes

Ingredients:

- 2 tablespoon olive oil
- 1 red onion, chopped
- Salt and white pepper to the taste
- 3 gold potatoes, peeled and cubed
- 2 carrots, chopped

- 4 cups fish stock
- 4 ounces salmon fillets, boneless and cubed
- ½ cup heavy cream
- 1 tablespoon dill, chopped

Directions:

1. Heat up a pan with the oil over medium heat, add the onion, and sauté for 5 minutes.
2. Add the rest of the ingredients expect the cream, salmon and the dill, bring to a simmer and cook for 5-6 minutes more.
3. Add the salmon, cream and the dill, simmer for 5 minutes more, divide into bowls and serve.

Nutrition:

- calories 214, fat 16.3, fiber 1.5, carbs 6.4, protein 11.8

Oat Risotto With Mushrooms, Kale, And Chicken

Servings:4

Cooking Time:30 Minutes

Ingredients:

- 4 cups reduced-sodium chicken broth
- 1 tablespoon extra-virgin olive oil
- 1 small onion, finely chopped
- 1 pound sliced mushrooms
- 1 pound boneless, skinless chicken thighs, cut into bite-size pieces
- 1¼ cups quick-cooking steel-cut oats
- 1 (10-ounce) package frozen chopped kale (about 4 cups)
- ½ cup grated Parmesan cheese (optional)
- Freshly ground black pepper (optional)

Directions:

1. In a medium saucepan, bring the broth to a simmer over medium-low heat.
2. Warm the olive oil in a large, nonstick skillet over medium-high heat. Sauté the onion and mushrooms until the onion is translucent, about 5 minutes. Push the vegetables to the side, and add the chicken. Let it sit untouched until it browns, about 2 minutes.
3. Add the oats. Cook for 1 minute, stirring constantly. Add ½ cup of the hot broth, and stir until it is completely absorbed. Continue stirring in broth, ½ cup at a time, until it is absorbed and the oats and chicken are cooked, about 10 minutes. If you run out of broth, switch to hot water.

4. Stir in the frozen kale, and cook until it's warm. Top with Parmesan and black pepper, if you like.

5. FLAVOR BOOST: Garnish with minced parsley and red pepper flakes. You can also substitute ½ cup dry white wine for ½ cup of the chicken broth.

6. INGREDIENT TIP: All varieties of oats have similar amounts of fiber, vitamins, and minerals. The main difference is in how quickly they're digested, with the steel-cut and old-fashioned/rolled oats breaking down more slowly, which is helpful for blood sugar control. The quick-cooking steel-cut oats used in this risotto are simply cut into smaller pieces, enabling you to make this dish in under 30 minutes.

Nutrition:

- Calories: 470 ,Total Fat: 16g ,Saturated Fat: 4g ,Cholesterol: 118mg ,Sodium: 389mg ,Carbohydrates: 44g ,Fiber: 9g ,Protein: 40g

Chickpea Fried Eggplant Salad

Servings:3
Cooking Time:10 Minutes
Ingredients:

- 1 cup chopped dill
- 1 cup chopped parsley
- 1 cup cooked or canned chickpeas, drained
- 1 large eggplant, thinly sliced (no more than 1/4 inch in thickness)
- 1 small red onion, sliced in 1/2 moons
- 1/2 English cucumber, diced
- 3 Roma tomatoes, diced
- 3 tbsp Za'atar spice, divided
- oil for frying, preferably extra virgin olive oil
- Salt
- 1 large lime, juice of
- 1/3 cup extra virgin olive oil
- 1–2 garlic cloves, minced
- Salt & Pepper to taste

Directions:

1. On a baking sheet, spread out sliced eggplant and season with salt generously. Let it sit for 30 minutes. Then pat dry with paper towel.

2. Place a small pot on medium high fire and fill halfway with oil. Heat oil for 5 minutes. Fry eggplant in batches until golden brown, around 3 minutes per side. Place cooked eggplants on a paper towel lined plate.

3. Once eggplants have cooled, assemble the eggplant on a serving dish. Sprinkle with 1 tbsp of Za'atar.

4. Mix dill, parsley, red onions, chickpeas, cucumbers, and tomatoes in a large salad bowl. Sprinkle remaining Za'atar and gently toss to mix.

5. Whisk well the vinaigrette ingredients in a small bowl. Drizzle 2 tbsp of the dressing over the fried eggplant. Add remaining dressing over the chickpea salad and mix.

6. Add the chickpea salad to the serving dish with the fried eggplant.

7. Serve and enjoy.

Nutrition:

- Calories per serving: 642; Protein: 16.6g; Carbs: 25.9g; Fat: 44.0g

Broccoli And Brown Rice Pasta Shells With Garlic

Servings:3
Cooking Time:8 Minutes
Ingredients:

- 1 large head broccoli, cut into chunks and florets (peel the stem and cut into chunks)
- 1 pound brown rice pasta shells
- 1/3 cup extra-virgin olive oil
- 2-3 large garlic cloves, minced
- crushed red pepper flakes to taste
- low sodium salt and fresh ground pepper to taste

Directions:

1. Fill a large pasta pot 3/4 full with low sodium salted water and bring to a boil. Add pasta shells and bring back to boiling.

2. Add broccoli stem chunks and let cook for about 1 minute, then add florets. Continue boiling until pasta is cooked. Strain and return to pot.

3. Meanwhile, in a large frying pan over medium heat, combine olive oil, garlic, red pepper, salt and pepper and heat until almost sizzling, but don't let the garlic brown.

4. Pour the garlic mixture over the broccoli/pasta mixture and toss until a moist sauce starts to form.

5. You can sprinkle a little bit of parmesan on top of it while serving.

Nutrition:

- Calories: 384, Fat: 19.8g, Total Carbs: 42.9g, Sugars: 3.6g, Protein: 11.7g

Easy Mozzarella & Pesto Chicken Casserole

Servings:4
Cooking Time:30 Minutes
Ingredients:

- ¼ - cup pesto
- 8 - Oz cream cheese softened
- ¼ - ½ - cup heavy cream
- 8 - Oz mozzarella cubed
- 2 - Lb cooked cubed chicken breasts
- 8 - Oz mozzarella shredded

Directions:

1. Preheat stove to 400. Splash a vast meal dish with cooking shower.

2. Consolidate the initial three fixings and blend until smooth in an extensive bowl. Include the chicken and cubed mozzarella. Exchange to the goulash dish. Sprinkle the destroyed mozzarella to finish everything.

3. Preparation are for 25-30 minutes. Present with zoodles, spinach, or squashed cauliflower.

Nutrition:

- Calories: 404 ,Fat 23g ,Net carbs: 8g ,Protein: 31g

Mexican Quinoa Bake

Servings:4
Cooking Time:40 Minutes
Ingredients:

- 3 cups sweet potato, peeled, diced very small (about 1 large sweet potato)
- 2 cups cooked quinoa
- 1 cup shredded sharp cheddar cheese
- 2 Tbs chili powder
- T Tbs paprika
- 1 1/4 cup salsa of your choice
- 1 red bell pepper, diced
- 1 large carrot, diced
- 3 Tbs canned green chiles
- 1 small onion, diced
- 3 garlic cloves, minced
- 2 cups cooked black beans

Directions:

1. Preheat oven to 400oF.

2. Dice, chop, measure and preparation all ingredients.

3. Combine all ingredients in one big bowl and toss ingredients well.

4. Spray a 9 X 13-inch pan with cooking spray and pour all ingredients in.

5. Bake for 35-40 minutes or until sweet potato pieces are slightly mushy, cheese is melted and items are heated all the way through.

6. Let sit for about 5 minutes, scoop into bowls and enjoy!

Nutrition:

- Calories per serving: 414; Carbs: 56.6g; Protein: 22.0g; Fat: 13.0g

Spaghetti In Lemon Avocado White Sauce

Servings:3
Cooking Time:30 Minutes
Ingredients:

- Freshly ground black pepper
- Zest and juice of 1 lemon
- 1 avocado, pitted and peeled
- 1-pound spaghetti
- Salt
- 1 tbsp Olive oil
- 8 oz small shrimp, shelled and deveined
- ¼ cup dry white wine
- 1 large onion, finely sliced

Directions:

1. Let a big pot of water boil. Once boiling add the spaghetti or pasta and cook following manufacturer's instructions until al dente. Drain and set aside.

2. In a large fry pan, over medium fire sauté wine and onions for ten minutes or until onions are translucent and soft.

3. Add the shrimps into the fry pan and increase fire to high while constantly sautéing until shrimps are cooked around five minutes. Turn the fire off. Season with salt and add the oil right away. Then quickly toss in the cooked pasta, mix well.

4. In a blender, until smooth, puree the lemon juice and avocado. Pour into the fry pan of pasta, combine well. Garnish with pepper and lemon zest then serve.

Nutrition:

- Calories per Serving: 206; Carbs: 26.3g; Protein: 10.2g; Fat: 8.0g

Lipsmacking Chicken Tetrazzini

Servings:3

Cooking Time:3hours

Ingredients:

- Toasted French bread slices
- ¾ cup thinly sliced green onion
- 2/3 cup grated parmesan cheese
- 10 oz dried spaghetti or linguine, cooked and drained
- ¼ tsp ground nutmeg
- ¼ tsp ground black pepper
- 2 tbsp dry sherry
- ¼ cup chicken broth or water
- 1 16oz jar of Alfredo pasta sauce
- 2 4.5oz jars of sliced mushrooms, drained
- 2.5 lbs. skinless chicken breasts cut into ½ inch slices

Directions:

1. In a slow cooker, mix mushrooms and chicken.

2. In a bowl, mix well nutmeg, pepper, sherry, broth and alfredo sauce before pouring over chicken and mushrooms.

3. Set on high heat, cover and cook for two to three hours.

4. Once chicken is cooked, pour over pasta, garnish with green onion and serve with French bread on the side.

Nutrition:

- Calories per Serving: 505; Carbs: 24.7g; Protein: 35.1g; Fat: 30.2g

Red Cabbage Tilapia Taco Bowl

Servings:4

Cooking Time:20 Minutes

Ingredients:

- 2 cups caulis rice
- 2 tsp ghee
- 4 tilapia fillets, cut into cubes
- ¼ tsp taco seasoning
- Salt and chili pepper to taste
- ¼ head red cabbage, shredded
- 1 ripe avocado, pitted and chopped

Directions:

1. Sprinkle caulis rice in a bowl with a little water and microwave for 3 minutes. Fluff after with a fork and set aside. Melt ghee in a skillet over medium heat, rub the tilapia with the taco seasoning, salt, and chili pepper, and fry until brown on all sides, for about 8 minutes in total.

2. Transfer to a plate and set aside. In 4 serving bowls, share the caulis rice, cabbage, fish, and avocado. Serve with chipotle lime sour cream dressing.

Nutrition:

- Calories 269, ,Fat 24g ,Net Carbs 4g ,Protein 15g

Chicken Skillet

Servings:3

Cooking Time:35 Minutes

Ingredients:

- 6 chicken thighs, bone-in and skin-on
- Juice of 2 lemons
- 1 teaspoon oregano, dried
- 1 red onion, chopped
- Salt and black pepper to the taste
- 1 teaspoon garlic powder
- 2 garlic cloves, minced
- 2 tablespoons olive oil
- 2 and ½ cups chicken stock
- 1 cup white rice
- 1 tablespoon oregano, chopped
- 1 cup green olives, pitted and sliced
- 1/3 cup parsley, chopped
- ½ cup feta cheese, crumbled

Directions:

1. Heat up a pan with the oil over medium heat, add the chicken thighs skin side down, cook for 4 minutes on each side and transfer to a plate.

2. Add the garlic and the onion to the pan, stir and sauté for 5 minutes.

3. Add the rice, salt, pepper, the stock, oregano, and lemon juice, stir, cook for 1-2 minutes more and take off the heat.

4. Add the chicken to the pan, introduce the pan in the oven and bake at 375 degrees F for 25 minutes.

5. Add the cheese, olives and the parsley, divide the whole mix between plates and serve for lunch.

Nutrition:

- calories 435, fat 18.5, fiber 13.6, carbs 27.8, protein 25.6

Prosciutto Balls

Servings:4

Cooking Time:10 Minutes

Ingredients:

- 8 Mozzarella balls, cherry size
- 4 oz bacon, sliced
- ¼ teaspoon ground black pepper
- ¾ teaspoon dried rosemary
- 1 teaspoon butter

Directions:

1. Sprinkle the sliced bacon with ground black pepper and dried rosemary.
2. Wrap every Mozzarella ball in the sliced bacon and secure them with toothpicks.
3. Melt butter.
4. Brush wrapped Mozzarella balls with butter.
5. Line the tray with the baking paper and arrange Mozzarella balls in it.
6. Bake the meal for 10 minutes at 365F.

Nutrition:

- calories 323, fat 26.8, fiber 0.1, carbs 0.6, protein 20.6

Simple Penne Anti-pasto

Servings:5

Cooking Time:15 Minutes

Ingredients:

- ¼ cup pine nuts, toasted
- ½ cup grated Parmigiano-Reggiano cheese, divided
- 8oz penne pasta, cooked and drained
- 1 6oz jar drained, sliced, marinated and quartered artichoke hearts
- 1 7 oz jar drained and chopped sun-dried tomato halves packed in oil
- 3 oz chopped prosciutto
- 1/3 cup pesto
- ½ cup pitted and chopped Kalamata olives
- 1 medium red bell pepper

Directions:

1. Slice bell pepper, discard membranes, seeds and stem. On a foiled lined baking sheet, place bell pepper halves, press down by hand and broil in oven for eight minutes. Remove from oven, put in a sealed bag for 5 minutes before peeling and chopping.

2. Place chopped bell pepper in a bowl and mix in artichokes, tomatoes, prosciutto, pesto and olives.
3. Toss in ¼ cup cheese and pasta. Transfer to a serving dish and garnish with ¼ cup cheese and pine nuts. Serve and enjoy!

Nutrition:

- Calories per Serving: 606; Carbs: 70.3g; Protein: 27.2g; Fat: 27.6g

Bell Peppers 'n Tomato-chickpea Rice

Servings:4

Cooking Time:35 Minutes

Ingredients:

- 2 tablespoons olive oil
- 1/2 chopped red bell pepper
- 1/2 chopped green bell pepper
- 1/2 chopped yellow pepper
- 1/2 chopped red pepper
- 1 medium onion, chopped
- 1 clove garlic, minced
- 2 cups cooked jasmine rice
- 1 teaspoon tomato paste
- 1 cup chickpeas
- salt to taste
- 1/2 teaspoon paprika
- 1 small tomato, chopped
- Parsley for garnish

Directions:

1. In a large mixing bowl, whisk well olive oil, garlic, tomato paste, and paprika. Season with salt generously.
2. Mix in rice and toss well to coat in the dressing.
3. Add remaining ingredients and toss well to mix.
4. Let salad rest to allow flavors to mix for 15 minutes.
5. Toss one more time and adjust salt to taste if needed.
6. Garnish with parsley and serve.

Nutrition:

- Calories per serving: 490; Carbs: 93.0g; Protein: 10.0g; Fat: 8.0g

Chicken With Potatoes Olives & Sprouts

Servings:4
Cooking Time:35 Minutes
Ingredients:

- 1 lb. chicken breasts, skinless, boneless, and cut into pieces
- ¼ cup olives, quartered
- 1 tsp oregano
- 1 ½ tsp Dijon mustard
- 1 lemon juice
- 1/3 cup vinaigrette dressing
- 1 medium onion, diced
- 3 cups potatoes cut into pieces
- 4 cups Brussels sprouts, trimmed and quartered
- ¼ tsp pepper
- ¼ tsp salt

Directions:

1. Warm-up oven to 400 F. Place chicken in the center of the baking tray, then place potatoes, sprouts, and onions around the chicken.
2. In a small bowl, mix vinaigrette, oregano, mustard, lemon juice, and salt and pour over chicken and veggies. Sprinkle olives and season with pepper.
3. Bake in preheated oven for 20 minutes. Transfer chicken to a plate. Stir the vegetables and roast for 15 minutes more. Serve and enjoy.

Nutrition:

- Calories: 397 ,Fat: 13g ,Protein: 38.3g ,Carbs: 31.4g ,Sodium 175 mg

Spiced Seared Scallops With Lemon Relish

Servings:3
Cooking Time:40 Minutes
Ingredients:

- 2 pounds scallops, cleaned
- ½ teaspoon cumin powder
- ¼ teaspoon ground ginger
- ½ teaspoon ground coriander
- ½ teaspoon smoked paprika
- ½ teaspoon salt
- 3 tablespoons olive oil

Directions:

1. Pat the scallops dry with a paper towel.
2. Sprinkle them with spices and salt.
3. Heat the oil in a skillet and place half of the scallops in the hot oil. Cook for 1-2 minutes per side, just until the scallops look golden brown on the sides.
4. Remove the scallops and place the remaining ones in the hot oil.
5. Serve the scallops warm and fresh with your favorite side dish.

Nutrition:

- Per Serving:Calories:292 Fat:12.3g Protein:38.2g Carbohydrates:5.7g

Squash And Eggplant Casserole

Servings:2
Cooking Time:45 Minutes
Ingredients:

- ½ cup dry white wine
- 1 eggplant, halved and cut to 1-inch slices
- 1 large onion, cut into wedges
- 1 red bell pepper, seeded and cut to julienned strips
- 1 small butternut squash, cut into 1-inch slices
- 1 tbsp olive oil
- 12 baby corn
- 2 cups low sodium vegetable broth
- Salt and pepper to taste
- ¼ cup parmesan cheese, grated
- 1 cup instant polenta
- 2 tbsp fresh oregano, chopped
- 1 garlic clove, chopped
- 2 tbsp slivered almonds
- 5 tbsp parsley, chopped
- Grated zest of 1 lemon

Directions:

1. Preheat the oven to 350 degrees Fahrenheit.
2. In a casserole, heat the oil and add the onion wedges and baby corn. Sauté over medium high heat for five minutes. Stir occasionally to prevent the onions and baby corn from sticking at the bottom of the pan.
3. Add the butternut squash to the casserole and toss the vegetables. Add the eggplants and the red pepper.
4. Cover the vegetables and cook over low to medium heat.

5. Cook for about ten minutes before adding the wine. Let the wine sizzle before stirring in the broth. Bring to a boil and cook in the oven for 30 minutes.

6. While the casserole is cooking inside the oven, make the topping by spreading the slivered almonds on a baking tray and toasting under the grill until they are lightly browned.

7. Place the toasted almonds in a small bowl and mix the remaining ingredients for the toppings.

8. Preparation are the polenta. In a large saucepan, bring 3 cups of water to boil over high heat.

9. Add the polenta and continue whisking until it absorbs all the water.

10. Reduce the heat to medium until the polenta is thick. Add the parmesan cheese and oregano.

11. Serve the polenta on plates and add the casserole on top. Sprinkle the toppings on top.

Nutrition:

- Calories per Serving: 579.3; Carbs: 79.2g; Protein: 22.2g; Fat: 19.3g

Vegetable Ribbon Noodles With Chicken Breast Fillet

Servings:2
Cooking Time:30 Minutes
Ingredients:

- 250 g chicken breast fillet
- 1 medium-sized carrot
- 2 small zucchini
- 2 medium-sized tomatoes
- 1 tbsp tomato paste
- 50 ml vegetable broth
- 1 tbsp olive oil
- ½ teaspoon paprika powder
- Salt and pepper

Directions:

1. Cut the chicken breast fillet into bite-sized pieces. Heat the olive oil in a pan and add the paprika powder. Now sear the meat until it is completely cooked through. Season with a little salt and pepper.

2. In the meantime, wash and peel the carrots and cut lengthways into thin strips. Wash the zucchini and cut lengthways into thin strips.

3. Take the chicken out of the pan and sear the vegetable noodles in the remaining gravy for 3-4 minutes.

4. Wash tomatoes and cut into small pieces. Then add to the vegetable noodles together with the tomato paste. Simmer for 3-4 minutes over medium heat. Season to taste with salt and pepper.

5. Add the chicken pieces and sear everything for 2-3 minutes.

6. Arrange on two plates and serve.

Nutrition:

- Calories: 300 Total Fat: 17g Saturated Fat: 4g Cholesterol: 16mg Sodium: 59mg Total Carbohydrates: 34g Fiber: 2g Protein: 7g

Chicken Stuffed Peppers

Servings:6
Cooking Time:10 Minutes
Ingredients:

- 1 cup Greek yogurt
- 2 tablespoons mustard
- Salt and black pepper to the taste
- 1 pound rotisserie chicken meat, cubed
- 4 celery stalks, chopped
- 2 tablespoons balsamic vinegar
- 1 bunch scallions, sliced
- ¼ cup parsley, chopped
- 1 cucumber, sliced
- 3 red bell peppers, halved and deseeded
- 1 pint cherry tomatoes, quartered

Directions:

1. In a bowl, mix the chicken with the celery and the rest of the ingredients except the bell peppers and toss well.

2. Stuff the peppers halves with the chicken mix and serve for lunch.

Nutrition:

- calories 266, fat 12.2, fiber 4.5, carbs 15.7, protein 3.7

Herbed Roasted Cod

Servings:3
Cooking Time:45 Minutes
Ingredients:

- 4 cod fillets
- 4 parsley sprigs
- 2 cilantro sprigs
- 2 basil sprigs

- 1 lemon, sliced
- Salt and pepper to taste
- 2 tablespoons olive oil

Directions:

1. Place the parsley, cilantro, basil and lemon slices at the bottom of a deep dish baking pan.

2. Place the cod over the herbs and cook in the preheated oven at 350F for 15 minutes.

3. Serve the cod warm and fresh with your favorite side dish.

Nutrition:

- Per Serving:Calories:192 Fat:8.1g Protein:28.6g Carbohydrates:0.1g

Tasty Lime Cilantro Cauliflower Rice

Servings:3
Cooking Time:10 Minutes

Ingredients:

- 1 head cauliflower, rinsed
- 1 tablespoon extra-virgin olive oil
- 2 garlic cloves, minced
- 2 scallions, chopped
- ½ teaspoon sea salt
- Pinch of pepper
- 4 tablespoons fresh lime juice
- 1/4 cup chopped fresh cilantro

Directions:

1. Chop cauliflower into florets and transfer to a food processor; pulse into rice texture.

2. Heat a large skillet over medium heat and add olive oil; sauté garlic and scallions for about 4 minutes or until fragrant and tender.

3. Increase heat to medium high and stir in cauliflower rice; cook, covered, for about 6 minutes or until cauliflower is crispy on outside and soft inside.

4. Season with salt and pepper and transfer to a bowl. Toss with freshly squeezed lime juice and cilantro and serve right away.

Nutrition:

- Calories: 300 Total Fat: 17g Saturated Fat: 4g Cholesterol: 16mg Sodium: 59mg Total Carbohydrates: 34g Fiber: 2g Protein: 7g

Garlic Clove Roasted Chicken

Servings:5
Cooking Time:40 Minutes

Ingredients:

- 8 chicken legs
- 40 garlic cloves, crushed
- 1 shallot, sliced
- ½ cup white wine
- 1 bay leaf
- 1 thyme sprig
- Salt and pepper to taste

Directions:

1. Season the chicken with salt and pepper.

2. Combine it with the rest of the ingredients in a deep dish baking pan.

3. Cover the pan with aluminum foil and cook in the preheated oven at 350F for 1 hour.

4. Serve the chicken warm and fresh.

Nutrition:

- Per Serving:Calories:225 Fat:7.5g Protein:29.9g Carbohydrates:5.6g

Quinoa & Black Bean Stuffed Sweet Potatoes

Servings:8
Cooking Time:60 Minutes

Ingredients:

- 4 sweet potatoes
- ½ onion, diced
- 1 garlic glove, crushed and diced
- ½ large bell pepper diced (about 2/3 cups)
- Handful of diced cilantro
- ½ cup cooked quinoa
- ½ cup black beans
- 1 tbsp olive oil
- 1 tbsp chili powder
- ½ tbsp cumin
- ½ tbsp paprika
- ½ tbsp oregano
- 2 tbsp lime juice
- 2 tbsp honey
- Sprinkle salt
- 1 cup shredded cheddar cheese
- Chopped spring onions, for garnish (optional)

Directions:

1. Preheat oven to 400oF.

2. Wash and scrub outside of potatoes. Poke with fork a few times and then place on parchment paper on cookie sheet. Bake for 40-45 minutes or until it is cooked.

3. While potatoes are baking, sauté onions, garlic, olive oil and spices in a pan on the stove until onions are translucent and soft.

4. In the last 10 minutes while the potatoes are cooking, in a large bowl combine the onion mixture with the beans, quinoa, honey, lime juice, cilantro and ½ cup cheese. Mix well.

5. When potatoes are cooked, remove from oven and let cool slightly. When cool to touch, cut in half (hot dog style) and scoop out most of the insides. Leave a thin ring of potato so that it will hold its shape. You can save the sweet potato guts for another recipe, such as my veggie burgers (recipe posted below).

6. Fill with bean and quinoa mixture. Top with remaining cheddar cheese.

7. (If making this a freezer meal, stop here. Individually wrap potato skins in plastic wrap and place on flat surface to freeze. Once frozen, place all potatoes in large zip lock container or Tupperware.)

8. Return to oven for an additional 10 minutes or until cheese is melted

Nutrition:

*   Calories per serving: 243; Carbs: 37.6g; Protein: 8.5g; Fat: 7.3g

Halloumi, Grape Tomato And Zucchini Skewers With Spinach-basil Oil

Servings:3

Cooking Time:10 Minutes

Ingredients:

*   1 large zucchini, halved lengthways, cut into 8 pieces
*   16 grape tomatoes
*   180 g halloumi cheese, cut into 16 pieces
*   Olive oil spray
*   For the spinach-basil oil:
*   2 cups baby spinach leaves
*   2 cups fresh basil leaves
*   185 ml (3/4 cup) extra-virgin olive oil
*   125 ml (1/2 cup) light olive oil

Directions:

1. In a saucepan of boiling water, cook the spinach and the basil for about 30 seconds or until just wilted. Drain and cool under running cold water.

2. Place the cooked spinach and basil into a food processor. Add the light olive oil and the extra-virgin olive oil; process until the mixture is smooth. Transfer into an airtight container, refrigerate for 8 hours to develop the flavors.

3. Preheat the barbecue grill to medium-high.

4. Thread a piece of zucchini, halloumi cheese, and tomato into each skewer. Lightly spray with the olive oil spray.

5. Grill for about4 minutes per side or until cooked through and golden brown.

6. Arrange the grilled skewers on to serving platter; serve immediately with the preparation ared spinach-basil oil.

Nutrition:

*   192.2Cal, 20 g total fat (4 g sat. fat), 1 g carb., 1 g fiber, 1 g sugar, 3 g protein, and 328.8 mg sodium.

Low Carb Berry Salad With Citrus Dressing

Servings:3

Cooking Time:10 Minutes

Ingredients:

*   Salad:
*   ¼ cup blueberries
*   ½ cup chopped strawberries
*   1 cup mixed greens (kale and chard)
*   2 cups baby spinach
*   2 chopped green onions
*   ½ cup chopped avocado
*   1 shredded carrots
*   Citrus Dressing:
*   1 tablespoon extra-virgin olive oil
*   2 tablespoons apple cider vinegar
*   ¼ cup fresh orange juice
*   5 strawberries chopped

Directions:

1. In a blender, blend together all dressing ingredients until very smooth; set aside.

2. Combine all salad ingredients in a large bowl; drizzle with dressing and toss to coat well before serving.

Nutrition:

- Calories: 300 Total Fat: 17g Saturated Fat: 4g Cholesterol: 16mg Sodium: 59mg Total Carbohydrates: 34g Fiber: 2g Protein: 7g

Cajun Garlic Shrimp Noodle Bowl

Servings:2

Cooking Time:15 Minutes

Ingredients:

- ½ teaspoon salt
- 1 onion, sliced
- 1 red pepper, sliced
- 1 tablespoon butter
- 1 teaspoon garlic granules
- 1 teaspoon onion powder
- 1 teaspoon paprika
- 2 large zucchinis, cut into noodle strips
- 20 jumbo shrimps, shells removed and deveined
- 3 cloves garlic, minced
- 3 tablespoon ghee
- A dash of cayenne pepper
- A dash of red pepper flake

Directions:

1. Preparation are the Cajun seasoning by mixing the onion powder, garlic granules, pepper flakes, cayenne pepper, paprika and salt. Toss in the shrimp to coat in the seasoning.
2. In a skillet, heat the ghee and sauté the garlic. Add in the red pepper and onions and continue sautéing for 4 minutes.
3. Add the Cajun shrimp and cook until opaque. Set aside.
4. In another pan, heat the butter and sauté the zucchini noodles for three minutes.
5. Assemble by the placing the Cajun shrimps on top of the zucchini noodles.

Nutrition:

- Calories: 712 ,Fat: 30.0g ,Protein: 97.8g ,Carbs: 20.2g

Tarragon Cod Fillets

Servings:4

Cooking Time:12 Minutes

Ingredients:

- 4 cod fillets, boneless
- ¼ cup capers, drained

- 1 tablespoon tarragon, chopped
- Sea salt and black pepper to the taste
- 2 tablespoons olive oil
- 2 tablespoons parsley, chopped
- 1 tablespoon olive oil
- 1 tablespoon lemon juice

Directions:

1. Heat up a pan with the oil over medium-high heat, add the fish and cook for 3 minutes on each side.
2. Add the rest of the ingredients, cook everything for 7 minutes more, divide between plates and serve.

Nutrition:

- Calories 162 ,Fat 9.6 g ,Fiber 4.3 g ,Carbs 12.4 g ,Protein 16.5 g

Kidney Bean And Parsley-lemon Salad

Servings:6

Cooking Time:10 Minutes

Ingredients:

- ¼ cup lemon juice (about 1 ½ lemons)
- ¼ cup olive oil
- ¾ cup chopped fresh parsley
- ¾ teaspoon salt
- 1 can (15 ounces) chickpeas, rinsed and drained, or 1 ½ cups cooked chickpeas
- 1 medium cucumber, peeled, seeded and diced
- 1 small red onion, diced
- 2 cans (15 ounces each) red kidney beans, rinsed and drained, or 3 cups cooked kidney beans
- 2 stalks celery, sliced in half or thirds lengthwise and chopped
- 2 tablespoons chopped fresh dill or mint
- 3 cloves garlic, pressed or minced
- Small pinch red pepper flakes

Directions:

1. Whisk well in a small bowl the pepper flakes, salt, garlic, and lemon juice until emulsified.
2. In a serving bowl, combine the preparation ared kidney beans, chickpeas, onion, celery, cucumber, parsley and dill (or mint).
3. Drizzle salad with the dressing and toss well to coat.
4. Serve and enjoy.

Nutrition:

- Calories per serving: 228; Protein: 8.5g; Carbs: 26.2g; Fat: 11.0g

Garlic Mushroom Chicken

Servings:4

Cooking Time:15 Minutes

Ingredients:

- 3 garlic cloves, minced
- 1 onion, chopped
- 2 cups mushrooms, sliced
- 1 tbsp olive oil
- ½ cup chicken stock
- ¼ tsp pepper
- ½ tsp salt

Directions:

1. Season chicken with pepper and salt. Warm oil in a pan on medium heat, then put season chicken in the pan and cook for 5-6 minutes on each side. Remove and place on a plate.

2. Add onion and mushrooms to the pan and sauté until tender, about 2-3 minutes. Add garlic and sauté for a minute. Add stock and bring to boil. Stir well and cook for 1-2 minutes. Pour over chicken and serve.

Nutrition:

- Calories: 331 ,Fat: 14.5g ,Protein: 43.9g ,Carbs: 4.6g ,Sodium 420 mg

Pan Roasted Chicken With Olives And Lemon

Servings:4

Cooking Time:50 Minutes

Ingredients:

- 4 chicken legs
- Salt and pepper to taste
- 3 tablespoons olive oil
- 1 lemon, juiced
- 1 orange, juiced
- 1 jalapeno, sliced
- 2 garlic cloves, chopped
- ½ cup green olives, sliced
- ¼ cup black olives, pitted and sliced
- 1 thyme sprig
- 1 rosemary sprig

Directions:

1. Season the chicken with salt and pepper.

2. Heat the oil in a skillet and add the chicken.

3. Cook on each side for 5 minutes until golden brown then add the rest of the ingredients and continue cooking on medium heat for15 minutes.

4. Serve the chicken and the sauce warm

Nutrition:

- Per Serving:Calories:319 Fat:18.9g Protein:29.7g Carbohydrates:8.0g

Green Smoothie Bowl

Servings:3

Cooking Time:15 Inutes

Ingredients:

- 200 g natural yogurt (1.5% fat)
- 1 medium apple
- 4 apricots
- 2 tbsp oatmeal
- 50 g fresh baby spinach
- 1 tbsp ground flaxseed

Directions:

1. Wash the spinach, remove the dead leaves and pat dry with a piece of kitchen paper. Wash apricots, remove stones and cut into small pieces. Wash, quarter and core the apple. Then cut into small pieces.

2. Put the spinach and fruit in a bowl and puree with a hand blender.

3. Divide the yoghurt into two bowls and pour the green mixture over them. Sprinkle with the oatmeal and flaxseed and serve.

Nutrition:

- Calories: 300 Total Fat: 17g Saturated Fat: 4g Cholesterol: 16mg Sodium: 59mg Total Carbohydrates: 34g Fiber: 2g Protein: 7g

Chicken Souvlaki 2

Servings:3

Cooking Time:30 Minutes

Ingredients:

- 4-6 chicken breasts, boneless, skinless
- For the marinade:
- 1 tablespoon dried oregano (use Greek or Turkish oregano)
- 1 tablespoon garlic, finely minced (or garlic puree from a jar)
- 1 tablespoon red wine vinegar
- 1 teaspoon dried thyme

- 1/2 cup lemon juice, freshly squeezed
- 1/2 cup olive oil

Directions:

1. If there are any visible fat on the chicken, trim them off. Cut each breasts into 5-6 pieces 1-inch thick crosswise strips. Put them in a Ziploc bag or a container with tight lid.

2. Whisk the marinade ingredients together until combined. Pour into the bag or container with the chicken, seal, and shake the bag or the container to coat the chicken. Marinade for 6 to 8 hours or more in the refrigerator.

3. When marinated, remove the chicken from the fridge, let thaw to room temperature, and drain; discard the marinade. Thread the chicken strips into skewers, about 6 pieces on each skewer, the meat folded over to it would not spin around on the skewers.

4. Mist the grill with olive oil. Preheat the charcoal or gas grill to medium high.

5. Grill the skewers for about 12-15 minutes, turning once as soon as you see grill marks. Souvlaki is done when the chicken is slightly browned and firm, but not hard to the touch.

Nutrition:

- 360 cal., 26 g total fat (4.5 g sat fat), 90 mg chol., 170 mg sodium, 570 mg potassium, 3 g carb., 0 g fiber, <1 g sugar, and 30 g protein.

Salmon Parmesan Gratin

Servings:3

Cooking Time:45 Minutes

Ingredients:

- 4 salmon fillets, cubed
- 2 garlic cloves, chopped
- 1 fennel bulb, sliced
- ½ teaspoon ground coriander
- ½ teaspoon Dijon mustard
- ½ cup vegetable stock
- 1 cup heavy cream
- 2 eggs
- Salt and pepper to taste
- 1 cup grated Parmesan cheese

Directions:

1. Combine the salmon, garlic, fennel, coriander and mustard in a small deep dish baking pan.

2. Mix the eggs with cream and stock and pour the mixture over the fish.

3. Top with Parmesan cheese and bake in the preheated oven at 350F for 25 minutes.

4. Serve the gratin right away.

Nutrition:

- Per Serving:Calories:414 Fat:25.9g Protein:41.0g Carbohydrates:6.1g

Flank Steak

Servings:3

Cooking Time:40 Minutes

Ingredients:

- 4 flank steaks
- 1 lemon, juiced
- 1 orange, juiced
- 4 garlic cloves, chopped
- 1 teaspoon Dijon mustard
- 1 teaspoon chopped thyme
- 1 teaspoon dried sage
- 2 tablespoons olive oil
- Salt and pepper to taste

Directions:

1. Combine the flank steaks and the rest of the ingredients in a zip lock bag.

2. Refrigerate for 30 minutes.

3. Heat a grill pan over medium flame and place the steaks on the grill.

4. Cook on each side for 6-7 minutes.

5. Serve the steaks warm and fresh.

Nutrition:

- Per Serving:Calories:234 Fat:13.4g Protein:21.6g Carbohydrates:6.7g

Grilled Basil-lemon Tofu Burgers

Servings:5

Cooking Time:6 Minutes

Ingredients:

- 6 slices (1/4-inch thick each) tomato
- 6 pieces (1 1/2-ounce) whole-wheat hamburger buns
- 1 pound tofu, firm or extra-firm, drained
- 1 cup watercress, trimmed
- Cooking spray
- 1/3 cup fresh basil, finely chopped
- 2 tablespoons Dijon mustard

- 2 tablespoons honey
- 1/4 cup freshly squeezed lemon juice
- 2 teaspoons grated lemon rind
- 1 tablespoon olive oil, extra-virgin,
- 1/2 teaspoon salt
- 1/4 teaspoon black pepper (freshly ground)
- 3 garlic cloves, minced
- 1 garlic cloves, minced
- 1/3 cup Kalamata olives, finely, chopped pitted
- 3 tablespoons sour cream, reduced-fat
- 3 tablespoons light mayonnai

Directions:

1. Combine the marinade ingredients in a small-sized bowl. In a crosswise direction, cut the tofu into 6 slices. Pat each piece dry using paper towels. Place them in a jelly roll pan and brush both sides of the slices with the marinade mixture; reserve any leftover marinade. Marinate for 1 hour.

2. Preheat the grill and coated the grill rack with cooking spray. Place the tofu slices; grill for about 3 minutes per side, brushing the tofu with the reserved marinade mixture.

3. In a small-sized bowl, combine the garlic-olive mayonnaise ingredients. Spread about 1 1/2 tablespoons of the mixture over the bottom half of the hamburger buns. Top each with 1 slice tofu, 1 slice tomato, about 2 tablespoons of watercress, and top with the top buns.

Nutrition:

- 276 Cal, 11.3 g total fat (1.9 g sat. fat, 5.7 g mono fat, 2.2 g poly fat), 10.5 g protein, 34.5 g carb., 1.5 g fiber, 5 mg chol., 2.4 mg iron, 743 mg sodium, and 101 mg calcium.

Cleansing Vegetable Broth

Servings:6
Cooking Time:20 Minutes
Ingredients:

- 1/4 cup water
- 2 cloves garlic, minced
- 1/2 cup chopped red onion
- 1 tablespoon minced fresh ginger
- 1 cup chopped tomatoes
- 1 small head of broccoli, chopped into florets
- 3 medium carrots, diced
- 3 celery stalks, diced

- 1/8 teaspoon cayenne pepper
- 1/4 teaspoon cinnamon
- 1 teaspoon turmeric
- Sea salt and pepper
- 6 cups vegetable broth
- ¼ cup fresh lemon juice
- 1 cup chopped purple cabbage
- 2 cups chopped kale

Directions:

1. Boil ¼ cup of water in a large pot; add garlic and onion and sauté for about 2 minutes, stirring.

2. Stir in ginger, tomatoes, broccoli, carrots and celery and cook for about 3 minutes. Stir in spices.

3. Add in vegetable broth and bring the mixture to a boil; lower heat and simmer for about 15 minutes or until veggies are tender.

4. Stir in lemon juice, cabbage and kale and cook for about 2 minutes or until kale is wilted. Adjust the seasoning and serve hot.

Nutrition:

- Calories: 300 Total Fat: 17g Saturated Fat: 4g Cholesterol: 16mg Sodium: 59mg Total Carbohydrates: 34g Fiber: 2g Protein: 7g

Italian White Bean Soup

Servings:4
Cooking Time:50 Minutes
Ingredients:

- 1 (14 ounce) can chicken broth
- 1 bunch fresh spinach, rinsed and thinly sliced
- 1 clove garlic, minced
- 1 stalk celery, chopped
- 1 tablespoon lemon juice
- 1 tablespoon vegetable oil
- 1 onion, chopped
- 1/4 teaspoon ground black pepper
- 1/8 teaspoon dried thyme
- 2 (16 ounce) cans white kidney beans, rinsed and drained
- 2 cups water

Directions:

1. Place a pot on medium high fire and heat pot for a minute. Add oil and heat for another minute.

2. Stir in celery and onion. Sauté for 7 minutes.

3. Stir in garlic and cook for another minute.

4. Add water, thyme, pepper, chicken broth, and beans. Cover and simmer for 15 minutes.

5. Remove 2 cups of the bean and celery mixture with a slotted spoon and set aside.

6. With an immersion blender, puree remaining soup in pot until smooth and creamy.

7. Return the 2 cups of bean mixture. Stir in spinach and lemon juice. Cook for 2 minutes until heated through and spinach is wilted.

8. Serve and enjoy.

Nutrition:

- Calories per serving: 245; Protein: 12.0g; Carbs: 38.1g; Fat: 4.9g

Turkey Fritters And Sauce

Servings:3
Cooking Time:30 Minutes

Directions:

1. Heat up a pan with 1 tablespoon oil over medium heat, add the onion and the garlic, sauté for 5 minutes, cool down and transfer to a bowl.

2. Add the meat, turkey, oregano and pepper flakes, stir and shape medium fritters out of this mix.

3. Heat up another pan greased with cooking spray over medium-high heat, add the turkey fritters and brown for 5 minutes on each side.

4. Introduce the pan in the oven and bake the fritters at 375 degrees F for 15 minutes more.

5. Meanwhile, in a bowl, mix the yogurt with the cucumber, oil, garlic powder, lemon juice and parsley and whisk really well.

6. Divide the fritters between plates, spread the sauce all over and serve for lunch.

Nutrition:

- calories 364, fat 16.8, fiber 5.5, carbs 26.8, protein 23.4

Cream Cheese Tart

Servings:6
Cooking Time:20 Minutes

Ingredients:

- 1 cup wheat flour, whole grain
- ½ teaspoon salt
- 1/3 cup butter, softened
- 1 cup Mozzarella, shredded
- 3 tablespoons chives, chopped
- 1 tablespoon cream cheese
- ½ teaspoon ground paprika
- 4 eggs, beaten
- 1 teaspoon dried oregano

Directions:

1. In the mixer bowl combine together flour and salt. Add butter and blend the mixture until you get non-sticky dough or knead it with the help of the fingertips.

2. Roll up the dough and arrange it in the round tart mold.

3. Flatten it gently and bake for 10 minutes at 365F.

4. Meanwhile, mix up together eggs with Mozzarella cheese, cream cheese, and chives.

5. Remove the tart crust from the oven and chill for 5-10 minutes.

6. Then place the cheese mixture in the tart crust and flatten it well with the help of a spatula.

7. Bake the tart for 10 minutes.

8. Use the kitchen torch to make the grilled tart surface.

9. Chill the cooked tart well and only after this slice it onto the servings.

Nutrition:

- calories 229, fat 14.8, fiber 0.8, carbs 16.7, protein 7.5

Beef Bourguignon

Servings:3
Cooking Time:2 Hours

Ingredients:

- 3 tablespoons olive oil
- 2 pounds beef roast, cubed
- 1 tablespoon all-purpose flour
- 3 sweet onions, chopped
- 2 carrots, sliced
- 4 garlic cloves, minced
- 1 chili pepper, sliced
- 1 pound button mushrooms
- 1 ½ cups beef stock
- ½ cup dark beer
- 2 bay leaves
- 1 thyme sprig
- 1 rosemary sprig
- Salt and pepper to taste

Directions:

1. Sprinkle the beef with flour.

2. Heat the oil in a deep heavy pot and add the beef roast.

3. Cook on all sides for 5 minutes or until browned.

4. Add the onions, carrots and chili and cook for 5 more minutes.

5. Add the mushrooms, stock, beer, bay leaves, thyme, rosemary, salt and pepper.

6. Cover the pot and cook on low heat for 1 ½ hours.

7. Serve the stew warm and fresh.

Nutrition:

- Per Serving:Calories:306 Fat:12.6g Protein:37.6g Carbohydrates:9.0g

Fried Chicken With Tzatziki Sauce

Servings:4

Cooking Time:30 Minutes

Ingredients:

- 4 chicken breasts, cubed
- 4 tablespoons olive oil
- 1 teaspoon dried basil
- 1 teaspoon dried oregano
- ½ teaspoon chili flakes
- Salt and pepper to taste
- 1 cup Greek yogurt
- 1 cucumber, grated
- 4 garlic cloves, minced
- 1 teaspoon lemon juice
- 1 teaspoon chopped mint
- 2 tablespoons chopped parsley

Directions:

1. Season the chicken with salt, pepper, basil, oregano and chili.

2. Heat the oil in a skillet and add the chicken. Cook on each side for 5 minutes on high heat just until golden brown.

3. Cover the chicken with a lid and continue cooking for 15-20 more minutes.

4. For the sauce, mix the yogurt, cucumber, garlic, lemon juice, mint and parsley, as well as salt and pepper.

5. Serve the chicken and the sauce fresh.

Nutrition:

- Per Serving:Calories:366 Fat:22.6g Protein:34.8g Carbohydrates:6.2g

Blackened Fish Tacos With Slaw

Servings:4

Cooking Time:20 Minutes

Ingredients:

- 1 tbsp olive oil
- 1 tsp chili powder
- 2 tilapia fillets
- 1 tsp paprika
- 4 low carb tortillas
- Slaw: ½ cup red cabbage, shredded
- 1 tbsp lemon juice
- 1 tsp apple cider vinegar
- 1 tbsp olive oil
- Salt and black pepper to taste

Directions:

1. Season the tilapia with chili powder and paprika. Heat the olive oil in a skillet over medium heat.

2. Add tilapia and cook until blackened, about 3 minutes per side. Cut into strips. Divide the tilapia between the tortillas. Combine

Nutrition:

- Calories 268, ,Fat: 20g ,Net Carbs: 5g ,Protein: 18g

Pan-seared Salmon Salad With Snow Peas & Grapefruit

Servings:3

Cooking Time:10 Minutes

Ingredients:

- 4 (100g) skin-on salmon fillets
- 1/8 teaspoon sea salt
- 2 teaspoons extra virgin olive oil
- 4 cups arugula
- 8 leaves Boston lettuce, washed and dried
- 1 cup snow peas, cooked
- 2 avocados, diced
- For Grapefruit-Dill Dressing:
- 1/4 cup grapefruit juice
- 1/4 cup extra virgin olive oil
- 1 teaspoon raw honey
- 1 tablespoon Dijon mustard
- 1 tablespoon chopped fresh dill
- 2 garlic cloves, minced
- 1/2 teaspoon pepper

Directions:

1. Sprinkle fish with about 1/8 teaspoon salt and cook in 2 teaspoons of olive oil over medium heat for about 4 minutes per side or until golden.

2. In a small bowl, whisk together al dressing ingredients and set aside. Divide arugula and lettuce among four serving plates.

3. Divide lettuce and arugula among 4 plates and add the remaining salad ingredients; top each with seared fish and drizzle with dressing. Enjoy!

Barbecued Spiced Tuna With Avocado-mango Salsa

Servings:4
Cooking Time:10 Minutes

Ingredients:

- 4 (120g each) skinless tuna fillets
- 1 teaspoon dried oregano
- 1 teaspoon onion powder
- 1 teaspoon ground paprika
- 1 teaspoon ground coriander
- 1 teaspoon ground cumin
- 1 tablespoon olive oil
- Thinly shaved fennel
- Baby rocket leaves
- Avocado-Mango Salsa:
- 1/2 red onion, chopped
- 1 cucumber, chopped
- 1 avocado, diced
- 1 mango, diced
- 1 long red chilli, chopped
- 2 tablespoons lime juice
- 1/2 cup chopped coriander

Directions:

1. In a bowl, mix together onion powder, paprika, coriander, cumin, and oil until well combined; add in tuna and turn until well coated; sprinkle with salt and pepper.

2. Preheat the BBQ grill on medium high and grill the fish for about 3 minutes per side or until cooked to your liking. Wrap in foil and let set for at least 5 minutes.

3. In the meantime, in a bowl, mix together avocado, mango, red onion, cucumber, chili, coriander, and fresh lime juice until well combined.

4. Divide fennel and rocket on serving plates and top each with the grilled tuna and mango-avocado salsa. Serve right away.

Nutrition:

- Calories: 300 Total Fat: 17g Saturated Fat: 4g Cholesterol: 16mg Sodium: 59mg Total Carbohydrates: 34g Fiber: 2g Protein: 7g

Caramelized Shallot Steaks

Servings:7
Cooking Time:45 Minutes

Ingredients:

- 6 flank steaks
- Salt and pepper to taste
- 1 teaspoon dried oregano
- 1 teaspoon dried basil
- 6 shallots, sliced
- 4 tablespoons olive oil
- ¼ cup dry white wine

Directions:

1. Season the steaks with salt, pepper, oregano and basil.

2. Heat a grill pan over medium flame and place the steaks on the grill.

3. Cook on each side for 6-7 minutes.

4. Heat the oil in a skillet and stir in the shallots. Cook for 15 minutes, stirring often, until the shallots are caramelized.

5. Add the wine and cook for another 5 minutes.

6. Serve the steaks with shallots.

Nutrition:

- Per Serving:Calories:258 Fat:16.3g Protein:23.5g Carbohydrates:2.1g

Cod And Mushrooms Mix

Servings:4
Cooking Time:25 Minutes

Ingredients:

- 2 cod fillets, boneless
- 4 tablespoons olive oil
- 4 ounces mushrooms, sliced
- Sea salt and black pepper to the taste
- 12 cherry tomatoes, halved
- 8 ounces lettuce leaves, torn
- 1 avocado, pitted, peeled and cubed
- 1 red chili pepper, chopped
- 1 tablespoon cilantro, chopped
- 2 tablespoons balsamic vinegar
- 1 ounce feta cheese, crumbled

Directions:

1. Put the fish in a roasting pan, brush it with 2 tablespoons oil, sprinkle salt and pepper all over and broil under medium-high heat for 15 minutes. Meanwhile, heat up a pan with the rest of the oil over medium heat, add the mushrooms, stir and sauté for 5 minutes.

2. Add the rest of the ingredients, toss, cook for 5 minutes more and divide between plates.

3. Top with the fish and serve right away.

Nutrition:

- Calories 257 ,Fat 10 g ,Fiber 3.1 g ,Carbs 24.3 g ,Protein 19.4 g

Balsamic Steak With Feta, Tomato, And Basil

Servings:4
Cooking Time:20 Minutes
Ingredients:

- 1 tablespoon balsamic vinegar
- 1/4 cup basil leaves
- 175 g Greek fetta, crumbled
- 2 tablespoons olive oil
- 2 teaspoons baby capers
- 4 sirloin steaks, trimmed
- 4 whole garlic cloves, skin on
- 6 roma tomatoes, halved
- Olive oil spray
- Salt and cracked black pepper

Directions:

1. Preheat the oven to 200C.

2. Line a baking tray with baking paper. Place the tomatoes and then scatter with the capers, crumbled feta, and the garlic cloves. Drizzle with 1 tablespoon of the olive oil and season with salt and pepper; cook for about 15 minutes or until the tomatoes are soft. Remove from the oven, set aside.

3. In a large non-metallic bowl, toss the steak with the remaining 1 tablespoon of olive oil, vinegar, salt and pepper; cover and refrigerate for 5 minutes.

4. Preheat the grill pan to high heat; grill the steaks for about 4 minutes per side or until cooked to your preference.

5. Serve with the preparation ared tomato mixture and sprinkle with basil.

Nutrition:

- 520.3 Cal, 30 g total fat (12 g sat. fat), 3 g carb., 2 g fiber, 2 g sugar, 59 g protein, and 622.82 mg sodium

Crispy Pollock And Gazpacho

Servings:3
Cooking Time:15 Minutes
Ingredients:

- 85 g whole-wheat bread, torn into chunks
- 4 tablespoons olive oil
- 4 pieces Pollock fillets, skinless
- 4 large tomatoes, cut into chunks
- 3/4 cucumber, cut into chunks
- 2 tablespoons sherry vinegar
- 2 garlic cloves, crushed
- 1/2 red onion, thinly sliced
- 1 yellow pepper, deseeded, cut into chunks

Directions:

1. Preheat the oven to 200C, gas to 6, or fan to 180C.

2. Over a baking tray, scatter the chunks of bread. Toss with 1 tablespoon of the olive oil and bake for about 10 minutes, or until golden and crispy.

3. Meanwhile, mix the cucumber, tomatoes, onion, pepper, crushed garlic, sherry vinegar, and 2 tablespoons of the olive oil; season well.

4. Heat a non-stick large frying pan. Add the remaining 1 tablespoon of the olive oil and heat. When the oil is hot, add the fish; cook for about 4 minutes or until golden. Flip the fillet; cook for additional 1 to 2 minutes or until the fish cooked through.

5. In a mixing bowl, quickly toss the salad and the croutons; divide among 4 plates and then serve with the fish.

Nutrition:

- 296 Cal, 13 g total fat (2 g sat. fat), 19 g carb., 9 g sugar, 3 g fiber, 27 g protein, and 0.67 g sodium.

Grilled Chicken And Rustic Mustard Cream

Servings:3
Cooking Time:12 Minutes
Ingredients:

- 1 tablespoon plus 1 teaspoon whole-grain Dijon mustard, divided
- 1 tablespoon water
- 1 teaspoon fresh rosemary, chopped

- 1/4 teaspoon black pepper
- 1/4 teaspoon of salt
- 1 tablespoon olive oil
- 3 tablespoons light mayonnaise
- 4 pieces (6-ounces each) chicken breast halves, skinless, boneless
- Rosemary sprigs (optional)
- Cooking spray

Directions:

1. Preheat the grill.
2. In a small-sized bowl, combine the olive oil, 1-teaspoon of mustard; brush evenly over each chicken breast.
3. Coat the grill rack with the cooking spray, place and chicken, and grill for 6 minutes per side or until cooked.
4. While the chicken is grilling, combine the mayonnaise, the 1 tablespoon of mustard, and the water in a bowl.
5. Serve the grilled chicken with the mustard cream. If desired garnish with some rosemary sprigs.

Nutrition:

- 262 Cal, 10 g total fat (1 g sat. fat, 4 g mono fat, 3 g poly fat), 39.6 g protein, 1.7 g carb., 0.2 g fiber, 102 mg chol., 1.4 mg iron, 448 mg sodium, and 25 mg calcium.

Mushroom Pilaf

Servings:3
Cooking Time:50 Minutes

Ingredients:

- 2 tablespoons olive oil
- 1 shallot, chopped
- 2 garlic cloves, minced
- 1 pound button mushrooms
- 1 cup brown rice
- 2 cups chicken stock
- 1 bay leaf
- 1 thyme sprig
- Salt and pepper to taste

Directions:

1. Heat the oil in a skillet and stir in the shallot and garlic. Cook for 2 minutes until softened and fragrant.
2. Add the mushrooms and rice and cook for 5 minutes.
3. Add the stock, bay leaf and thyme, as well as salt and pepper and continue cooking for 20 more minutes on low heat.

4. Serve the pilaf warm and fresh.

Nutrition:

- Per Serving:Calories:265 Fat:8.9g Protein:7.6g Carbohydrates:41.2g

Pastitsio An Italian Dish

Servings:8
Cooking Time:30 Minutes

Ingredients:

- 2 tbsp chopped fresh flat leaf parsley
- ¾ cup shredded mozzarella cheese
- 1 3oz package of fat free cream cheese
- ½ cup 1/3 less fat cream cheese
- 1 can 14.5-oz of diced tomatoes, drained
- 2 cups fat free milk
- 1 tbsp all-purpose flour
- ¾ tsp kosher salt
- 5 garlic cloves, minced
- 1 ½ cups chopped onion
- 1 tbsp olive oil
- 1 lb. ground sirloin
- Cooking spray
- 8 oz penne, cooked and draine

Directions:

1. On medium high fire, place a big nonstick saucepan and for five minutes sauté beef. Keep on stirring to break up the pieces of ground meat. Once cooked, remove from pan and drain fat.
2. Using same pan, heat oil and fry onions until soft around four minutes while occasionally stirring.
3. Add garlic and continue cooking for another minute while constantly stirring.
4. Stir in beef and flour, cook for another minute. Mix constantly.
5. Add the fat free cream cheese, less fat cream cheese, tomatoes and milk. Cook until mixture is smooth and heated. Toss in pasta and mix well.
6. Transfer pasta into a greased rectangular glass dish and top with mozzarella. Cook in a preheated broiler for four minutes. Remove from broiler and garnish with parsley before serving.

Nutrition:

- Calories per Serving: 263; Carbs: 17.8g; Protein: 24.1g; Fat: 10.6g

Spiced Grilled Flank Steak

Servings:3

Cooking Time:40 Minutes

Ingredients:

- 4 flank steaks
- 1 teaspoon chili powder
- 1 teaspoon ground coriander
- 1 teaspoon ground cumin
- 1 teaspoon mustard powder
- Salt and pepper to taste

Directions:

1. Season the steaks with salt and pepper then sprinkle with chili, coriander, cumin and mustard powder.
2. Allow to rest for 20 minutes then heat a grill pan over medium flame and place the steaks on the grill.
3. Cook on each side for 5-7 minutes and serve the steaks warm and fresh.

Nutrition:

- Per Serving:Calories:202 Fat:8.8g Protein:28.2g Carbohydrates:0.9g

Spiced Eggplant Stew

Servings:4

Cooking Time:45 Minutes

Ingredients:

- 4 eggplants, cubed
- Salt and black pepper to the taste
- 2 yellow onions, chopped
- 2 red bell peppers, chopped
- 30 ounces canned tomatoes, chopped
- 1 cup black olives, pitted and chopped
- ¼ teaspoon allspice, ground
- ½ teaspoon cinnamon powder
- 1 teaspoon oregano, dried
- A drizzle of olive oil
- A pinch of red chili flakes
- 3 tablespoons Greek yogurt

Directions:

1. Heat up a pot with the oil over medium high heat, add the onions, bell pepper, oregano, cinnamon and the allspice and sauté fro 5 minutes.
2. Add the rest of the ingredients except the flakes and the yogurt, bring to a simmer and cook over medium heat for 40 minutes.

3. Divide the stew into bowls, top each serving with the flakes and the yogurt and serve.

Nutrition:

- calories 256, fat 3.5, fiber 25.4, carbs 53.3, protein 8.8

Turkey With Leeks And Radishes

Servings:2

Cooking Time:10 Minutes

Ingredients:

- 1-pound turkey breast, skinless, boneless and cubed
- 1 leek, sliced
- 1 cup radishes, sliced
- 1 red onion, chopped
- 1 tablespoon olive oil
- A pinch of salt and black pepper
- 1 cup chicken stock
- ½ teaspoon sweet paprika
- ½ teaspoon coriander, ground
- 1 tablespoon cilantro, chopped

Directions:

1. In your slow cooker, combine the turkey with the leek, radishes, onion and the other ingredients toss, put the lid on and cook on High for 6 hours.
2. Divide everything between plates and serve.

Nutrition:

- Calories 226, ,Fat 9g ,Fiber 1g ,Carbs 6g, ,Protein 12g

Blue Cheese And Grains Salad

Servings:4

Cooking Time:40 Minutes

Ingredients:

- ¼ cup thinly sliced scallions
- ½ cup millet, rinsed
- ½ cup quinoa, rinsed
- 1 ½ tsp olive oil
- 1 Bartlett pear, cored and diced
- 1/8 tsp ground black pepper
- 2 cloves garlic, minced
- 2 oz blue cheese
- 2 tbsp fresh lemon juice
- 2 tsp dried rosemary
- 4 4-oz boneless, skinless chicken breasts
- 6 oz baby spinach

- olive oil cooking spray
- ¼ cup fresh raspberries
- 1 tbsp pure maple syrup
- 1 tsp fresh thyme leaf
- 2 tbsp grainy mustard
- 6 tbsp balsamic vinegar

Directions:

1. Bring millet, quinoa, and 2 ¼ cups water on a small saucepan to a boil. Once boiling, slow fire to a simmer and stir once. Cover and cook until water is fully absorbed and grains are soft around 15 minutes. Turn off fire, fluff grains with a fork and set aside to cool a bit.

2. Arrange one oven rack to highest position and preheat broiler. Line a baking sheet with foil, and grease with cooking spray.

3. Whisk well pepper, oil, rosemary, lemon juice and garlic. Rub onto chicken.

4. Place chicken on preparation ared pan, pop into the broiler and broil until juices run clear and no longer pin inside around 12 minutes.

5. Meanwhile, make the dressing by combining all ingredients in a blender. Blend until smooth.

6. Remove chicken from oven, cool slightly before cutting into strips, against the grain.

7. To assemble, place grains in a large salad bowl. Add in dressing and spinach, toss to mix well.

8. Add scallions and pear, mix gently and evenly divide into four plates. Top each salad with cheese and chicken.

9. Serve and enjoy.

Nutrition:

- Calories per Serving: 530.4; Carbs: 77g; Protein: 21.4g; Fat: 15.2g

Filling Macaroni Soup

Servings:6
Cooking Time:45 Minutes

Ingredients:

- 1 cup of minced beef or chicken or a combination of both
- 1 cup carrots, diced
- 1 cup milk
- ½ medium onion, sliced thinly
- 3 garlic cloves, minced
- Salt and pepper to taste
- 2 cups broth (chicken, vegetable or beef)
- ½ tbsp olive oil

- 1 cup uncooked whole wheat pasta like macaroni, shells, even angel hair broken to pieces
- 1 cup water

Directions:

1. In a heavy bottomed pot on medium high fire heat oil.

2. Add garlic and sauté for a minute or two until fragrant but not browned.

3. Add onions and sauté for 3 minutes or until soft and translucent.

4. Add a cup of minced meat. You can also use whatever leftover frozen meat you have.

5. Sauté the meat well until cooked around 8 minutes. While sautéing, season meat with pepper and salt.

6. Add water and broth and bring to a boil.

7. Once boiling, add pasta. I use any leftover pasta that I have in the pantry. If all you have left is spaghetti, lasagna, angel hair or fettuccine, just break them into pieces—around 1-inch in length before adding to the pot.

8. Slow fire to a simmer and cook while covered until pasta is soft.

9. Halfway through cooking the pasta, around 8 minutes I add the carrots.

10. Once the pasta is soft, turn off fire and add milk.

11. Mix well and season to taste again if needed.

12. Serve and enjoy.

Nutrition:

- Calories per Serving: 125; Carbs: 11.4g; Protein: 10.1g; Fat: 4.3g

Feta, Eggplant And Sausage Penne

Servings:6
Cooking Time:30 Minutes

Ingredients:

- ¼ cup chopped fresh parsley
- ½ cup crumbled feta cheese
- 6 cups hot cooked penne
- 1 14.5oz can diced tomatoes
- ¼ tsp ground black pepper
- 1 tsp dried oregano
- 2 tbsp tomato paste
- 4 garlic cloves, minced
- ½ lb. bulk pork breakfast sausage
- 4 ½ cups cubed peeled eggplant

Directions:

1. On medium high fire, place a nonstick, big fry pan and cook for seven minutes garlic, sausage and eggplant

or until eggplants are soft and sausage are lightly browned.

2. Stir in diced tomatoes, black pepper, oregano and tomato paste. Cover and simmer for five minutes while occasionally stirring.

3. Remove pan from fire, stir in pasta and mix well.

4. Transfer to a serving dish, garnish with parsley and cheese before servin

Nutrition:

- Calories per Serving: 376; Carbs: 50.8g; Protein: 17.8g; Fat: 11.6g

Creamy Artichoke Lasagna

Servings:3

Cooking Time:70 Minutes

Ingredients:

- 1 cup shredded mozzarella cheese
- 2 cups light cream
- ¼ cup all-purpose flour
- 1 cup vegetable broth
- ¾ tsp salt
- 1 egg
- 1 cup snipped fresh basil
- 1 cup finely shredded Parmesan cheese
- 1 15-oz carton ricotta cheese
- 4 cloves garlic, minced
- ½ cup pine nuts
- 3 tbsp olive oil
- 9 dried lasagna noodles, cooked, rinsed in cold water and drained
- 15 fresh baby artichokes
- ¼ cup lemon juice
- 3 cups water

Directions:

1. Preparation are in a medium bowl lemon juice and water. Put aside. Slice off artichoke base and remove yellowed outer leaves and cut into quarters. Immediately soak sliced artichokes in preparation ared liquid and drain after a minute.

2. Over medium fire, place a big saucepan with 2 tbsp oil and fry half of garlic, pine nuts and artichokes. Stir frequently and cook until artichokes are soft around ten minutes. Turn off fire and transfer mixture to a big bowl and quickly stir in salt, egg, ½ cup of basil, ½ cup of parmesan cheese and ricotta cheese. Mix thoroughly.

3. In a small bowl mix flour and broth. In same pan, add 1 tbsp oil and fry remaining garlic for half a minute. Add light cream and flour mixture. Stir constantly and cook until thickened. Remove from fire and stir in ½ cup of basil.

4. In a separate bowl mix ½ cup parmesan and mozzarella cheese.

5. Assemble the lasagna by layering the following in a greased rectangular glass dish: lasagna, 1/3 of artichoke mixture, 1/3 of sauce, sprinkle with the dried cheeses and repeat layering procedure until all ingredients are used up.

6. For forty minutes, bake lasagna in a pre-heated oven of 350oF. Remove lasagna from oven and before serving, let it stand for fifteen minutes.

Nutrition:

- Calories per Serving: 425; Carbs: 41.4g; Protein: 21.3g; Fat: 19.8g

Salmon And Corn Salad

Servings:4

Cooking Time:5 Minutes

Ingredients:

- ½ cup pecans, chopped
- 2 cups baby arugula
- 1 cup corn
- ¼ pound smoked salmon, skinless, boneless and cut into small chunks
- 2 tablespoons olive oil
- 2 tablespoon lemon juice
- Sea salt and black pepper to the taste

Directions:

1. In a salad bowl, combine the salmon with the corn and the rest of the ingredients, toss and serve right away

Nutrition:

- Calories 284 ,Fat 18.4 g ,Fiber 5.4 g ,Carbs 22.6 g .Protein 17.4 g

Berries And Grilled Calamari

Servings:4

Cooking Time:5 Minutes

Ingredients:

- ¼ cup dried cranberries
- ¼ cup extra virgin olive oil
- ¼ cup olive oil
- ¼ cup sliced almonds
- ½ lemon, juiced

- ¾ cup blueberries
- 1 ½ pounds calamari tube, cleaned
- 1 granny smith apple, sliced thinly
- 1 tablespoon fresh lemon juice
- 2 tablespoons apple cider vinegar
- 6 cups fresh spinach
- Freshly grated pepper to taste
- Sea salt to taste

Directions:

1. In a small bowl, make the vinaigrette by mixing well the tablespoon of lemon juice, apple cider vinegar, and extra virgin olive oil. Season with pepper and salt to taste. Set aside.

2. Turn on the grill to medium fire and let the grates heat up for a minute or two.

3. In a large bowl, add olive oil and the calamari tube. Season calamari generously with pepper and salt.

4. Place seasoned and oiled calamari onto heated grate and grill until cooked or opaque. This is around two minutes per side.

5. As you wait for the calamari to cook, you can combine almonds, cranberries, blueberries, spinach, and the thinly sliced apple in a large salad bowl. Toss to mix.

6. Remove cooked calamari from grill and transfer on a chopping board. Cut into ¼-inch thick rings and throw into the salad bowl.

7. Drizzle with vinaigrette and toss well to coat salad.

8. Serve and enjoy!

Nutrition:

- Calories: 567 ,Fat: 24.5g ,Protein: 54.8g ,Carbs: 30.6g

Grilled Salmon With Cucumber Dill Sauce

Servings:4
Cooking Time:30 Minutes
Ingredients:

- 4 salmon fillets
- 1 teaspoon smoked paprika
- 1 teaspoon dried sage
- Salt and pepper to taste
- 4 cucumbers, sliced
- 2 tablespoons chopped dill

- ½ cup Greek yogurt
- 1 tablespoon lemon juice
- 1 tablespoon olive oil

Directions:

1. Season the salmon with salt, pepper, paprika and sage.

2. Heat a grill pan over medium flame and place the salmon on the grill.

3. Cook on each side for 4 minutes.

4. For the sauce, mix the cucumbers, dill, yogurt, lemon juice and oil in a bowl. Add salt and pepper and mix well.

5. Serve the salmon with the cucumber sauce.

Nutrition:

- Per Serving:Calories:224 Fat:10.3g Protein:26.3g Carbohydrates:8.9g

Shrimp Pancakes

Servings:4
Cooking Time:10 Minutes
Ingredients:

- 4 eggs, beaten
- 4 teaspoons sour cream
- 1 cup shrimps, peeled, boiled
- 1 teaspoon butter
- 1 teaspoon olive oil
- 1/3 cup Mozzarella, shredded
- ½ teaspoon salt
- 1 teaspoon dried oregano

Directions:

1. In the mixing bowl, combine together sour cream, eggs, salt, and dried oregano.

2. Place butter and olive oil in the crepe skillet and heat the ingredients up.

3. Separate the egg liquid into 4 parts.

4. Ladle the first part of the egg liquid in the skillet and flatten it in the shape of crepe.

5. Sprinkle the egg crepe with ¼ part of shrimps and a small amount of Mozzarella.

6. Roast the crepe for 2 minutes from one side and then flip it onto another.

7. Cook the crepe for 30 seconds more.

8. Repeat the same steps with all remaining ingredients.

Nutrition:

- calories 148, fat 8.5, fiber 0.2, carbs 1.5, protein 16.1

SNACK

Pita Chips

Servings:3

Cooking Time:30 Minutes

Ingredients:

- 6 whole wheat pitas, cut each into 8 wedges
- 2 tsp. olive oil
- Red chili powder, to taste
- Garlic powder, to taste
- Pinch of salt

Directions:

1. Preheat the oven to 400 degrees F.
2. In the bottom of a large baking sheet, place the pita wedges.
3. Brush the both sides of each with oil and sprinkle with chili powder, garlic powder and salt.
4. Now, arrange the pita wedges in a single layer.
5. Bake for about 8 minutes or until golden brown.
6. Serve with your favorite dip

Nutrition:

- 242 Calories 25g carbs 12g fat 13g protein

Light & Creamy Garlic Hummus

Servings:10

Cooking Time:40 Minutes

Ingredients:

- 1 1/2 cups dry chickpeas, rinsed
- 2 1/2 tbsp fresh lemon juice
- 1 tbsp garlic, minced
- 1/2 cup tahini
- 6 cups of water
- Pepper
- Salt

Directions:

1. Add water and chickpeas into the instant pot.
2. Seal pot with a lid and select manual and set timer for 40 minutes.
3. Once done, allow to release pressure naturally. Remove lid.
4. Drain chickpeas well and reserved 1/2 cup chickpeas liquid.
5. Transfer chickpeas, reserved liquid, lemon juice, garlic, tahini, pepper, and salt into the food processor and process until smooth.
6. Serve and enjoy

Nutrition:

- Calories 152 Fat 6.9 g Carbohydrates 17.6 g Sugar 2.8 g Protein 6.6 g Cholesterol 0 mg

Baked Sweet-potato Fries

Servings:6

Cooking Time: 20 Minutes

Ingredients:

- 1 1/2 teaspoons dried oregano
- 1 teaspoon dried thyme
- 1 teaspoon garlic powder
- 1/2 teaspoon salt
- 2 large sweet potatoes (about 2 pounds), skins on, scrubbed, cut into 1/2-inch thick 4-inch long sticks
- 3 large egg whites (a scant 1/2 cup)
- Vegetable oil, for the parchment
- For the Mediterranean spice:
- Oregano
- Thyme
- Garlic

Directions:

1. Place all of the Mediterranean spice ingredients in a small food processor or a spice grinder; briefly grind or process to blend.
2. Place the oven racks in the middle and upper position; preheat the oven to 450F.
3. Line 2 baking sheets with parchment paper; rub the paper with the oil.
4. Put the potatoes in a microwavable container, cover, and microwave for 2 minutes. Stir gently, cover, and microwave for about 1-2 minutes more or until the pieces are pliable; let rest for about 5 minutes covered. Pour into a platter.
5. In a large-sized bowl, whisk the eggs until frothy. Add the spice mix and whisk again to blend.
6. Working in batches, toss the sweet potatoes in the seasoned egg whites letting the excess liquid drip back into the bowl. Arrange the coated potatoes in a single layer on the preparation ared baking sheets.

7. Bake for 10 minutes; flip the pieces over using a spatula. Rotate the baking sheets from back to front and one to the other; bake for about 15 minutes or until dark golden brown. Serve immediately.

Nutrition:

- 100 cal., 4 g total fat (0 g sat. fat), 0 mg chol., 60 mg sodium, 230 mg pot., 12 g total carbs., 2 g fiber, 2 g sugar, 3 g protein, 150% vitamin A, 2% vitamin C, 4% calcium, and 6% iron.

Basil & Walnut Pesto

Servings:1
Cooking Time:30 Minutes

Ingredients:

- 2oz fresh basil
- 2oz walnuts
- 1oz pine nuts
- 3 cloves of garlic, crushed
- 2 tablespoons Parmesan, grated
- 4 tablespoons olive oil

Directions:

1. Place the pesto ingredients into a food processor and process until it becomes a smooth paste.
2. Serve with meat, fish, salad and pasta dishes.

Nutrition:

- Calories: 136 ,Sodium: 23 mg, ,Dietary Fiber: 1.2 g ,Total Fat: 3.1 g, ,Total Carbs: 14.3 g ,Protein: 1.4 g

Spiced Spinach Bites

Servings:3
Cooking Time:20 Minutes

Ingredients:

- 12 baby spinach leaves
- 2 chopped limes
- ½ chopped chilli
- 1 sliced shallot
- 1 teaspoon chopped ginger
- 2 tablespoons peanuts
- A pinch of sea salt
- 1 tablespoon coriander

Directions:

1. In a bowl, combine peanuts, chilli, shallot, ginger, limes, and coriander; season with a sprinkle of sea salt. Lay spinach leaves on a plate and add a spoonful of the mixture on each; roll them up to make round wraps.

Nutrition:

- 448 Calories 27g fat 41g carbs 15g protein

Tuna Salad

Servings:6
Cooking Time:30 Minutes

Ingredients:

- 1 can (5 ounce) albacore tuna, solid white
- 1 to 2 tablespoons mayo or Greek yogurt
- 1 whole-wheat crackers (I used sleeve Ritz®)
- 1/4 cup chickpeas, rinsed, drained (or preferred white beans)
- 1/4 cup Kalamata olives, quartered
- 1/4 cup roughly chopped marinated artichoke hearts

Directions:

1. Flake the tuna out of the can into medium-sized bowl.
2. Add the chickpeas, olives, and artichoke hearts; toss to combine.
3. Add mayo or Greek yogurt according to your taste; stir until well combined.
4. Spoon the salad mixture onto crackers; serve

Nutrition:

- 130 cal., 5 g total fat (0.5 g sat. fat), 25 mg chol., 240 mg sodium, 240 mg pot., 8 g total carbs., 1 g fiber, <1 g sugar, 12 g protein, 2% vitamin A, 2% vitamin C, 4% calcium, and 6% iron.

Parsley Nachos

Servings:3
Cooking Time:10 Minutes

Ingredients:

- 3 oz tortilla chips
- ¼ cup Greek yogurt
- 1 tablespoon fresh parsley, chopped
- ¼ teaspoon minced garlic
- 2 kalamata olives, chopped
- 1 teaspoon paprika
- ¼ teaspoon ground thyme

Directions:

1. In the mixing bowl mix up together Greek yogurt, parsley, minced garlic, olives, paprika, and thyme.
2. Then add tortilla chips and mix up gently.
3. The snack should be served immediately.

Nutrition:

- calories 81, fat 1.6, fiber 2.2, carbs 14.1, protein 3.5

Grilled Tuna

Servings:3

Cooking Time:6 Minutes

Ingredients:

- 3 tuna fillets
- 3 teaspoons teriyaki sauce
- ½ teaspoon minced garlic
- 1 teaspoon olive oil

Directions:

1. Whisk together teriyaki sauce, minced garlic, and olive oil.
2. Bruhs every tuna fillet with teriyaki mixture.
3. Preheat grill to 390F.
4. Grill the fish for 3 minutes from each side.

Nutrition:

- calories 382, fat 32.6, fiber 0, carbs 1.1, protein 21.4

Basil Tilapia

Servings:3

Cooking Time:20 Minutes

Ingredients:

- 12 oz tilapia fillet
- 2 oz Parmesan, grated
- 1 tablespoon olive oil
- ½ teaspoon ground black pepper
- 1 cup fresh basil
- 3 tablespoons avocado oil
- 1 tablespoon pine nuts
- 1 garlic clove, peeled
- ¾ teaspoon white pepper

Directions:

1. Make pesto sauce: blend the avocado oil, fresh basil, pine nuts, garlic clove, and white pepper until smooth.
2. After this, cut the tilapia fillet on 3 servings.
3. Sprinkle every fish serving with olive oil and ground black pepper.
4. Roast the fillets over the medium heat for 2 minutes from each side.
5. Meanwhile, line the baking tray with baking paper.
6. Arrange the roasted tilapia fillets in the tray.
7. Then top them with pesto and Parmesan.
8. Bake the fish for 15 minutes at 365F.

Nutrition:

- calories 321, fat 17, fiber 1.2, carbs 4.4, protein 37.4

Cod With Lentils

Servings:4

Cooking Time:30 Minutes

Ingredients:

- 1 red pepper, chopped
- 1 yellow onion, diced
- 1 teaspoon ground black pepper
- 1 teaspoon butter
- 1 jalapeno pepper, chopped
- ½ cup lentils
- 3 cups chicken stock
- 1 teaspoon salt
- 1 tablespoon tomato paste
- 1 teaspoon chili pepper
- 3 tablespoons fresh cilantro, chopped
- 8 oz cod, chopped

Directions:

1. Place butter, red pepper, onion, and ground black pepper in the saucepan.
2. Roast the vegetables for 5 minutes over the medium heat.
3. Then add chopped jalapeno pepper, lentils, and chili pepper.
4. Mix up the mixture well and add chicken stock and tomato paste.
5. Stir until homogenous. Add cod.
6. Close the lid and cook chili for 20 minutes over the medium heat

Nutrition:

- calories 187, fat 2.3, fiber 8.8, carbs 21.3, protein 20.6

Popcorn-pine Nut Mix

Servings:3

Cooking Time:10 Minutes

Ingredients:

- 1 tablespoon olive oil
- 1/2 cup pine nuts
- 1/2 teaspoon Italian seasoning
- 1/4 cup popcorn, white kernels, popped
- 1/4 teaspoon salt
- 2 tablespoons honey
- 1/2 lemon zest

Directions:

1. Place the popped corn in a medium bowl.

2. In a dry pan or skillet over low heat, toast the pine nuts, stirring frequently for about 4 to 5 minutes, until fragrant and some begin to brown; remove from the heat.

3. Stir the oil in; add honey, the Italian seasoning, the lemon zest, and the salt. Stir to mix and pour over the popcorn; toss the ingredients to coat the popcorn kernels with the honey syrup.

4. It's alright if most of the nuts sink in the bowl bottom.

5. Let the mixture sit for about 2 minutes to allow the honey to cool and to get stickier.

6. Transfer the bowl contents into a Servings: bowl so the nuts are on the top. Gently stir and serve.

Nutrition:

- 80 cal, 6 g total fat (0.5 g sat. fat), 0 mg chol., 105 mg sodium, 60 mg pot., 5 total carbs., <1 g fiber, 4 g sugar, 2 g protein, 2% vitamin A, 8% vitamin C, 4% calcium, and 4% iron.

Collard Greens And Tomatoes

Servings:3
Cooking Time:12 Minutes

Ingredients:

- 1-pound collard greens
- 3 bacon strips, chopped
- ¼ cup cherry tomatoes, halved
- 1 tbsp. apple cider vinegar
- 2 tbsp. chicken stock
- Salt and ground black pepper to taste

Directions:

1. Heat a pan over medium heat, add the bacon, stir, and cook until it browns. Add the tomatoes, collard greens, vinegar, stock, salt, and pepper, stir, and cook for 8 minutes.

2. Add more salt, and pepper, stir again gently, divide onto plates, and serve

Nutrition:

- Calories 120 ,Fat 8 g ,Carbs 3 g ,Protein 7 g

Deviled Avocado Eggs

Servings:3
Cooking Time:30 Minutes

Ingredients:

- 6 large organic eggs
- 1 medium avocado, peeled, pitted and chopped
- 2 tsp. fresh lime juice
- Salt, to taste

- Cayenne pepper, to taste

Directions:

1. In a pan of water, add eggs and cook for about 15-20 minutes.

2. Drain and keep aside to cool completely.

3. Peel the eggs and with a sharp knife, slice them in half vertically.

4. Scoop out the yolks.

5. In a bowl, add half of egg yolks, avocado, lime juice and salt and with a fork, mash until well combined.

6. Scoop the avocado mixture in the egg halves evenly.

7. Serve with the sprinkling of cayenne peppe

Nutrition:

- 448 Calories 27g fat 41g carbs 15g protein

Yogurt Dip

Servings:5
Cooking Time:10 Minutes

Ingredients:

- 2 cups Greek yogurt
- 2 tablespoons pistachios, toasted and chopped
- A pinch of salt and white pepper
- 2 tablespoons mint, chopped
- 1 tablespoon kalamata olives, pitted and chopped
- ¼ cup za'atar spice
- ¼ cup pomegranate seeds
- 1/3 cup olive oil

Directions:

1. In a bowl, combine the yogurt with the pistachios and the rest of the ingredients, whisk well, divide into small cups and serve with pita chips on the side.

Candied Ginger

Servings:3
Cooking Time:40 Minutes

Ingredients:

- 2 1/2 cups salted pistachios, shelled
- 1 1/4 tsp. powdered ginger
- 3 tbsp. pure maple syrup

Directions:

1. Add 1 1/4 tsp. of powdered ginger to a bowl with pistachios. Stir well until combined. There

2. Should be no lumps.

3. Drizzle with 3 tbsp. of maple syrup and stir well.

4. Transfer to a baking sheet lined with parchment paper and spread evenly.

5. Cook into a preheated oven at 275°F for about 20 minutes.

6. Take it out from the oven, stir, and cook again for 10–15 minutes.

7. Let it cool for about a few minutes until crispy. Enjoy!

Nutrition:

- Calories: 378 ,Fats: 27.6 g ,Carbs: 26 g ,Protein: 13 g

Trail Mix

Servings:3

Cooking Time:10 Minutes

Ingredients:

- ¼ cup unsalted roasted peanuts
- ¼ cup whole shelled almonds
- ¼ cup chopped pitted dates
- ¼ cup dried cranberries
- 2 ounces dried apricots

Directions:

1. In a medium bowl, mix together all the ingredients until well combined. Enjoy!

Nutrition:

- 448 Calories 27g fat 41g carbs 15g protein

Baked Goat Cheese Caprese Salad

Servings:3

Cooking Time:15 Minutes

Ingredients:

- 1 (log 4 ounce) fresh goat cheese, halved
- 1 pinch cayenne pepper, or to taste
- 16 cherry tomatoes, diagonally cut into halves
- 2 tablespoons olive oil, divided
- 3 tablespoons basil chiffonade (thinly sliced fresh basil leaves), divided
- Freshly ground black pepper, to taste

Directions:

1. Preheat the oven to 400F or 200C.

2. Drizzle about 1 1/2 teaspoons olive oil into the bottom of 2 pieces 6-ounch ramekin. Sprinkle about 1 tablespoon of basil per ramekin.

3. Place 1 goat half over each ramekin; surround with cherry tomato halves.

4. Sprinkle with the black pepper and the cayenne. Spread the remaining basil on top of each.

5. Place the ramekins on a baking sheet. Drizzle each serve with the remaining olive oil; bake for about 15 minutes or until bubbling. Serve warm.

Nutrition:

- 178 cal., 15.5 g total fat (6.8 sat. fat), 22 mg chol., 152 mg sodium, 4.1 g total carbs., 0.9 g fiber, 0.7 g sugar, and 6.8 g protein.

Crunchy Veggie Chips

Servings:3

Cooking Time:17 Minutes

Ingredients:

- 1 cup thinly sliced portobello mushrooms
- 1 cup thinly sliced zucchini
- 1 cup thinly sliced sweet potatoes
- 1 tablespoon extra-virgin olive oil
- Pinch of sea salt
- Pinch of pepper

Directions:

1. Place veggies in a baking dish and drizzle with olive oil; sprinkle with salt and pepper and toss to coat well; bake at 325°F for about 12 minutes or until crunchy. Enjoy!

Nutrition:

- 448 Calories 27g fat 41g carbs 15g protein

Cucumber-basil Salsa On Halibut Pouches

Servings:3

Cooking Time:17 Minutes

Ingredients:

- 1 lime, thinly sliced into 8 pieces
- 2 cups mustard greens, stems removed
- 2 tsp olive oil
- 4 – 5 radishes trimmed and quartered
- 4 4-oz skinless halibut filets
- 4 large fresh basil leaves
- Cayenne pepper to taste – optional
- Pepper and salt to taste
- 1 ½ cups diced cucumber
- 1 ½ finely chopped fresh basil leaves
- 2 tsp fresh lime juice
- Pepper and salt to taste

Directions:

1. Preheat oven to 400oF.

2. Preparation are parchment papers by making 4 pieces of 15 x 12-inch rectangles. Lengthwise, fold in half and unfold pieces on the table.

3. Season halibut fillets with pepper, salt and cayenne—if using cayenne.

4. Just to the right of the fold going lengthwise, place ½ cup of mustard greens. Add a basil leaf on center of mustard greens and topped with 1 lime slice. Around the greens, layer ¼ of the radishes. Drizzle with ½ tsp of oil, season with pepper and salt. Top it with a slice of halibut fillet.

5. Just as you would make a calzone, fold parchment paper over your filling and crimp the edges of the parchment paper beginning from one end to the other end. To seal the end of the crimped parchment paper, pinch it.

6. Repeat process to remaining ingredients until you have 4 pieces of parchment papers filled with halibut and greens.

7. Place pouches in a baking pan and bake in the oven until halibut is flaky, around 15 to 17 minutes.

8. While waiting for halibut pouches to cook, make your salsa by mixing all salsa ingredients in a medium bowl.

9. Once halibut is cooked, remove from oven and make a tear on top. Be careful of the steam as it is very hot. Equally divide salsa and spoon ¼ of salsa on top of halibut through the slit you have created.

10. Serve and enjoy

Nutrition:

- Calories per serving: 335.4; Protein: 20.2g; Fat: 16.3g; Carbs: 22.1g

Jalapeno Chickpea Hummus

Servings:3

Cooking Time:20 Minutes

Ingredients:

- 1 cup dry chickpeas, soaked overnight and drained
- 1 tsp ground cumin
- 1/4 cup jalapenos, diced
- 1/2 cup fresh cilantro
- 1 tbsp tahini
- 1/2 cup olive oil
- Pepper
- Salt

Directions:

1. Add chickpeas into the instant pot and cover with vegetable stock.

2. Seal pot with lid and cook on high for 25 minutes.

3. Once done, allow to release pressure naturally. Remove lid.

4. Drain chickpeas well and transfer into the food processor along with remaining ingredients and process until smooth.

5. Serve and enjoy.

Nutrition:

- Calories 425 Fat 30.4 g Carbohydrates 31.8 g Sugar 5.6 g Protein 10.5 g Cholesterol 0 mg

Tomato Olive Salsa

Servings:3

Cooking Time:5 Minutes

Ingredients:

- 2 cups olives, pitted and chopped
- 1/4 cup fresh parsley, chopped
- 1/4 cup fresh basil, chopped
- 2 tbsp green onion, chopped
- 1 cup grape tomatoes, halved
- 1 tbsp olive oil
- 1 tbsp vinegar
- Pepper
- Salt

Directions:

1. Add all ingredients into the inner pot of instant pot and stir well.

2. Seal pot with lid and cook on high for 5 minutes.

3. Once done, allow to release pressure naturally for 5 minutes then release remaining using quick release. Remove lid.

4. Stir well and serve

Nutrition:

- Calories 119 Fat 10.8 g Carbohydrates 6.5 g Sugar 1.3 g Protein 1.2 g Cholesterol 0 mg

Shrimp And Mushrooms Mix

Servings:4

Cooking Time:30 Minutes

Ingredients:

- 1 pound shrimp, peeled and deveined
- 2 green onions, sliced
- ½ pound white mushrooms, sliced
- 2 tablespoons balsamic vinegar
- 2 tablespoons sesame seeds, toasted

- 2 teaspoons ginger, minced
- 2 teaspoons garlic, minced
- 3 tablespoons olive oil
- 2 tablespoons dill, chopped

Directions:

1. Heat up a pan with the oil over medium-high heat, add the green onions and the garlic and sauté for 2 minutes.

2. Add the rest of the ingredients except the shrimp and cook for 6 minutes more.

3. Add the shrimp, cook for 4 minutes, divide everything between plates and serve.

Nutrition:

- calories 245, fat 8.5, fiber 45.8, carbs 11.8, protein 17.7

Lavash Roll Ups

Servings:4

Cooking Time:10 Minutes

Ingredients:

- 2 lavash wraps (whole-wheat)
- 1/4 cup roasted red peppers, sliced
- 1/4 cup black olives, sliced
- 1/2 cup hummus of choice
- 1/2 cup grape tomatoes, halved
- 1 Medium cucumber, sliced
- Fresh dill, for garnish

Directions:

1. Lay out the lavash wraps on a clean surface. Evenly spread hummus over each piece.

2. Layer the cucumbers across the wraps, about 1/2-inch from each other, leaving about 2-icnh empty space at the bottom of the wrap for rolling purposes.

3. Place the roasted pepper slices around the cucumbers. Sprinkle with black olives and the tomatoes. Garnish with freshly chopped dill.

4. Tightly roll each wrap, using the hummus at the end to almost glue the wrap into a roll.

5. Slice each roll into 4 equal pieces. Secure each piece by sticking a toothpick through the center of each roll slice.

6. Lay each on a serving bowl or tray; garnish more with fresh dill.

Nutrition:

- 250 cal, 8 g total fat (0.5 g sat. fat), 0 mg chol., 440 mg sodium, 340 mg pot., 43 total carbs., 40 g fiber, 3 g

sugar, 10 g protein, 15% vitamin A, 25% vitamin C, 6% calcium, and 8% iron.

Chicken Kale Wraps

Servings:4

Cooking Time:10 Minutes

Ingredients:

- 4 kale leaves
- 4 oz chicken fillet
- ½ apple
- 1 tablespoon butter
- ¼ teaspoon chili pepper
- ¾ teaspoon salt
- 1 tablespoon lemon juice
- ¾ teaspoon dried thyme

Directions:

1. Chop the chicken fillet into the small cubes.

2. Then mix up together chicken with chili pepper and salt.

3. Heat up butter in the skillet.

4. Add chicken cubes. Roast them for 4 minutes.

5. Meanwhile, chop the apple into small cubes and add it in the chicken.

6. Mix up well.

7. Sprinkle the ingredients with lemon juice and dried thyme.

8. Cook them for 5 minutes over the medium-high heat.

9. Fill the kale leaves with the hot chicken mixture and wrap

Nutrition:

- calories 106, fat 5.1, fiber 1.1, carbs 6.3, protein 9

Crazy Saganaki Shrimp

Servings:4

Cooking Time:10 Minutes

Ingredients:

- ¼ tsp salt
- ½ cup Chardonnay
- ½ cup crumbled Greek feta cheese
- 1 medium bulb. fennel, cored and finely chopped
- 1 small Chile pepper, seeded and minced
- 1 tbsp extra virgin olive oil
- 12 jumbo shrimps, peeled and deveined with tails left on
- 2 tbsp lemon juice, divided

- 5 scallions sliced thinly
- Pepper to taste

Directions:

1. In medium bowl, mix salt, lemon juice and shrimp.
2. On medium fire, place a saganaki pan (or large nonstick saucepan) and heat oil.
3. Sauté Chile pepper, scallions, and fennel for 4 minutes or until starting to brown and is already soft.
4. Add wine and sauté for another minute.
5. Place shrimps on top of fennel, cover and cook for 4 minutes or until shrimps are pink.
6. Remove just the shrimp and transfer to a plate.
7. Add pepper, feta and 1 tbsp lemon juice to pan and cook for a minute or until cheese begins to melt.
8. To serve, place cheese and fennel mixture on a serving plate and top with shrimps.

Nutrition:

- Calories per serving: 310; Protein: 49.7g; Fat: 6.8g; Carbs: 8.4g

Apple Chips

Servings:4
Cooking Time:45 Minutes

Ingredients:

- 2 Golden Delicious apples, cored and thinly sliced
- 1 1/2 teaspoons white sugar
- 1/2 teaspoon ground cinnamon

Directions:

1. Set your oven to 225 degrees F.
2. Place apple slices on a baking sheet.
3. Sprinkle sugar an
4. d cinnamon over apple slices.
5. Bake for 45 minutes.
6. Serve

Nutrition:

- Calories 127 ,Total Fat 3.5 g ,Saturated Fat 0.5 g ,Cholesterol 162 mg ,Sodium 142 mg ,Total Carbs 33.6g ,Fiber 0.4 g ,Sugar 0.5 g ,Protein 4.5 g

Honey Halibut

Servings:3
Cooking Time:15 Minutes

Ingredients:

- 1-pound halibut
- 1 teaspoon lime zest
- ½ teaspoon honey
- 1 teaspoon olive oil
- ½ teaspoon lime juice
- ¼ teaspoon salt
- ¼ teaspoon chili flakes

Directions:

1. Cut the fish on the sticks and sprinkle with salt and chili flakes.
2. Whisk together lime zest, honey, olive oil, and lime juice.
3. Brush the halibut sticks with the honey mixture from each side.
4. Line the baking tray with baking paper and place the fish inside.
5. Bake the halibut for 15 minutes at 375F. Flip the fish on another side after 7 minutes of cooking.

Nutrition:

- calories 254, fat 19, fiber 0, carbs 0.7, protein 18.8

Healthy Spinach Dip

Servings:4
Cooking Time:8 Minutes

Ingredients:

- 14 oz spinach
- 2 tbsp fresh lime juice
- 1 tbsp garlic, minced
- 2 tbsp olive oil
- 2 tbsp coconut cream
- Pepper
- Salt

Directions:

1. Add all ingredients except coconut cream into the instant pot and stir well.
2. Seal pot with lid and cook on low pressure for 8 minutes.
3. Once done, allow to release pressure naturally for 5 minutes then release remaining using quick release. Remove lid.
4. Add coconut cream and stir well and blend spinach mixture using a blender until smooth.
5. Serve and enjoy.

Nutrition:

- Calories 109 Fat 9.2 g Carbohydrates 6.6 g Sugar 1.1 g Protein 3.2 g Cholesterol 0 mg

Chickpeas And Eggplant Bowls

Servings:5

Cooking Time:30 Minutes

Ingredients:

- 2 eggplants, cut in half lengthwise and cubed
- 1 red onion, chopped
- Juice of 1 lime
- 1 tablespoon olive oil
- 28 ounces canned chickpeas, drained and rinsed
- 1 bunch parsley, chopped
- A pinch of salt and black pepper
- 1 tablespoon balsamic vinegar

Directions:

1. Spread the eggplant cubes on a baking sheet lined with parchment paper, drizzle half of the oil all over, season with salt and pepper and cook at 425 degrees F for 10 minutes.

2. Cool the eggplant down, add the rest of the ingredients, toss, divide between appetizer plates and serve.

Nutrition:

- calories 263, fat 12, fiber 9.3, carbs 15.4, protein 7.5

Stuffed Mackerel

Servings:5

Cooking Time:30 Minutes

Ingredients:

- 4 teaspoons capers, drained
- 1-pound whole mackerel, peeled, trimmed
- 1 teaspoon garlic powder
- ½ teaspoon ground coriander
- ½ teaspoon salt
- 1 tablespoon lime juice
- ¼ teaspoon chili flakes
- ½ white onion, sliced
- 4 teaspoons butter
- 3 tablespoons water

Directions:

1. Rub the fish with salt, garlic powder, and chili flakes.

2. Then sprinkle it with lime juice.

3. Line the baking tray with parchment and arrange the fish inside.

4. Fill the mackerel with capers and butter.

5. Then sprinkle fish with water.

6. Cover the fish with foil and secure the edges.

7. Bake the mackerel for 30 minutes at 365F.

Nutrition:

- calories 262, fat 17.5, fiber 0.4, carbs 1.8, protein 25.5

Feta Tomato Sea Bass

Servings:3

Cooking Time:8 Minutes

Ingredients:

- 4 sea bass fillets
- 1 1/2 cups water
- 1 tbsp olive oil
- 1 tsp garlic, minced
- 1 tsp basil, chopped
- 1 tsp parsley, chopped
- 1/2 cup feta cheese, crumbled
- 1 cup can tomatoes, diced
- Pepper
- Salt

Directions:

1. Season fish fillets with pepper and salt.

2. Pour 2 cups of water into the instant pot then place steamer rack in the pot.

3. Place fish fillets on steamer rack in the pot.

4. Seal pot with lid and cook on high for 5 minutes.

5. Once done, release pressure using quick release. Remove lid.

6. Remove fish fillets from the pot and clean the pot.

7. Add oil into the inner pot of instant pot and set the pot on sauté mode.

8. Add garlic and sauté for 1 minute.

9. Add tomatoes, parsley, and basil and stir well and cook for 1 minute.

10. Add fish fillets and top with crumbled cheese and cook for a minute.

11. Serve and enjoy

Nutrition:

- Calories 219 Fat 10.1 g Carbohydrates 4 g Sugar 2.8 g Protein 27.1 g Cholesterol 70 mg

Avocado & Pea Dip With Carrots

Servings:3
Cooking Time:10 Minutes
Ingredients:

- 1 avocado, peeled and seed removed
- 1 1/2 cups steamed snow peas
- 1/4 teaspoon cayenne pepper
- 2 tablespoons lime juice
- 1 clove of garlic, diced
- Carrots to serve

Directions:

1. Combine together all ingredients in a blender and blend until very smooth. Serve with fresh carrots.

Nutrition:

- 448 Calories 27g fat 41g carbs 15g protein

Avocado Dip

Servings:8
Cooking Time:10 Minutes
Ingredients:

- ½ cup heavy cream
- 1 green chili pepper, chopped
- Salt and pepper to the taste
- 4 avocados, pitted, peeled and chopped
- 1 cup cilantro, chopped
- ¼ cup lime juice

Directions:

1. In a blender, combine the cream with the avocados and the rest of the ingredients and pulse well.
2. Divide the mix into bowls and serve cold as a party dip

Nutrition:

- calories 200, fat 14.5, fiber 3.8, carbs 8.1, protein 7.6

Tasty Black Bean Dip

Servings:3
Cooking Time:18 Minutes
Ingredients:

- 2 cups dry black beans, soaked overnight and drained
- 1 1/2 cups cheese, shredded
- 1 tsp dried oregano
- 1 1/2 tsp chili powder
- 2 cups tomatoes, chopped
- 2 tbsp olive oil

- 1 1/2 tbsp garlic, minced
- 1 medium onion, sliced
- 4 cups vegetable stock
- Pepper
- Salt

Directions:

1. Add all ingredients except cheese into the instant pot.
2. Seal pot with lid and cook on high for 18 minutes.
3. Once done, allow to release pressure naturally. Remove lid. Drain excess water.
4. Add cheese and stir until cheese is melted.
5. Blend bean mixture using an immersion blender until smooth.
6. Serve and enjoy.

Nutrition:

- Calories 402 Fat 15.3 g Carbohydrates 46.6 g Sugar 4.4 g Protein 22.2 g Cholesterol 30 mg

Za'atar Fries

Servings:3
Cooking Time:35 Minutes
Ingredients:

- 1 teaspoon Za'atar spices
- 3 sweet potatoes
- 1 tablespoon dried dill
- 1 teaspoon salt
- 3 teaspoons sunflower oil
- ½ teaspoon paprika

Directions:

1. Pour water in the crockpot. Peel the sweet potatoes and cut them into the fries.
2. Line the baking tray with parchment.
3. Place the layer of the sweet potato in the tray.
4. Sprinkle the vegetables with dried dill, salt, and paprika.
5. Then sprinkle sweet potatoes with Za'atar and mix up well with the help of the fingertips.
6. Sprinkle the sweet potato fries with sunflower oil.
7. Preheat the oven to 375F.
8. Bake the sweet potato fries for 35 minutes. Stir the fries every 10 minutes.

Nutrition:

- calories 28, fat 2.9, fiber 0.2, carbs 0.6, protein 0.2

Stuffed Zucchinis

Servings:6

Cooking Time:30 Minutes

Ingredients:

- 6 zucchinis, halved lengthwise and insides scooped out
- 2 garlic cloves, minced
- 2 tablespoons oregano, chopped
- Juice of 2 lemons
- Salt and black pepper to the taste
- 2 tablespoons olive oil
- 8 ounces feta cheese, crumbed

Directions:

1. Arrange the zucchini halves on a baking sheet lined with parchment paper, divide the cheese and the rest of the ingredients in each zucchini half and bake at 450 degrees F for 40 minutes.

2. Arrange the stuffed zucchinis on a platter and serve as an appetizer.

Nutrition:

- 242 Calories 25g carbs 12g fat 13g protein

Plum Wraps

Servings:3

Cooking Time:10 Minutes

Ingredients:

- 4 plums
- 4 prosciutto slices
- ¼ teaspoon olive oi

Directions:

1. Preheat the oven to 375F.

2. Wrap every plum in prosciutto slice and secure with a toothpick (if needed).

3. Place the wrapped plums in the oven and bake for 10 minutes.

Nutrition:

- calories 62, fat 2.2, fiber 0.9, carbs 8, protein 4.3

Polenta Cups Recipe

Servings:3

Cooking Time:20 Minutes

Ingredients:

- 1 cup yellow cornmeal
- 1 garlic clove, minced
- 1/2 teaspoon fresh thyme, minced or 1/4 teaspoon dried thyme
- 1/2 teaspoon salt
- 1/4 cup feta cheese, crumbled
- 1/4 teaspoon pepper
- 2 tablespoons fresh basil, chopped
- 4 cups water
- 4 plum tomatoes, finely chopped

Directions:

1. In a heavy, large saucepan, bring the water and the salt to a boil; reduce the heat to a gentle boil. Slowly whisk in the cornmeal; cook, stirring with a wooden spoon for about 15 to 20 minutes, or until the polenta is thick and pulls away cleanly from the sides of the pan. Remove from the heat; stir in the pepper and the thyme.

2. Grease miniature muffin cups with cooking spray. Spoon a heaping tablespoon of the polenta mixture into each muffin cups.

3. With the back of a spoon, make an indentation in the center of each; cover and chill until the mixture is set.

4. Meanwhile, combine the feta cheese, tomatoes, garlic, and basil in a small-sized bowl.

5. Unmold the chilled polenta cups; place them on an ungreased baking sheet. Tops each indentation with 1 heaping tablespoon of the feta mixture. Broil the cups 4 inches from the heat source for about 5 to 7 minutes, or until heated through.

Nutrition:

- 26 cal, 1 mg chol., 62 mg sodium, 5 g carbs., 1 g fiber, and 1 g protein.

Carrot Chips

Servings:3

Cooking Time:10 Minutes

Ingredients:

- 6 large carrots
- 2 tablespoons extra virgin olive oil
- ½ teaspoon black pepper

Directions:

1. Chop the carrots into 2-inch sections and then cut each section into thin sticks.

2. Toss together the carrots sticks with extra virgin olive oil and pepper in a bowl and spread into a baking sheet lined with parchment paper.

3. Bake the carrot sticks at 425° for about 20 minutes or until browned.

Nutrition:
- 448 Calories 27g fat 41g carbs 15g protein

Asparagus Frittata

Servings:4

Cooking Time:15 Minutes

Ingredients:
- ¼ cup onion, chopped
- Drizzle of olive oil
- 1-pound asparagus spears, cut into 1-inch pieces
- Salt and ground black pepper to taste
- 4 eggs, whisked
- 1 cup cheddar cheese, grated

Directions:
1. Heat a pan with the oil over medium-high heat, add the onions, stir, and cook for 3 minutes. Add the asparagus, stir, and cook for 6 minutes. Add the eggs, stir, and cook for 3 minutes.
2. Add the salt and pepper sprinkle with the cheese, put in an oven, and broil for 3 minutes.
3. Divide the frittata onto plates and serve.

Nutrition:
- Calories 200 ,Fat 12 g ,Carbs 5 g ,Protein 14 g

Superfood Spiced Apricot-sesame Bliss Balls

Servings:3

Cooking Time:30 Minutes

Ingredients:
- 2 tablespoons sesame seeds
- 1 cup apricots
- 1 cup natural gluten-free muesli
- 1 cup almonds
- 2 tablespoons raw honey
- 1 teaspoon ground cinnamon

Directions:
1. In a food processor, process almonds until finely chopped; add in raw honey, muesli, apricots, and cinnamon and process until very smooth.
2. Add sesame seeds in a shallow dish. Roll two tablespoons of the almond mixture into bite-sized balls and then roll them into the sesame seeds until well coated.
3. Arrange them on a tray and refrigerate until set. Serve and store the rest in an airtight container.

Nutrition:

- 448 Calories 27g fat 41g carbs 15g protein

Meat-filled Phyllo (samboosek)

Servings:1

Cooking Time:10 Minutes

Ingredients:
- 1 lb. ground beef or lamb
- 1 medium yellow onion, finely chopped
- 1 TB. seven spices
- 1 tsp. salt
- 1 pkg. frozen phyllo dough (12 sheets)
- 2/3 cup butter, melted

Directions:
1. In a medium skillet over medium heat, brown beef for 3 minutes, breaking up chunks with a wooden spoon.
2. Add yellow onion, seven spices, and salt, and cook for 5 to 7 minutes or until beef is browned and onions are translucent. Set aside, and let cool.
3. Place first sheet of phyllo on your work surface, brush with melted butter, lay second sheet of phyllo on top, and brush with melted butter. Cut sheets into 3-inch-wide strips.
4. Spoon 2 tablespoons meat filling at end of each strip, and fold end strip to cover meat and form a triangle. Fold pointed end up and over to the opposite end, and you should see a triangle forming. Continue to fold up and then over until you come to the end of strip.
5. Place phyllo pies on a baking sheet, seal side down, and brush tops with butter. Repeat with remaining phyllo and filling.
6. Bake for 10 minutes or until golden brown.
7. Remove from the oven and set aside for 5 minutes before serving warm or at room temperature

Nutrition:
- 242 Calories 25g carbs 12g fat 13g protein

Rosemary & Garlic Kale Chips

Servings:1

Cooking Time:30 Minutes

Ingredients:
- 9oz kale chips, chopped into 2inch
- 2 sprigs of rosemary
- 2 cloves of garlic
- 2 tablespoons olive oil
- Sea salt
- Freshly ground black pepper

Directions:

1. Gently warm the olive oil, rosemary and garlic over a low heat for 10 minutes. Remove it from the heat and set aside to cool.
2. Take the rosemary and garlic out of the oil and discard them.
3. Toss the kale leaves in the oil, making sure they are well coated.
4. Season with salt and pepper.
5. Spread the kale leaves onto 2 baking sheets and bake them in the oven at 170C/325F for 15 minutes, until crispy.

Nutrition:

- Calories: 249 ,Sodium: 36 mg ,Dietary Fiber: 1.7 g ,Total Fat: 4.3 g ,Total Carbs: 15.3 g ,Protein: 1.4 g

Sardine Meatballs

Servings:3

Cooking Time:10 Minutes

Ingredients:

- 11 oz sardines, canned, drained
- 1/3 cup shallot, chopped
- 1 teaspoon chili flakes
- ½ teaspoon salt
- 2 tablespoon wheat flour, whole grain
- 1 egg, beaten
- 1 tablespoon chives, chopped
- 1 teaspoon olive oil
- 1 teaspoon butter

Directions:

1. Put the butter in the skillet and melt it.
2. Add shallot and cook it until translucent.
3. After this, transfer the shallot in the mixing bowl.
4. Add sardines, chili flakes, salt, flour, egg, chives, and mix up until smooth with the help of the fork.
5. Make the medium size cakes and place them in the skillet.
6. Add olive oil.
7. Roast the fish cakes for 3 minutes from each side over the medium heat.
8. Dry the cooked fish cakes with the paper towel if needed and transfer in the serving plates.

Nutrition:

- calories 221, fat 12.2, fiber 0.1, carbs 5.4, protein 21.3

Honey Garlic Shrimp

Servings:3

Cooking Time:5 Minutes

Ingredients:

- 1 lb shrimp, peeled and deveined
- 1/4 cup honey
- 1 tbsp garlic, minced
- 1 tbsp ginger, minced
- 1 tbsp olive oil
- 1/4 cup fish stock
- Pepper
- Salt

Directions:

1. Add shrimp into the large bowl. Add remaining ingredients over shrimp and toss well.
2. Transfer shrimp into the instant pot and stir well.
3. Seal pot with lid and cook on high for 5 minutes.
4. Once done, release pressure using quick release. Remove lid.
5. Serve and enjoy.

Nutrition:

- Calories 240 Fat 5.6 g Carbohydrates 20.9 g Sugar 17.5 g Protein 26.5 g Cholesterol 239 mg

Orange Salsa

Servings:3

Cooking Time:30 Minutes

Ingredients:

- 1½ C. fresh mango, cut into chunks
- 1½ C. fresh pineapple, peeled, pitted and cubed
- ¼ C. red onion, chopped
- 2 tbsp. fresh cilantro, chopped
- 2 tbsp. fresh orange juice
- Salt and freshly ground black pepper, to taste
- 2 tbsp. unsweetened coconut, shredded

Directions:

1. In a large bowl, add all ingredients except coconut and gently toss to coat well.
2. Serve immediately with the topping of coconut.

Nutrition:

- 448 Calories 27g fat 41g carbs 15g protein

Cod And Cabbage

Servings:4

Cooking Time:15 Minutes

Ingredients:

- 3 cups green cabbage, shredded
- 1 sweet onion, sliced
- A pinch of salt and black pepper
- ½ cup feta cheese, crumbled
- 4 teaspoons olive oil
- 4 cod fillets, boneless
- ¼ cup green olives, pitted and chopped

Directions:

1. Grease a roasting pan with the oil, add the fish, the cabbage and the rest of the ingredients, introduce in the pan and cook at 450 degrees F for 15 minutes.

2. Divide the mix between plates and serve

Nutrition:

- calories 270, fat 10, fiber 3, carbs 12, protein 31

Blueberry Cauliflower

Servings:1

Cooking Time:5 Minutes

Ingredients:

- ¼ cup frozen strawberries
- 2 tsp. maple syrup
- ¾ cup unsweetened cashew milk
- 1 tsp. vanilla extract
- ½ cup plain cashew yogurt
- 5 tbsp. powdered peanut butter
- ¾ cup frozen wild blueberries
- ½ cup cauliflower florets, coarsely chopped

Directions:

1. Add all the smoothie ingredients to a high-speed blender.

2. Quickly combine until smooth.

3. Pour into a chilled glass and serve.

Nutrition:

- Calories: 340 ,Fats: 11 g ,Carbs: 48 g ,Protein: 16 g

Honey Chili Nuts

Servings:1

Cooking Time:30 Minutes

Ingredients:

- 5oz walnuts
- 5oz pecan nuts
- 2oz softened butter
- 1 tablespoon honey
- ½ bird's-eye chili, very finely chopped and de-seeded

Directions:

1. Preheat the oven to 180C/360F.

2. Combine the butter, honey and chili in a bowl, then add the nuts and stir them well.

3. Spread the nuts onto a lined baking sheet and roast them in the oven for 10 minutes, stirring once halfway through.

4. Remove from the oven and allow them to cool before eating.

Nutrition:

- Calories: 295 ,Sodium: 28 mg ,Dietary Fiber: 1.6 g ,Total Fat: 4.7 g ,Total Carbs: 14.6 g ,Protein: 1.3 g

Shrimp And Lemon Sauce

Servings:4

Cooking Time:15 Minutes

Ingredients:

- 1 pound shrimp, peeled and deveined
- 1/3 cup lemon juice
- 4 egg yolks
- 2 tablespoons olive oil
- 1 cup chicken stock
- Salt and black pepper to the taste
- 1 cup black olives, pitted and halved
- 1 tablespoon thyme, chopped

Directions:

1. In a bowl, mix the lemon juice with the egg yolks and whisk well.

2. Heat up a pan with the oil over medium heat, add the shrimp and cook for 2 minutes on each side and transfer to a plate.

3. Heat up a pan with the stock over medium heat, add some of this over the egg yolks and lemon juice mix and whisk well.

4. Add this over the rest of the stock, also add salt and pepper, whisk well and simmer for 2 minutes.

5. Add the shrimp and the rest of the ingredients, toss and serve right away.

Nutrition:

- calories 237, fat 15.3, fiber 4.6, carbs 15.4, protein 7.6

Chili-lime Cucumber, Jicama, & Apple Sticks

Servings:3

Cooking Time:10 Minutes

Ingredients:

- 6 spears cucumber
- 6 spears very ripe apple
- 6 spears jicama (you can use mango instead)
- 1 teaspoon chili lime seasoning
- 2 lime wedges

Directions:

1. In a bowl, mix together cucumber, apple, jicama, lime juice, chili lime seasoning until well combined. Serve garnished with lime wedges. Enjoy!

Nutrition:

- 324 Calories 24g fat 20g protein 7g carbs

Roasted Chickpeas

Servings:3

Cooking Time:30 Minutes

Ingredients:

- 1 C. cooked chickpeas
- 1 small garlic clove, minced
- ½ tsp. dried oregano, crushed
- 1/8 tsp. ground cumin
- 1/8 tsp. smoked paprika
- Pinch of cayenne pepper
- Salt, to taste
- ½ tbsp. olive oil

Directions:

1. Preheat the oven to 400 degrees F. Grease a large baking sheet.
2. Place chickpeas in the preparation ared baking sheet in a single layer.
3. Roast for about 30 minutes, stirring the after every 10 minutes.
4. Meanwhile, in a small mixing bowl, mix together garlic, thyme and spices.
5. Remove the baking sheet from oven.
6. Add the garlic mixture and oil and toss to coat well.
7. Roast for about 10-15 minutes more.
8. Now, turn the oven off but keep the baking sheet in oven for about 10 minutes

Nutrition:

- 242 Calories 25g carbs 12g fat 13g protein

Chicken Bites

Servings:5

Cooking Time:5 Minutes

Ingredients:

- ½ cup coconut flakes
- 8 oz chicken fillet
- ¼ cup Greek yogurt
- 1 teaspoon dried dill
- 1 teaspoon salt
- 1 teaspoon ground black pepper
- 1 tablespoon tomato sauce
- 1 teaspoon honey
- 4 tablespoons sunflower oil

Directions:

1. Chop the chicken fillet on the small cubes (popcorn cubes)
2. Sprinkle them with dried dill, salt, and ground black pepper.
3. Then add Greek yogurt and stir carefully.
4. After this, pour sunflower oil in the skillet and heat it up.
5. Coat chicken cubes in the coconut flakes and roast in the hot oil for 3-4 minutes or until the popcorn cubes are golden brown.
6. Dry the popcorn chicken with the help of the paper towel.
7. Make the sweet sauce: whisk together honey and tomato sauce.
8. Serve the popcorn chicken hot or warm with sweet sauce.

Nutrition:

- calories 107, fat 5.2, fiber 0.8, carbs 2.8, protein 12.1

Walnut & Spiced Apple Tonic

Servings:1

Cooking Time:15 Minutes

Ingredients:

- 6 walnuts halves
- 1 apple, cored
- 1 banana
- ½ teaspoon matcha powder
- ½ teaspoon cinnamon
- Pinch of ground nutmeg

Directions:

1. Place ingredients into a blender and add sufficient water to cover them. Blitz until smooth and creamy.

Nutrition:

- Calories: 124 ,Sodium: 22 mg ,Dietary Fiber: 1.4 g ,Total Fat: 2.1 g ,Total Carbs: 12.3 g ,Protein: 1.2 g

Roasted Radishes

Servings:2

Cooking Time:35 Minutes

Ingredients:

- 2 cups radishes cut in quarters
- Salt and ground black pepper to taste
- 2 tbsp. butter, melted
- 1 tbsp. fresh chives, chopped
- 1 tbsp. lemon zest

Directions:

1. Spread the radishes on a lined baking sheet. Add the salt, pepper, chives, lemon zest, and butter, toss to coat, and bake in the oven at 375ºF for 35 minutes.
2. Divide onto plates and serve.

Nutrition:

- Calories 122 ,Fat 12 g ,Carbs 3 g ,Protein 14 g

Pepper Salmon Skewers

Servings:5

Cooking Time:15 Minutes

Ingredients:

- 1.5-pound salmon fillet
- ½ cup Plain yogurt
- 1 teaspoon paprika
- 1 teaspoon turmeric
- 1 teaspoon red pepper
- 1 teaspoon salt
- 1 teaspoon dried cilantro
- 1 teaspoon sunflower oil
- ½ teaspoon ground nutmeg

Directions:

1. For the marinade: mix up together Plain yogurt, paprika, turmeric red pepper, salt, and ground nutmeg.
2. Chop the salmon fillet roughly and put it in the yogurt mixture.
3. Mix up well and marinate for 25 minutes.
4. Then skew the fish on the skewers.
5. Sprinkle the skewers with sunflower oil and place in the tray.

6. Bake the salmon skewers for 15 minutes at 375F.

Nutrition:

- calories 217, fat 9.9, fiber 0.6, carbs 4.2, protein 28.1

Raw Broccoli Poppers

Servings:4

Cooking Time:8 Minutes

Ingredients:

- 1/8 cup water
- 1/8 tsp. fine sea salt
- 4 cups broccoli florets, washed and cut into 1-inch pieces
- 1/4 tsp. turmeric powder
- 1 cup unsalted cashews, soaked overnight or at least 3-4 hours and drained
- 1/4 tsp. onion powder
- 1 red bell pepper, seeded and
- 2 tbsp. nutritional heaping
- 2 tbsp. lemon juice

Directions:

1. Transfer the drained cashews to a high-speed blender and pulse for about 30 seconds. Add in the chopped pepper and pulse again for 30 seconds.
2. Add 2 tbsp. of lemon juice, 1/8 cup of water, 2 tbsp. of nutritional yeast/ heaping, ¼ tsp. of onion powder, 1/8 of tsp. fine sea salt, and 1/4 tsp. of turmeric powder. Pulse for about 45 seconds until smooth.
3. Handover the broccoli into a bowl and add in the chopped cheesy cashew mixture. Toss well until coated.
4. Transfer the pieces of broccoli to the trays of a yeast dehydrator.
5. Follow the dehydrator's instructions and dehydrate for about 8 minutes at 125°F or until crunchy.

Nutrition:

- Calories: 408 .Fats: 32 g ,Carbs: 22 g ,Protein: 15 g

Eggplant Dip

Servings:3

Cooking Time:40 Minutes

Ingredients:

- 1 eggplant, poked with a fork
- 2 tablespoons tahini paste
- 2 tablespoons lemon juice
- 2 garlic cloves, minced
- 1 tablespoon olive oil

- Salt and black pepper to the taste
- 1 tablespoon parsley, chopped

Directions:

1. Put the eggplant in a roasting pan, bake at 400 degrees F for 40 minutes, cool down, peel and transfer to your food processor.

2. Add the rest of the ingredients except the parsley, pulse well, divide into small bowls and serve as an appetizer with the parsley sprinkled on top.

Nutrition:

- calories 121, fat 4.3, fiber 1, carbs 1.4, protein 4.3

Berry & Veggie Gazpacho

Servings:3
Cooking Time:30 Minutes

Ingredients:

- 1½ lb. fresh strawberries, hulled and sliced
- ½ C. red bell pepper, seeded and chopped
- 1 small cucumber, peeled, seeded and chopped
- ¼ C. onion, chopped
- ¼ C. fresh basil leaves
- 1 small garlic clove, chopped
- ¼ of small jalapeño pepper, seeded and chopped
- 1 tbsp. olive oil
- 3 tbsp. balsamic vinegar

Directions:

1. In a high-speed blender, add all ingredients and pulse until smooth.

2. Transfer the gazpacho into a large bowl.

3. Cover and refrigerate to chill completely before serving.

Nutrition:

- 448 Calories 27g fat 41g carbs 15g protein

Seafood Stew Cioppino

Servings:6
Cooking Time:40 Minutes

Ingredients:

- ¼ cup Italian parsley, chopped
- ¼ tsp dried basil
- ¼ tsp dried thyme
- ½ cup dry white wine like pinot grigio
- ½ lb. King crab legs, cut at each joint
- ½ onion, chopped
- ½ tsp red pepper flakes (adjust to desired spiciness)

- 1 28-oz can crushed tomatoes
- 1 lb. mahi mahi, cut into ½-inch cubes
- 1 lb. raw shrimp
- 1 tbsp olive oil
- 2 bay leaves
- 2 cups clam juice
- 50 live clams, washed
- 6 cloves garlic, minced
- Pepper and salt to taste

Directions:

1. On medium fire, place a stockpot and heat oil.

2. Add onion and for 4 minutes sauté until soft.

3. Add bay leaves, thyme, basil, red pepper flakes and garlic. Cook for a minute while stirring a bit.

4. Add clam juice and tomatoes. Once simmering, place fire to medium low and cook for 20 minutes uncovered.

5. Add white wine and clams. Cover and cook for 5 minutes or until clams have slightly opened.

6. Stir pot then add fish pieces, crab legs and shrimps. Do not stir soup to maintain the fish's shape. Cook while covered for 4 minutes or until clams are fully opened; fish and shrimps are opaque and cooked.

7. Season with pepper and salt to taste.

8. Transfer Cioppino to serving bowls and garnish with parsley before serving.

Nutrition:

- Calories per Serving: 371; Carbs: 15.5 g; Protein: 62 g; Fat: 6.8 g

Crab Stew

Servings:2
Cooking Time:13 Minutes

Ingredients:

- 1/2 lb lump crab meat
- 2 tbsp heavy cream
- 1 tbsp olive oil
- 2 cups fish stock
- 1/2 lb shrimp, shelled and chopped
- 1 celery stalk, chopped
- 1/2 tsp garlic, chopped
- 1/4 onion, chopped
- Pepper
- Salt

Directions:

1. Add oil into the inner pot of instant pot and set the pot on sauté mode.
2. Add onion and sauté for 3 minutes.
3. Add garlic and sauté for 30 seconds.
4. Add remaining ingredients except for heavy cream and stir well.
5. Seal pot with lid and cook on high for 10 minutes.
6. Once done, release pressure using quick release. Remove lid.
7. Stir in heavy cream and serve

Nutrition:
- Calories 376 Fat 25.5 g Carbohydrates 5.8 g Sugar 0.7 g Protein 48.1 g Cholesterol 326 mg

Savory Pita Chips

Servings:1
Cooking Time:10 Minutes

Ingredients:
- 3 pitas
- 1/4 cup extra-virgin olive oil
- 1/4 cup zaatar

Directions:
1. Preheat the oven to 450°F.
2. Cut pitas into 2-inch pieces, and place in a large bowl.
3. Drizzle pitas with extra-virgin olive oil, sprinkle with zaatar, and toss to coat.
4. Spread out pitas on a baking sheet, and bake for 8 to 10 minutes or until lightly browned and crunchy.
5. Let pita chips cool before removing from the baking sheet. Store in an airtight container for up to 1 month.

Nutrition:
- 242 Calories 25g carbs 12g fat 13g protein

Raw Turmeric Cashew Nut & Coconut Balls

Servings:3
Cooking Time:10 Minutes

Ingredients:
- 1 cup raw cashews
- 1 1/2 cup shredded coconut
- 1 tablespoon raw honey
- 3 teaspoons ground turmeric
- 1 teaspoon cinnamon
- 1 teaspoon ground ginger
- 1 teaspoon black pepper

- 1/2 teaspoon sea salt

Directions:
1. In a food processor, process coconut until almost oily; add in the rest of the ingredients and process until cashews are finely chopped.
2. Press the mixture into bite-sized balls and arrange them on a baking tray. Refrigerate until firm before serving

Nutrition:
- 324 Calories 24g fat 20g protein 7g carbs

Mozzarella Cauliflower Bars

Servings:12
Cooking Time:40 Minutes

Ingredients:
- 1 big cauliflower head, riced
- ½ cup low-fat mozzarella cheese, shredded
- ¼ cup egg whites
- 1 teaspoon Italian seasoning
- Black pepper to the taste

Directions:
1. Spread the cauliflower rice on a lined baking sheet, cook in the oven at 375 degrees F for 20 minutes, transfer to a bowl, add black pepper, cheese, seasoning, and egg whites, stir well, spread into a rectangle pan and press on the bottom.
2. Introduce in the oven at 375 degrees F, bake for 20 minutes, cut into 12 bars, and serve as a snack.

Nutrition:
- Calories 140 ,Fat 1 g ,Carbohydrate 6 g ,Protein 6 g

Creamy Curry Salmon

Servings:2
Cooking Time:30 Minutes

Ingredients:
- 2 salmon fillets, boneless and cubed
- 1 tablespoon olive oil
- 1 tablespoon basil, chopped
- Sea salt and black pepper to the taste
- 1 cup Greek yogurt
- 2 teaspoons curry powder
- 1 garlic clove, minced
- ½ teaspoon mint, chopped

Directions:

1. Heat up a pan with the oil over medium-high heat, add the salmon and cook for 3 minutes.
2. Add the rest of the ingredients, toss, cook for 15 minutes more, divide between plates and serve.

Nutrition:
- calories 284, fat 14.1, fiber 8.5, carbs 26.7, protein 31.4

Veggie Balls

Servings:3
Cooking Time:30 Minutes

Ingredients:
- 2 medium sweet potatoes, peeled and cubed into ½-inch size
- 2 tbsp. unsweetened coconut milk
- 1 C. fresh kale leaves, trimmed and chopped
- 1 medium shallot, chopped finely
- 1 tsp. ground cumin
- ½ tsp. granulated garlic
- ¼ tsp. ground turmeric
- Salt and freshly ground black pepper, to taste
- Ground flax seeds, as require

Directions:
1. Preheat the oven to 400 degrees F. Line a baking sheet with parchment paper.
2. In a pan of water, arrange a steamer basket.
3. Place the sweet potato in steamer basket and steam for about 10-15 minutes.
4. In a large bowl, place the sweet potato with the coconut milk and mash well.
5. Add remaining ingredients except flax seeds and mix till well combined.
6. Make about 1½-2-inch balls from the mixture.
7. Arrange the balls onto preparation ared baking sheet in a single layer and sprinkle with flax seeds.
8. Bake for about 20-25 minutes.

Nutrition:
- 448 Calories 27g fat 41g carbs 15g protein

Lime Pea Guacamole

Servings:3
Cooking Time:10 Minutes

Ingredients:
- 2 cups thawed frozen green peas
- ¼ cup fresh lime juice

- 1 teaspoon crushed garlic
- ½ teaspoon cumin
- 1/8 teaspoon hot sauce
- ½ cup chopped cilantro
- 4 green onions, chopped
- 1 tomato, chopped
- Black pepper

Directions:
1. In a food processor, blend together peas, lime juice, garlic, and cumin until very smooth; transfer to a large bowl and stir in hot sauce, cilantro, green onion, tomato and pepper. Refrigerate, covered, for about 30 minutes for flavors to blend. Enjoy!

Nutrition:
- 324 Calories 24g fat 20g protein 7g carbs

Zucchini Cakes

Servings:4
Cooking Time:10 Minutes

Ingredients:
- 1 zucchini, grated
- ¼ carrot, grated
- ¼ onion, minced
- 1 teaspoon minced garlic
- 3 tablespoons coconut flour
- 1 teaspoon Italian seasonings
- 1 egg, beaten
- 1 teaspoon coconut oil

Directions:
1. In the mixing bowl combine together grated zucchini, carrot, minced onion, and garlic.
2. Add coconut flour, Italian seasoning, and egg.
3. Stir the mass until homogenous.
4. Heat up coconut oil in the skillet.
5. Place the small zucchini fritters in the hot oil. Make them with the help of the spoon.
6. Roast the zucchini fritters for 4 minutes from each side.

Nutrition:
- calories 65, fat 3.3, fiber 3, carbs 6.3, protein 3.3

Healthy Guacamole

Servings:3
Cooking Time:30 Minutes
Ingredients:

- 2 medium ripe avocados, peeled, pitted and chopped
- 1 small red onion, chopped
- 1 garlic clove, minced
- 1 Serrano pepper, seeded and chopped
- 1 tomato, seeded and chopped
- 2 tbsp. fresh cilantro leaves, chopped
- 1 tbsp. fresh lime juice
- Salt, to taste

Directions:

1. In a large bowl, add avocado and with a fork, mash it completely.
2. Add remaining all ingredients and gently stir to combine.
3. Serve immediately

Nutrition:

- 448 Calories 27g fat 41g carbs 15g protein

Honey Balsamic Salmon

Servings:2
Cooking Time:3 Minutes
Ingredients:

- 2 salmon fillets
- 1/4 tsp red pepper flakes
- 2 tbsp honey
- 2 tbsp balsamic vinegar
- 1 cup of water
- Pepper
- Salt

Directions:

1. Pour water into the instant pot and place trivet in the pot.
2. In a small bowl, mix together honey, red pepper flakes, and vinegar.
3. Brush fish fillets with honey mixture and place on top of the trivet.
4. Seal pot with lid and cook on high for 3 minutes.
5. Once done, release pressure using quick release. Remove lid.
6. Serve and enjoy.

Nutrition:

- Calories 303 Fat 11 g Carbohydrates 17.6 g Sugar 17.3 g Protein 34.6 g Cholesterol 78 mg

Leeks And Calamari Mix

Servings:6
Cooking Time:15 Minutes
Ingredients:

- 2 tablespoon avocado oil
- 2 leeks, chopped
- 1 red onion, chopped
- Salt and black to the taste
- 1 pound calamari rings
- 1 tablespoon parsley, chopped
- 1 tablespoon chives, chopped
- 2 tablespoons tomato paste

Directions:

1. Heat up a pan with the avocado oil over medium heat, add the leeks and the onion, stir and sauté for 5 minutes.
2. Add the rest of the ingredients, toss, simmer over medium heat for 10 minutes, divide into bowls and serve

Nutrition:

- calories 238, fat 9, fiber 5.6, carbs 14.4, protein 8.4

Chili Mango And Watermelon Salsa

Servings:8
Cooking Time:10 Minutes
Ingredients:

- 1 red tomato, chopped
- Salt and black pepper to the taste
- 1 cup watermelon, seedless, peeled and cubed
- 1 red onion, chopped
- 2 mangos, peeled and chopped
- 2 chili peppers, chopped
- ¼ cup cilantro, chopped
- 3 tablespoons lime juice
- Pita chips for serving

Directions:

1. In a bowl, mix the tomato with the watermelon, the onion and the rest of the ingredients except the pita chips and toss well.
2. Divide the mix into small cups and serve with pita chips on the side.

Nutrition:

- calories 62, fat 4.7, fiber 1.3, carbs 3.9, protein 2.3

Olive, Pepperoni, And Mozzarella Bites

Servings:2

Cooking Time:30 Minutes

Ingredients:

- 1 pound block Mozzarella cheese
- 1 package pepperoni
- 1 can whole medium black olives

Directions:

1. Slice the block of mozzarella cheese into 1/2x1/2-inch cubes. Drain the olives from the liquid.
2. With a toothpick, skewer the olive, pushing it 1/3 way up the toothpick.
3. Fold a pepperoni into half or quarters and skewer after the olive.
4. Finally, skewer a mozzarella cheese, not pushing all the way through the cube, about only half way through. Repeat with the remaining olives, pepperoni, and mozzarella cubes.

Nutrition:

- 75 cal., 5.6 g total fat (2.5 g sat. fat), 14 mg chol., 221 mg sodium, 16 mg pot., 0.8 g total carbs., 0 g fiber, 0 g sugar, 5.6 g protein, 3% vitamin A, 0% vitamin C, 11% calcium, and 1% iron.

Ginger Tahini Dip With Veggies

Servings:3

Cooking Time:10 Minutes

Ingredients:

- ½ cup tahini
- 1 teaspoon grated garlic
- 2 teaspoons ground turmeric
- 1 tablespoon grated fresh ginger
- ¼ cup apple cider vinegar
- ¼ cup water
- ½ teaspoon salt

Directions:

1. In a bowl, whisk together tahini, turmeric, ginger, water, vinegar, garlic, and salt until well blended. Serve with assorted veggies

Nutrition:

- 448 Calories 27g fat 41g carbs 15g protein

Roasted Red Endive With Caper Butter

Servings:4

Cooking Time:25 Minutes

Ingredients:

- 10 – 12 red endives
- 2 teaspoons extra virgin olive oil
- 2–5 anchovy fillets, packed in oil
- 1 small lemon, juiced
- 3 tablespoons capers, drained
- 5 tablespoons cold butter, cut into cubes
- 1 tablespoon fresh parsley, chopped
- Salt and pepper as needed

Directions:

1. Preheat the oven to 425 degrees F.
2. Toss endives with olive oil, salt, and pepper, and spread out on to a baking sheet cut side down. Bake for about 20-25 minutes or until caramelized.
3. While they're roasting, add the anchovies to a large pan over medium heat and use a fork to mash them until broken up.
4. Add lemon juice and mix well, then add capers.
5. Lower the heat and slowly stir in the butter and parsley.
6. Drizzle butter over roasted endives, season as necessary and garnish with more fresh parsley.

Nutrition:

- Calories 109 ,Fat 8.6g ,Protein1.5 g, ,Carbohydrates 4.9 g, ,Fiber 4 g

Red Pepper Tapenade

Servings:3

Cooking Time:10 Minutes

Ingredients:

- 7 ounces roasted red peppers, chopped
- ½ cup parmesan, grated
- 1/3 cup parsley, chopped
- 14 ounces canned artichokes, drained and chopped
- 3 tablespoons olive oil
- ¼ cup capers, drained
- 1 and ½ tablespoons lemon juice
- 2 garlic cloves, minced

Directions:

1. In your blender, combine the red peppers with the parmesan and the rest of the ingredients and pulse well.
2. Divide into cups and serve as a snack

Nutrition:

- calories 200, fat 5.6, fiber 4.5, carbs 12.4, protein 4.6

Tomato Triangles

Servings:6
Cooking Time: 10 Minutes
Ingredients:
- 6 corn tortillas
- 1 tablespoon cream cheese
- 1 tablespoon ricotta cheese
- ½ teaspoon minced garlic
- 1 tablespoon fresh dill, chopped
- 2 tomatoes, sliced

Directions:
1. Cut every tortilla into 2 triangles.
2. Then mix up together cream cheese, ricotta cheese, minced garlic, and dill.
3. Spread 6 triangles with cream cheese mixture.
4. Then place sliced tomato on them and cover with remaining tortilla triangles.

Nutrition:
- calories 71, fat 1.6, fiber 2.1, carbs 12.8, protein 2.3

Tomato Cod Mix

Servings:2
Cooking Time:5 Hours 30 Minutes
Ingredients:
- 1 teaspoon tomato paste
- 1 teaspoon garlic, diced
- 1 white onion, sliced
- 1 jalapeno pepper, chopped
- 1/3 cup chicken stock
- 7 oz Spanish cod fillet
- 1 teaspoon paprika
- 1 teaspoon salt

Directions:
1. Pour chicken stock in the saucepan.
2. Add tomato paste and mix up the liquid until homogenous.
3. Add garlic, onion, jalapeno pepper, paprika, and salt.
4. Bring the liquid to boil and then simmer it.
5. Chop the cod fillet and add it in the tomato liquid.
6. Close the lid and simmer the fish for 10 minutes over the low heat.
7. Serve the fish in the bowls with tomato sauce.

Nutrition:

- calories 113, fat 1.2, fiber 1.9, carbs 7.2, protein 18.9

Marinated Cheese

Servings:3
Cooking Time:10 Minutes
Ingredients:
- 8 ounces cream cheese
- 6 sprigs fresh thyme
- 3 sprigs fresh rosemary
- 2 garlic cloves, sliced
- 1/2 cup sun-dried tomato vinaigrette dressing
- 1 teaspoon black pepper
- 1 lemon peel, cut into thin strips

Directions:
1. Cut the cream cheese into 36 cubes. Place on a serving tray.
2. Combine the remaining ingredients together.
3. Pour the dressing over the cheese; toss lightly.
4. Refrigerate for at least 1 hour to marinate.

Nutrition:
- 44 cal., 4.3 g total fat (2.4 sat. fat), 13.9 mg chol., 40.6 mg sodium, 0.7 g total carbs., 0 g fiber, 0.4 g sugar, and 0.8 g protein.

Pecan Salmon Fillets

Servings:6
Cooking Time:30 Minutes
Ingredients:
- 3 tablespoons olive oil
- 3 tablespoons mustard
- 5 teaspoons honey
- 1 cup pecans, chopped
- 6 salmon fillets, boneless
- 1 tablespoon lemon juice
- 3 teaspoons parsley, chopped
- Salt and pepper to the taste

Directions:
1. In a bowl, mix the oil with the mustard and honey and whisk well.
2. Put the pecans and the parsley in another bowl.
3. Season the salmon fillets with salt and pepper, arrange them on a baking sheet lined with parchment paper, brush with the honey and mustard mix and top with the pecans mix.

4. Introduce in the oven at 400 degrees F, bake for 15 minutes, divide between plates, drizzle the lemon juice on top and serve.

Nutrition:

- calories 282, fat 15.5, fiber 8.5, carbs 20.9, protein 16.8

Radish Hash Browns

Servings:4

Cooking Time:10 Minutes

Ingredients:

- ½ tsp. onion powder
- 1-pound radishes, shredded
- ½ tsp. garlic powder
- Salt and ground black pepper to taste
- 4 eggs
- ⅓ Cup Parmesan cheese, grated

Directions:

1. In a bowl, mix the radishes with salt, pepper, onion, and garlic powder, eggs, and Parmesan cheese, and stir well.
2. Spread on a lined baking sheet, put in an oven at 375°F, and bake for 10 minutes.
3. Divide the hash browns onto plates and serve.

Nutrition:

- Calories 80 ,Fat 5 g ,Carbs 5 g ,Protein 7 g

Chia Crackers

Servings:24

Cooking Time:

Ingredients:

- 1/2 cup pecans, chopped
- 1/2 cup chia seeds
- 1/2 tsp. cayenne pepper
- 1 cup water
- 1/4 cup nutritional yeast
- 1/2 cup pumpkin seeds
- 1/4 cup ground flax
- Salt and pepper, to taste

Directions:

1. Mix around 1/2 cup of chia seeds and 1 cup of water. Keep it aside.
2. Take another bowl and combine all the remaining ingredients. Combine well and stir in the chia water mixture until you obtained dough.

3. Transfer the dough onto a baking sheet and roll it out into a ¼"-thick dough.
4. Transfer into a preheated oven at 325°F and bake for about ½ hour.
5. Take out from the oven, flip over the dough, and cut it into desired cracker shaped-squares.
6. Spread and back again for a further half an hour, or until crispy and browned.
7. Once done, take them out from the oven and let them cool at room temperature. Enjoy!

Nutrition:

- Calories: 41 ,Fats: 3.1 g ,Carbs: 2 g ,Protein: 2 g

Blueberry Granola Bars

Servings:3

Cooking Time:10 Minutes

Ingredients:

- ½ C. rolled oats
- 2 tbsp. flaxseeds
- 1 tbsp. sunflower seeds
- 1 tbsp. walnuts, chopped
- 2 tbsp. raisins
- ¾ C. fresh blueberries
- 1 banana, peeled and mashed
- 2 tbsp. dates, pitted and chopped finely
- 1 tbsp. fresh pomegranate juice

Directions:

1. Preheat your oven to 350 degrees F. Lightly, grease an 8-inch baking dish.
2. In a large bowl, add all ingredients and mix until well combined.
3. Place the mixture into preparation ared baking dish evenly and with the back of a spoon, smooth the surface.
4. Bake for about 25 minutes.
5. Remove from oven and keep onto a wire rack to cool.
6. With a sharp knife, cut into desired size bars and serve.

Nutrition:

- 448 Calories 27g fat 41g carbs 15g protein

Potato Chips

Servings:4

Cooking Time:5 Minutes

Ingredients:

- 1 tablespoon vegetable oil
- 1 potato, sliced paper thin
- Sea salt, to taste

Directions:

1. Toss potato with oil and sea salt.
2. Spread the slices in a baking dish in a single layer.
3. Cook in a microwave for 5 minutes until golden brown.
4. Serve.

Nutrition:

- Calories 80 ,Total Fat 3.5 g ,Saturated Fat 0.1 g ,Cholesterol 320 mg ,Sodium 350 mg ,Total Carbs 11.6 g ,Fiber 0.7 g ,Sugar 0.7 g ,Protein 1.2 g

Halibut And Quinoa Mix

Servings:4

Cooking Time:30 Minutes

Ingredients:

- 4 halibut fillets, boneless
- 2 tablespoons olive oil
- 1 teaspoon rosemary, dried
- 2 teaspoons cumin, ground
- 1 tablespoons coriander, ground
- 2 teaspoons cinnamon powder
- 2 teaspoons oregano, dried
- A pinch of salt and black pepper
- 2 cups quinoa, cooked
- 1 cup cherry tomatoes, halved
- 1 avocado, peeled, pitted and sliced
- 1 cucumber, cubed
- ½ cup black olives, pitted and sliced
- Juice of 1 lemon

Directions:

1. In a bowl, combine the fish with the rosemary, cumin, coriander, cinnamon, oregano, salt and pepper and toss.
2. Heat up a pan with the oil over medium heat, add the fish, and sear for 2 minutes on each side.
3. Introduce the pan in the oven and bake the fish at 425 degrees F for 7 minutes.
4. Meanwhile, in a bowl, mix the quinoa with the remaining ingredients, toss and divide between plates.

5. Add the fish next to the quinoa mix and serve right away.

Nutrition:

- calories 364, fat 15.4, fiber 11.2, carbs 56.4, protein 24.5

Homemade Nutella

Servings:3

Cooking Time:10 Minutes

Ingredients:

- 3/4 cup toasted hazelnuts
- 3 tablespoons peanut oil
- 2 tablespoons cocoa powder
- 3 scoops protein powder
- 1/2 teaspoon vanilla extract
- 2 tablespoons raw honey
- Pinch salt

Directions:

1. Add hazelnuts to your food processor and grind until finely ground; add in peanut oil and process the mixture into butter; add in the remaining ingredients and process until creamy and smooth. Serve with celery or carrot sticks.

Nutrition:

- 324 Calories 24g fat 20g protein 7g carbs

Superfood Raw Bars

Servings:6

Cooking Time:5 Minutes

Ingredients:

- 1/2 cup toasted pistachios
- 1/4 cup goji berries + 2 tablespoons more
- 1/2 cup roasted almonds
- 1/4 cup chia seeds
- 3/4 cup blackcurrants
- 3/4 cup coconut flakes, toasted
- 1/3 cup ginger
- 1 tablespoon raw cacao nibs
- 1 tablespoon coconut oil
- 500g chopped dark chocolate
- Pinch of sea salt

Directions:

1. Preparation are a baking pan by greasing and lining with baking paper.

2. In a large bowl, combine 1/3 cup of pistachios, blackcurrants, ½ cup of coconut flakes, goji berries, almond, chia pieces, and ginger until well mixed.

3. In another bowl, stir together cacao nibs, the remaining pistachios and coconut flakes, and more goji berries.

4. In a saucepan, stir together oil, chocolate and salt until chocolate is melted. Pour the chocolate mixture into the pistachio mixture and stir until well coated; transfer to the pan and sprinkle with the cacao mixture.

5. Refrigerate for at least 4 hours or until firm. Cut into 24 squares and serve, storing the rest in the refrigerator for up two weeks

Nutrition:

- 448 Calories 27g fat 41g carbs 15g protein

Kale Chips

Servings:3

Cooking Time:5 Minutes

Ingredients:

- 1 lb. fresh kale leaves, stemmed and torn
- ¼ tsp. cayenne pepper
- Salt, to taste
- 1 tbs. olive oil

Directions:

1. Preheat the oven to 350 degrees F. Line a large baking sheet with a parchment paper.

2. Place the kale pieces onto preparation ared baking sheet in a single layer.

3. Sprinkle the kale with cayenne and salt and drizzle with oil.

4. Bake for about 10-15 minutes.

Nutrition:

- 242 Calories 25g carbs 12g fat 13g protein

Wheat Crackers

Servings:4

Cooking Time:20 Minutes

Ingredients:

- 1 3/4 cups almond flour
- 1 1/2 cups coconut flour
- 3/4 teaspoon sea salt
- 1/3 cup vegetable oil
- 1 cup alkaline water
- Sea salt for sprinkling

Directions:

1. Set your oven to 350 degrees F.
2. Mix coconut flour, almond flour and salt in a bowl.
3. Stir in vegetable oil and water. Mix well until smooth.
4. Spread this dough on a floured surface into a thin sheet.
5. Cut small squares out of this sheet.
6. Arrange the dough squares on a baking sheet lined with parchment paper.
7. Bake for 20 minutes until light golden in color.
8. Serve

Nutrition:

- Calories 64 ,Total Fat 9.2 g ,Saturated Fat 2.4 g ,Cholesterol 110 mg ,Sodium 276 mg ,Total Carbs 9.2 g ,Fiber 0.9 g ,Sugar 1.4 g ,Protein 1.5 g

Parmesan Chips

Servings:4

Cooking Time:20 Minutes

Ingredients:

- 1 zucchini
- 2 oz Parmesan, grated
- ½ teaspoon paprika
- 1 teaspoon olive oil

Directions:

1. Trim zucchini and slice it into the chips with the help of the vegetable slices.

2. Then mix up together Parmesan and paprika.

3. Sprinkle the zucchini chips with olive oil.

4. After this, dip every zucchini slice in the cheese mixture.

5. Place the zucchini chips in the lined baking tray and bake for 20 minutes at 375F.

6. Flip the zucchini sliced onto another side after 10 minutes of cooking.

7. Chill the cooked chips well.

Nutrition:

- calories 64, fat 4.3, fiber 0.6, carbs 2.3, protein 5.2

Garlic Mussels

Servings:4

Cooking Time:10 Minutes

Ingredients:

- 1-pound mussels
- 1 chili pepper, chopped
- 1 cup chicken stock
- ½ cup milk

- 1 teaspoon olive oil
- 1 teaspoon minced garlic
- 1 teaspoon ground coriander
- ½ teaspoon salt
- 1 cup fresh parsley, chopped
- 4 tablespoons lemon juice

Directions:

1. Pour milk in the saucepan.
2. Add chili pepper, chicken stock, olive oil, minced garlic, ground coriander, salt, and lemon juice.
3. Bring the liquid to boil and add mussels.
4. Boil the mussel for 4 minutes or until they will open shells.
5. Then add chopped parsley and mix up the meal well.
6. Remove it from the heat

Nutrition:

- calories 136, fat 4.7, fiber 0.6, carbs 7.5, protein 15.3

Style Nachos Recipe

Servings:3
Cooking Time:10 Minutes

Ingredients:

- 6 pieces whole-wheat pita breads
- Cooking spray
- 1/2 teaspoon ground cumin
- 1/2 teaspoon ground coriander
- 1/2 teaspoon paprika
- 1/2 teaspoon pepper
- 1/2 teaspoons salt
- 1/2 cup hot water
- 1/2 teaspoon beef stock concentrate
- 1 pound ground lamb or beef
- 2 garlic cloves, minced
- 1 teaspoon cornstarch
- 2 medium cucumbers, peeled, seeded, grated
- 2 cups Greek yogurt, plain
- 2 tablespoons lemon juice
- 1/4 teaspoon grated lemon peel
- 1 teaspoon salt, divided
- 1/4 teaspoon pepper
- 1/2 cup pitted Greek olives, sliced
- 4 green onions, thinly sliced
- 1/2 cup crumbled feta cheese
- 2 cups torn romaine lettuce

- 2 medium tomatoes, seeded and chopped

Directions:

1. In a colander set over a bowl, toss the cucumbers with 1/2 teaspoon of the salt; let stand for 30 minutes, then squeeze and pat dry. Set aside.
2. In a small-sized bowl, combine the coriander, cumin, 1/2 teaspoon pepper, paprika, and 1/2 teaspoon salt; set aside.
3. Cut each pita bread into 8 wedges. Arrange them in a single layer on ungreased baking sheets. Sprits both sides of the wedges with cooking spray. Sprinkle with 3/4 teaspoon of the seasoning mix. Broil 3-4 inches from the heat source for about 3-4 minutes per side, or until golden brown. Transfer to wire racks, let cool.
4. Whisk hot water and beef stock cube in a 1-cup liquid measuring cup until blended. In a large-sized skillet, cook the lamb, seasoning with the remaining seasoning mix, over medium heat until the meat is no longer pink. Add the garlic; cook for 1 minute. Drain.
5. Stir in the cornstarch into the broth; mix until smooth. Gradually stir into the skillet; bring to a boil and cook, stirring, for 2 minutes or until thick.
6. In a small-sized bowl, combine the cucumbers, yogurt, lemon peel, lemon juice, and the remaining salt and 1/4 teaspoon pepper.
7. Arrange the pita wedges on a serving platter. Layer with the lettuce, lamb mixture, tomatoes, onions, olives, and cheese; serve immediately with the cucumber sauce.

Nutrition:

- 232 cal, 6.7 g total fat (2.9 g sat. fat), 42 mg chol., 630 mg sodium, 412 mg pot., 24 total carbs., 3.3 g fiber, 4.1 g sugar, 20.2 g protein, 8% vitamin A, 12% vitamin C, 11% calcium, and 15% iron.

Feta And Roasted Red Pepper Bruschetta

Servings:8
Cooking Time:15minutes

Ingredients:

- 6 Kalamata olives, pitted, chopped
- 2 tablespoons green onion, minced
- 1/4 cup Parmesan cheese, grated, divided
- 1/4 cup extra-virgin olive oil brushing, or as needed
- 1/4 cup cherry tomatoes, thinly sliced
- 1 teaspoon lemon juice
- 1 tablespoon extra-virgin olive oil

- 1 tablespoon basil pesto
- 1 red bell pepper, halved, seeded
- 1 piece (12 inch) whole-wheat baguette, cut into 1/2-inch thick slices
- 1 package (4 ounce) feta cheese with basil and sun-dried tomatoes, crumbled
- 1 clove garlic, minced

Directions:

1. Preheat the oven broiler. Place the oven rack 6 inches from the source of heat.

2. Brush both sides of the baguette slices, with the 1/4 cup olive oil. Arrange the bread slices on a baking sheet; toast for about 1 minute each side, carefully watching to avoid burning. Remove the toasted slices, transferring into another baking sheet.

3. With the cut sides down, place the red peppers in a baking sheet; broil for about 8 to 10 minutes or until the skin is charred and blistered. Transfer the roasted peppers into a bowl; cover with plastic wrap. Let cool, remove the charred skin. Discard skin and chop the roasted peppers.

4. In a bowl, mix the roasted red peppers, cherry tomatoes, feta cheese, green onion, olives, pesto, 1 tablespoon olive oil, garlic, and lemon juice.

5. Top each bread with 1 tablespoon of the roasted pepper mix, sprinkle lightly with the Parmesan cheese.

6. Return the baking sheet with the topped bruschetta; broil for about 1-2 minutes or until the topping is lightly browned.

Nutrition:

- 73 cal., 4.8 g total fat (1.4 sat. fat), 5 mg chol., 138 mg sodium, 5.3 g total carbs., 0.4 g fiber, 0.6 g sugar, and 2.1 g protein.

Vinegar Beet Bites

Servings:4
Cooking Time:30 Minutes
Ingredients:

- 2 beets, sliced
- A pinch of sea salt and black pepper
- 1/3 cup balsamic vinegar
- 1 cup olive oil

Directions:

1. Spread the beet slices on a baking sheet lined with parchment paper, add the rest of the ingredients, toss and bake at 350 degrees F for 30 minutes.

2. Serve the beet bites cold as a snack

Nutrition:

- calories 199, fat 5.4, fiber 3.5, carbs 8.5, protein 3.5

Rosemary Cauliflower Dip

Servings:3
Cooking Time:10 Minutes
Ingredients:

- 1 lb cauliflower florets
- 1 tbsp fresh parsley, chopped
- 1/2 cup heavy cream
- 1/2 cup vegetable stock
- 1 tbsp garlic, minced
- 1 tbsp rosemary, chopped
- 1 tbsp olive oil
- 1 onion, chopped
- Pepper
- Salt

Directions:

1. Add oil into the inner pot of instant pot and set the pot on sauté mode.

2. Add onion and sauté for 5 minutes.

3. Add remaining ingredients except for parsley and heavy cream and stir well.

4. Seal pot with lid and cook on high for 10 minutes.

5. Once done, allow to release pressure naturally for 10 minutes then release remaining using quick release. Remove lid.

6. Add cream and stir well. Blend cauliflower mixture using immersion blender until smooth.

7. Garnish with parsley and serve

Nutrition:

- Calories 128 Fat 9.4 g Carbohydrates 10.4 g Sugar 4 g Protein 3.1 g Cholesterol 21 mg

Paprika Salmon And Green Beans

Servings:3
Cooking Time:20 Minutes
Ingredients:

- ¼ cup olive oil
- ½ tablespoon onion powder
- ½ teaspoon bouillon powder
- ½ teaspoon cayenne pepper
- 1 tablespoon smoked paprika
- 1-pound green beans
- 2 teaspoon minced garlic

- 3 tablespoon fresh herbs
- 6 ounces of salmon steak
- Salt and pepper to taste

Directions:

1. Preheat the oven to 400F.
2. Grease a baking sheet and set aside.
3. Heat a skillet over medium low heat and add the olive oil. Sauté the garlic, smoked paprika, fresh herbs, cayenne pepper and onion powder. Stir for a minute then let the mixture sit for 5 minutes. Set aside.
4. Put the salmon steaks in a bowl and add salt and the paprika spice mixture. Rub to coat the salmon well.
5. Place the salmon on the baking sheet and cook for 18 minutes.
6. Meanwhile, blanch the green beans in boiling water with salt.
7. Serve the beans with the salmon.

Nutrition:

- Calories per Serving: 945.8; Fat: 66.6 g; Protein: 43.5 g; Carbs: 43.1 g

Zucchini Pepper Chips

Servings:4
Cooking Time:15 Minutes

Ingredients:

- 1 2/3 cups vegetable oil
- 1 teaspoon garlic powder
- 1 teaspoon onion powder
- 1/2 teaspoon black pepper
- 3 tablespoons crushed red pepper flakes
- 2 zucchinis, thinly sliced

Directions:

1. Mix oil with all the spices in a bowl.
2. Add zucchini slices and mix well.
3. Transfer the mixture to a Ziplock bag and seal it.
4. Refrigerate for 10 minutes.
5. Spread the zucchini slices on a greased baking sheet.
6. Bake for 15 minutes
7. Serve.

Nutrition:

- Calories 172 ,Total Fat 11.1 g ,Saturated Fat 5.8 g ,Cholesterol 610 mg ,Sodium 749 mg ,Total Carbs 19.9 g ,Fiber 0.2 g ,Sugar 0.2 g ,Protein 13.5 g

Roasted Asparagus

Servings:3
Cooking Time:10 Minutes

Ingredients:

- 1 asparagus bunch, trimmed
- 3 tsp. avocado oil
- A splash of lemon juice
- Salt and ground black pepper to taste
- 1 tbsp. fresh oregano, chopped

Directions:

1. Spread the asparagus spears on a lined baking sheet, season with salt, and pepper, drizzle with oil and lemon juice, sprinkle with oregano, and toss to coat well.
2. Put in an oven at 425°F, and bake for 10 minutes.
3. Divide onto plates and serve.

Nutrition:

- Calories 130 ,Fat 1 g ,Carbs 2 g ,Protein 3 g

Sage Salmon Fillet

Servings:1
Cooking Time: 30 Minutes

Ingredients:

- 4 oz salmon fillet
- ½ teaspoon salt
- 1 teaspoon sesame oil
- ½ teaspoon sage

Directions:

1. Rub the fillet with salt and sage.
2. Place the fish in the tray and sprinkle it with sesame oil.
3. Cook the fish for 25 minutes at 365F.
4. Flip the fish carefully onto another side after 12 minutes of cooking.

Nutrition:

- calories 191, fat 11.6, fiber 0.1, carbs 0.2, protein 2

Savory Trail Mix

Servings:3
Cooking Time:10 Minutes

Ingredients:

- ¼ cup chopped almonds
- 1/4 cup pumpkin seeds
- 1/4 cup sunflower seeds
- 1/2 teaspoon garlic powder
- 1/2 teaspoon onion powder
- 1/4 teaspoon cayenne pepper

Directions:

1. Mix everything and enjoy!

Nutrition:

- 324 Calories 24g fat 20g protein 7g carbs

Lavash Chips

Servings:3

Cooking Time:30 Minutes

Ingredients:

- 1 lavash sheet, whole grain
- 1 tablespoon canola oil
- 1 teaspoon paprika
- ½ teaspoon chili pepper
- ½ teaspoon salt

Directions:

1. In the shallow bowl whisk together canola oil, paprika, chili pepper, and salt.

2. Then chop lavash sheet roughly (in the shape of chips).

3. Sprinkle lavash chips with oil mixture and arrange in the tray to get one thin layer.

4. Bake the lavash chips for 10 minutes at 365F. Flip them on another side from time to time to avoid burning.

5. Cool the cooked chips well

Nutrition:

- calories 73, fat 4, fiber 0.7, carbs 8.4, protein 1.6

Healthy Poached Trout

Servings:2

Cooking Time:10 Minutes

Ingredients:

- 1 8-oz boneless, skin on trout fillet
- 2 cups chicken broth or water
- 2 leeks, halved
- 6-8 slices lemon
- salt and pepper to taste

Directions:

1. On medium fire, place a large nonstick skillet and arrange leeks and lemons on pan in a layer. Cover with soup stock or water and bring to a simmer.

2. Meanwhile, season trout on both sides with pepper and salt. Place trout on simmering pan of water. Cover and cook until trout is flaky, around 8 minutes.

3. In a serving platter, spoon leek and lemons on bottom of plate, top with trout and spoon sauce into plate. Serve and enjoy

Nutrition:

- Calories per serving: 360.2; Protein: 13.8g; Fat: 7.5g; Carbs: 51.5g

Rosemary Salmon

Servings:3

Cooking Time:10 Minutes

Ingredients:

- 2-pound salmon fillet
- 2 tablespoons avocado oil
- 2 teaspoons fresh rosemary, chopped
- ½ teaspoon minced garlic
- ½ teaspoon dried cilantro
- ½ teaspoon salt
- 1 teaspoon butter
- ½ teaspoon white pepper

Directions:

1. Whisk together avocado oil, fresh rosemary, minced garlic, dried cilantro, salt, and white pepper.

2. Rub the salmon fillet with the rosemary mixture generously and leave fish in the fridge for 20 minutes to marinate.

3. After this, put butter in the saucepan or big skillet and melt it.

4. Then put heat on maximum and place a salmon fillet in the hot butter.

5. Roast it for 1 minute from each side.

6. After this, preheat grill to 385F and grill the fillet for 8 minutes (for 4 minutes from each side).

7. Cut the cooked salmon on the servings

Nutrition:

- calories 257, fat 12.8, fiber 0.5, carbs 0.9, protein 35.3

Cucumber Rolls

Servings:3

Cooking Time:10 Minutes

Ingredients:

- 1 big cucumber, sliced lengthwise
- 1 tablespoon parsley, chopped
- 8 ounces canned tuna, drained and mashed
- Salt and black pepper to the taste
- 1 teaspoon lime juice

Directions:

1. Arrange cucumber slices on a working surface, divide the rest of the ingredients, and roll.

2. Arrange all the rolls on a platter and serve as an appetizer.

Nutrition:

- calories 200, fat 6, fiber 3.4, carbs 7.6, protein 3.5

Mahi Mahi And Pomegranate Sauce

Servings:4

Cooking Time:10 Minutes

Ingredients:

- 1 and ½ cups chicken stock
- 1 tablespoon olive oil
- 4 mahi mahi fillets, boneless
- 4 tablespoons tahini paste
- Juice of 1 lime
- Seeds from 1 pomegranate
- 1 tablespoon parsley, chopped

Directions:

1. Heat up a pan with the oil over medium-high heat, add the fish and cook for 3 minutes on each side.

2. Add the rest of the ingredients, flip the fish again, cook for 4 minutes more, divide everything between plates and serve.

Nutrition:

- calories 224, fat 11.1, fiber 5.5, carbs 16.7, protein 11.4

Oatmeal Cookies

Servings:3

Cooking Time:30 Minutes

Ingredients:

- ¾ C. whole wheat flour
- 1 C. instant oats
- 1½ tsp. organic baking powder
- 1½ tsp. ground cinnamon
- 1/8 tsp. salt
- 1 large organic egg, room temperature
- ½ C. organic honey
- 2 tbsp. coconut oil, melted
- 1 tsp. organic vanilla extract
- 1 C. red apple, cored and chopped finely

Directions:

1. In a large bowl, mix together flour, oats, baking powder, cinnamon and salt.

2. In another bowl, add remaining ingredients except apple and beat until well combined.

3. Add the flour mixture and mix until just combined.

4. Gently, fold in the apple.

5. Refrigerate for about 30 minutes.

6. Preheat the oven to 325 degrees F. Line a large baking sheet with parchment paper.

7. Place about 2 tbsp. of the mixture onto the preparation ared baking sheet in the shape of small mounds.

8. With the back of a spoon, flatten each cookie slightly

9. Bake for about 13-15 minutes.

10. Cool on the pan for 10 minutes before turning out onto a wire rack.

11. Remove from oven and keep onto a wire rack to cool for about 5 minutes.

12. Carefully invert the cookies onto the wire rack to cool completely before serving

Nutrition:

- 448 Calories 27g fat 41g carbs 15g protein

Grilled Shrimp Kabobs

Servings:4

Cooking Time:30 Minutes

Ingredients:

- 1 1/2 cups whole-wheat dry breadcrumbs
- 1 clove garlic, finely minced or pressed
- 1 teaspoon dried basil leaves
- 1/4 cup olive oil
- 2 pounds shrimp, peeled, deveined, leaving the tails on
- 2 tablespoons vegetable oil
- 2 teaspoons dried parsley flakes
- Salt and pepper
- 16 skewers, soaked for at least 20 minutes in water or until ready to use if using wooden

Directions:

1. Rinse the shrimps and dry.

2. Put the vegetable and the olive oil in a re-sealable plastic bag; add the shrimp and toss to coat with the oil mixture.

3. Add the breadcrumbs, parsley, garlic, basil, salt, and pepper; toss to coat with the dry mix.

4. Seal the bag, refrigerate for 1 hour. Thread the shrimps on the skewers.

5. Grill on preheated grill for about 2 minutes each side or until golden, making sure not to overcook

Nutrition:

- 502.7 cal., 24.8 g total fat (3.5 sat. fat), 285.8 mg chol., 1581.8 mg sodium, 31.7 g total carbs., 2 g fiber, 2.5 g sugar, and 36.4 g protein.

Healthy Carrot & Shrimp

Servings:4
Cooking Time:30 Minutes

Ingredients:

- 1 lb shrimp, peeled and deveined
- 1 tbsp chives, chopped
- 1 onion, chopped
- 1 tbsp olive oil
- 1 cup fish stock
- 1 cup carrots, sliced
- Pepper
- Salt

Directions:

1. Add oil into the inner pot of instant pot and set the pot on sauté mode.
2. Add onion and sauté for 2 minutes.
3. Add shrimp and stir well.
4. Add remaining ingredients and stir well.
5. Seal pot with lid and cook on high for 4 minutes.
6. Once done, release pressure using quick release. Remove lid.
7. Serve and enjoy.

Nutrition:

- Calories 197 Fat 5.9 g Carbohydrates 7 g Sugar 2.5 g Protein 27.7 g Cholesterol 239 mg

Easy Seafood French Stew

Servings:12
Cooking Time:45 Minutes

Ingredients:

- Pepper and Salt
- 1/2 lb. littleneck clams
- 1/2 lb. mussels
- 1 lb. shrimp, peeled and deveined
- 1 large lobster
- 2 lbs. assorted small whole fresh fish, scaled and cleaned
- 2 tbsp parsley, finely chopped
- 2 tbsp garlic, chopped
- 1 cup fennel, julienned
- Juice and zest of one orange
- 3 cups tomatoes, peeled, seeded, and chopped
- 1 cup leeks, julienned
- Pinch of Saffron
- 1 cup white wine
- Water
- 1 lb. fish bones
- 2 sprigs thyme
- 8 peppercorns
- 1 bay leaf
- 3 cloves garlic
- Salt and pepper
- 1/2 cup chopped celery
- 1/2 cup chopped onion
- 2 tbsp olive oil

Directions:

1. Do the stew: Heat oil in a large saucepan. Sauté the celery and onions for 3 minutes. Season with pepper and salt. Stir in the garlic and cook for about a minute. Add the thyme, peppercorns, and bay leaves. Stir in the wine, water and fish bones. Let it boil then before reducing to a simmer. Take the pan off the fire and strain broth into another container.

2. For the Bouillabaisse: Bring the strained broth to a simmer and stir in the parsley, leeks, orange juice, orange zest, garlic, fennel, tomatoes and saffron. Sprinkle with pepper and salt. Stir in the lobsters and fish. Let it simmer for eight minutes before stirring in the clams, mussels and shrimps. For six minutes, allow to cook while covered before seasoning again with pepper and salt.

3. Assemble in a shallow dish all the seafood and pour the broth over it.

Nutrition:

- Calories per serving: 348; Carbs: 20.0g; Protein: 31.8g; Fat: 15.2g

Orange-spiced Pumpkin Hummus

Servings:4

Cooking Time:5 Minutes

Ingredients:

- 1 tbsp. maple syrup
- 1/2 tsp. salt
- 1 can (16 oz.) garbanzo beans
- 1/8 tsp. ginger or nutmeg
- 1 cup canned pumpkin Blend,
- 1/8 tsp. cinnamon
- 1/4 cup tahini
- 1 tbsp. fresh orange juice
- Pinch of orange zest, for garnish
- 1 tbsp. apple cider vinegar

Directions:

1. Mix all the ingredients in a food processor or blender until slightly chunky.

2. Serve right away, and enjoy!

Nutrition:

- Calories: 291 ,Fats: 22.9 g ,Carbs: 15 g ,Protein: 12 g

DINNER RECIPES

Kibbeh In A Pan

Servings:3
Cooking Time:30 Minutes
Ingredients:

- 1/2 cup bulgur wheat, grind #1
- 1 cup water
- 1 large yellow onion, chopped
- 2 fresh basil leaves
- 1 lb. lean ground chuck beef
- 2 tsp. salt
- 1 tsp. ground black pepper
- 1/2 tsp. ground allspice
- 1/2 tsp. ground coriander
- 1/2 tsp. ground cumin
- 1/2 tsp. ground nutmeg
- 1/2 tsp. ground cloves
- 1/2 tsp. ground cinnamon
- 1/2 tsp. dried sage
- 1/2 lb. ground beef
- 4 TB. extra-virgin olive oil
- 1/2 cup pine nuts
- 1 tsp. seven spices

Directions:

1. In a small bowl, soak bulgur wheat in water for 30 minutes.
2. In a food processor fitted with a chopping blade, blend 1/2 of yellow onion and basil for 30 seconds. Add bulgur, and blend for 30 more seconds.
3. Add ground chuck, 11/2 teaspoons salt, black pepper, allspice, coriander, cumin, nutmeg, cloves, cinnamon, and sage, and blend for 1 minute.
4. Transfer mixture to a large bowl, and knead for 3 minutes.
5. In a medium skillet over medium heat, brown beef for 5 minutes, breaking up chunks with a wooden spoon.
6. Add remaining 1/2 of yellow onion, 2 tablespoons extra-virgin olive oil, remaining 1/2 teaspoon salt, pine nuts, and seven spices, and cook for 7 minutes.
7. Preheat the oven to 450ºF. Grease an 8×8-inch baking dish with extra-virgin olive oil.
8. Divide kibbeh dough in half, spread a layer of dough on bottom of the preparation ared baking dish, add a layer of sautéed vegetables, and top with remaining kibbeh dough.
9. Paint top of kibbeh with remaining 2 tablespoons extra-virgin olive oil, and cut kibbeh into 12 equal-size pieces. Bake for 25 minutes.
10. Let kibbeh rest for 15 minutes before serving.
Nutrition:

- Calories 476, Fat 40, Fiber 9, Carbs 33, Protein 6

Lemon Chicken Mix

Servings:3
Cooking Time:10 Minutes
Ingredients:

- 8 oz chicken breast, skinless, boneless
- 1 teaspoon Cajun seasoning
- 1 teaspoon balsamic vinegar
- 1 teaspoon olive oil
- 1 teaspoon lemon juice

Directions:

1. Cut the chicken breast on the halves and sprinkle with Cajun seasoning.
2. Then sprinkle the poultry with olive oil and lemon juice.
3. Then sprinkle the chicken breast with the balsamic vinegar.
4. Preheat the grill to 385F.
5. Grill the chicken breast halves for 5 minutes from each side.
6. Slice Cajun chicken and place in the serving plate.
Nutrition:

- calories 150, fat 5.2, fiber 0, carbs 0.1, protein 24.1

Chicken Cacciatore

Servings:6
Cooking Time:45 Minutes
Ingredients:

- 2 tablespoons extra virgin olive oil
- 6 chicken thighs
- 1 sweet onion, chopped
- 2 garlic cloves, minced
- 2 red bell peppers, cored and diced

- 2 carrots, diced
- 1 rosemary sprig
- 1 thyme sprig
- 4 tomatoes, peeled and diced
- ½ cup tomato juice
- ¼ cup dry white wine
- 1 cup chicken stock
- 1 bay leaf
- Salt and pepper to taste

Directions:

1. Heat the oil in a heavy saucepan.
2. Cook chicken on all sides until golden.
3. Stir in the onion and garlic and cook for 2 minutes.
4. Stir in the rest of the ingredients and season with salt and pepper.
5. Cook on low heat for 30 minutes.
6. Serve the chicken cacciatore warm and fresh.

Nutrition:

- Calories: 363 ,Fat: 14g ,Protein: 42g ,Carbohydrates: 9g

Cardamom Chicken And Apricot Sauce

Servings:3
Cooking Time:10 Minutes

Ingredients:

- Juice of ½ lemon
- Zest of ½ lemon, grated
- 2 teaspoons cardamom, ground
- Salt and black pepper to the taste
- 2 chicken breasts, skinless, boneless and halved
- 2 tablespoons olive oil
- 2 spring onions, chopped
- 2 tablespoons tomato paste
- 2 garlic cloves, minced
- 1 cup apricot juice
- ½ cup chicken stock
- ¼ cup cilantro, chopped

Directions:

1. In your slow cooker, combine the chicken with the lemon juice, lemon zest and the other ingredients except the cilantro, toss, put the lid on and cook on Low for 7 hours.

2. Divide the mix between plates, sprinkle the cilantro on top and serve.

Nutrition:

- calories 323, fat 12, fiber 11, carbs 23.8, protein 16.4

Beef And Grape Sauce

Servings:3
Cooking Time:30 Minutes

Ingredients:

- 1-pound beef sirloin
- 1 teaspoon molasses
- 1 tablespoon lemon zest, grated
- 1 teaspoon soy sauce
- 1 chili pepper, chopped
- ¼ teaspoon fresh ginger, minced
- 1 cup grape juice
- ½ teaspoon salt
- 1 tablespoon butter

Directions:

1. Sprinkle the beef sirloin with salt and minced ginger.
2. Heat up butter in the saucepan and add meat.
3. Roast it for 5 minutes from each side over the medium heat.
4. After this, add soy sauce, chili pepper, and grape juice.
5. Then add lemon zest and simmer the meat for 10 minutes.
6. Add molasses and mix up meat well.
7. Close the lid and cook meat for 5 minutes.
8. Serve the cooked beef with grape juice sauce

Nutrition:

- calories 267, fat 10, fiber 0.2, carbs 7.4, protein 34.9

Curry Chicken, Artichokes And Olives

Servings:3
Cooking Time:7 Hours

Ingredients:

- 2 pounds chicken breasts, boneless, skinless and cubed
- 12 ounces canned artichoke hearts, drained
- 1 cup chicken stock
- 1 red onion, chopped
- 1 tablespoon white wine vinegar
- 1 cup kalamata olives, pitted and chopped

- 1 tablespoon curry powder
- 2 teaspoons basil, dried
- Salt and black pepper to the taste
- ¼ cup rosemary, chopped

Directions:

1. In your slow cooker, combine the chicken with the artichokes, olives and the rest of the ingredients, put the lid on and cook on Low for 7 hours.

2. Divide the mix between plates and serve hot.

Nutrition:

- calories 275, fat 11.9, fiber 7.6, carbs 19.7, protein 18.7

Tasty Lamb Ribs

Servings:4
Cooking Time:30 Minutes

Ingredients:

- 2 garlic cloves, minced
- ¼ cup shallot, chopped
- 2 tablespoons fish sauce
- ½ cup veggie stock
- 2 tablespoons olive oil
- 1 and ½ tablespoons lemon juice
- 1 tablespoon coriander seeds, ground
- 1 tablespoon ginger, grated
- Salt and black pepper to the taste
- 2 pounds lamb ribs

Directions:

1. In a roasting pan, combine the lamb with the garlic, shallots and the rest of the ingredients, toss, introduce in the oven at 300 degrees F and cook for 2 hours.

2. Divide the lamb between plates and serve with a side salad.

Nutrition:

- calories 293, fat 9.1, fiber 9.6, carbs 16.7, protein 24.2

Chicken And Parsley Sauce

Servings:3
Cooking Time:25 Minutes

Ingredients:

- 1 cup ground chicken
- 2 oz Parmesan, grated
- 1 tablespoon olive oil
- 2 tablespoons fresh parsley, chopped

- 1 teaspoon chili pepper
- 1 teaspoon paprika
- ½ teaspoon dried oregano
- ¼ teaspoon garlic, minced
- ½ teaspoon dried thyme
- 1/3 cup crushed tomatoes

Directions:

1. Heat up olive oil in the skillet.

2. Add ground chicken and sprinkle it with chili pepper, paprika, dried oregano, dried thyme, and parsley. Mix up well.

3. Cook the chicken for 5 minutes and add crushed tomatoes. Mix up well.

4. Close the lid and simmer the chicken mixture for 10 minutes over the low heat.

5. Then add grated Parmesan and mix up.

6. Cook chicken bolognese for 5 minutes more over the medium heat.

Nutrition:

- calories 154, fat 9.3, fiber 1.1, carbs 3, protein 15.4

Chicken Burgers With Brussel Sprouts Slaw

Servings:3
Cooking Time:15 Minutes

Ingredients:

- ¼ cup apple, diced
- ¼ cup green onion, diced
- ½ avocado, cubed
- ½ pound Brussels sprouts, shredded
- 1 garlic clove, minced
- 1 tablespoon Dijon mustard
- 1/3 cup apple, sliced into strips
- 1/8 teaspoon red pepper flakes, optional
- 1-pound cooked ground chicken
- 3 slices bacon, cooked and diced
- Salt and pepper to tast

Directions:

1. In a mixing bowl, combine together chicken, green onion, Dijon mustard, garlic, apple, bacon and pepper flakes. Season with salt and pepper to taste. Mix the ingredients then form 4 burger patties.

2. Heat a grill pan over medium-high flame and grill the burgers. Cook for five minutes on side. Set aside.

3. In another bowl, toss the Brussels sprouts and apples.

4. In a small pan, heat coconut oil and add the Brussels sprouts mixture until everything is slightly wilted. Season with salt and pepper to taste.

5. Serve burger patties with the Brussels sprouts slaw.

Nutrition:

- Calories per Serving: 325.1; Carbs: 11.5g; Protein: 32.2g; Fat: 16.7g

Chicken And Lemongrass Sauce

Servings:3
Cooking Time:20 Minutes

Ingredients:

- 1 tablespoon dried dill
- 1 teaspoon butter, melted
- ½ teaspoon lemongrass
- ½ teaspoon cayenne pepper
- 1 teaspoon tomato sauce
- 3 tablespoons sour cream
- 1 teaspoon salt
- 10 oz chicken fillet, cubed

Directions:

1. Make the sauce: in the saucepan whisk together lemongrass, tomato sauce, sour cream, salt, and dried dill.

2. Bring the sauce to boil.

3. Meanwhile, pour melted butter in the skillet.

4. Add cubed chicken fillet and roast it for 5 minutes. Stir it from time to time.

5. Then place the chicken cubes in the hot sauce.

6. Close the lid and cook the meal for 10 minutes over the low heat.

Nutrition:

- calories 166, fat 8.2, fiber 0.2, carbs 1.1, protein 21

Fennel Wild Rice Risotto

Servings:6
Cooking Time:35 Minutes

Ingredients:

- 2 tablespoons extra virgin olive oil
- 1 shallot, chopped
- 2 garlic cloves, minced
- 1 fennel bulb, chopped
- 1 cup wild rice
- ¼ cup dry white wine
- 2 cups chicken stock
- 1 teaspoon grated orange zest
- Salt and pepper to taste

Directions:

1. Heat the oil in a heavy saucepan.

2. Add the garlic, shallot and fennel and cook for a few minutes until softened.

3. Stir in the rice and cook for 2 additional minutes then add the wine, stock and orange zest, with salt and pepper to taste.

4. Cook on low heat for 20 minutes.

5. Serve the risotto warm and fresh.

Nutrition:

- Calories: 162 ,Fat: 2g ,Protein: 8g ,Carbohydrates: 20g

Tasty Beef Goulash

Servings:3
Cooking Time:30 Minutes

Ingredients:

- 1/2 lb beef stew meat, cubed
- 1 tbsp olive oil
- 1/2 onion, chopped
- 1/2 cup sun-dried tomatoes, chopped
- 1/4 zucchini, chopped
- 1/2 cabbage, sliced
- 1 1/2 tbsp olive oil
- 2 cups chicken broth
- Pepper
- Salt

Directions:

1. Add oil into the instant pot and set the pot on sauté mode.

2. Add onion and sauté for 3-5 minutes.

3. Add tomatoes and cook for 5 minutes.

4. Add remaining ingredients and stir well.

5. Seal pot with lid and cook on high for 20 minutes.

6. Once done, allow to release pressure naturally for 10 minutes then release remaining using quick release. Remove lid.

7. Stir well and serve.

Nutrition:

- Calories 389 Fat 15.8 g Carbohydrates 19.3 g Sugar 10.7 g Protein 43.2 g Cholesterol 101 mg

Delicious Lemon Chicken Salad

Servings:4

Cooking Time:15 Minutes

Ingredients:

- 1 lb. chicken breast, cooked and diced
- 1 tbsp fresh dill, chopped
- 2 tsp olive oil
- 1/4 cup low-fat yogurt
- 1 tsp lemon zest, grated
- 2 tbsp onion, minced
- ¼ tsp pepper
- ¼ tsp salt

Directions:

1. Put all your fixing into the large mixing bowl and toss well. Season with pepper and salt. Cover and place in the refrigerator. Serve chilled and enjoy.

Nutrition:

- Calories: 165 ,Fat: 5.4g ,Protein: 25.2g ,Carbs: 2.2g ,Sodium 153mg

Buttery Chicken Spread

Servings:5

Cooking Time:20 Minutes

Ingredients:

- 8 oz chicken liver
- 3 tablespoon butter
- 1 white onion, chopped
- 1 bay leaf
- 1 teaspoon salt
- ½ teaspoon ground black pepper
- ½ cup of water

Directions:

1. Place the chicken liver in the saucepan.
2. Add onion, bay leaf, salt, ground black pepper, and water.
3. Mix up the mixture and close the lid.
4. Cook the liver mixture for 20 minutes over the medium heat.
5. Then transfer it in the blender and blend until smooth.
6. Add butter and mix up until it is melted.
7. Pour the pate mixture in the pate ramekin and refrigerate for 2 hours.

Nutrition:

- calories 122, fat 8.3, fiber 0.5, carbs 2.3, protein 9.5

Garlic Caper Beef Roast

Servings:3

Cooking Time:40 Minutes

Ingredients:

- 2 lbs beef roast, cubed
- 1 tbsp fresh parsley, chopped
- 1 tbsp capers, chopped
- 1 tbsp garlic, minced
- 1 cup chicken stock
- 1/2 tsp dried rosemary
- 1/2 tsp ground cumin
- 1 onion, chopped
- 1 tbsp olive oil
- Pepper
- Salt

Directions:

1. Add oil into the instant pot and set the pot on sauté mode.
2. Add garlic and onion and sauté for 5 minutes.
3. Add meat and cook until brown.
4. Add remaining ingredients and stir well.
5. Seal pot with lid and cook on high for 30 minutes.
6. Once done, allow to release pressure naturally. Remove lid.
7. Stir well and serve.

Nutrition:

- Calories 470 Fat 17.9 g Carbohydrates 3.9 g Sugar 1.4 g Protein 69.5 g Cholesterol 203 mg

Chipotle Turkey And Tomatoes

Servings:3

Cooking Time:1 Hour

Ingredients:

- 2 pounds cherry tomatoes, halved
- 3 tablespoons olive oil
- 1 red onion, roughly chopped
- 1 big turkey breast, skinless, boneless and sliced
- 3 garlic cloves, chopped
- 3 red chili peppers, chopped
- 4 tablespoons chipotle paste
- Zest of ½ lemon, grated
- Juice of 1 lemon
- Salt and black pepper to the taste
- A handful coriander, chopped

Directions:

1. Heat up a pan with the oil over medium-high heat, add the turkey slices, cook for 4 minutes on each side and transfer to a roasting pan.

2. Heat up the pan again over medium-high heat, add the onion, garlic and chili peppers and sauté for 2 minutes.

3. Add chipotle paste, sauté for 3 minutes more and pour over the turkey slices.

4. Toss the turkey slices with the chipotle mix, also add the rest of the ingredients except the coriander, introduce in the oven and bake at 400 degrees F for 45 minutes.

5. Divide everything between plates, sprinkle the coriander on top and serve.

Nutrition:

- calories 264, fat 13.2, fiber 8.7, carbs 23.9, protein 33.2

Olive Oil Drenched Lemon Chicken

Servings:3
Cooking Time:60 Minutes
Ingredients:

- 1 lemon, thinly sliced
- 1 red bell pepper, cut into 1-inch wide strips
- 1 red onion, cut into 1-inch wedges
- 1 tablespoon dried oregano
- 1/2 teaspoon coarsely ground black pepper
- 1/4 cup olive oil
- 2 tablespoons fresh lemon juice
- 2 tablespoons fresh lemon zest
- 3/4 teaspoon salt
- 4 large cloves garlic, pressed
- 4 skinless, boneless chicken breast halves
- 8 baby red potatoes, halved

Directions:

1. Preheat oven to 400oF.

2. In a bowl, mix well pepper, salt, oregano, garlic, lemon zest, lemon juice, and olive oil.

3. In a 9 x 13-inch casserole dish, evenly spread chicken in a single layer. Brush lemon juice mixture over chicken.

4. In a bowl mix well lemon slices, red onion, bell pepper, and potatoes. Drizzle remaining olive oil sauce and toss well to coat. Arrange vegetables and lemon slices around chicken breasts in baking dish.

5. Bake for 50 minutes; brush chicken and vegetables with pan drippings halfway through cooking time.

6. Let chicken rest for ten minutes befor

Nutrition:

- Calories per Serving: 517; Carbs: 65.1g; Protein: 30.8g; Fats: 16.7g

Steamed Chicken With Mushroom And Ginger

Servings:3
Cooking Time:10 Minutes
Ingredients:

- 4 x 150g chicken breasts
- 2 teaspoons extra-virgin olive oil
- 1 1/2 tablespoons balsamic vinegar
- 8cm piece ginger, cut into matchsticks
- 1 bunch broccoli
- 1 bunch carrots, diced
- 6 small dried shiitake mushrooms, chopped
- Spring onion, sliced
- Fresh coriander leaves,

Directions:

1. In a bowl, combine sliced chicken with salt, vinegar, and pepper; let marinate for at least 10 minutes.

2. Transfer the chicken to a baking dish and scatter with mushrooms and ginger; cook in a preheated oven at 350 degrees for about 15 minutes; place chopped broccoli and carrots on top of the chicken and return to the oven. Cook for another 3 minutes or until chicken is tender.

3. Divide the chicken, broccoli, and carrots on serving plates and drizzle each with olive oil and top with coriander and red onions. Enjoy!

Nutrition:

- Calories: 200, Fat: 6.0g, Total Carbs: 32.4g, Sugars: 15.3g, Protein: 11.7g

Grilled Chicken With Rainbow Salad Bowl

Servings:3
Cooking Time:10 Minutes
Ingredients:

- 300g grilled skinless chicken, shredded
- 2 cups mixed salad leaves
- 4 radishes, thinly sliced
- 1 cup chopped tomatoes
- 1 cup shredded carrot
- 1 cup podded edamame

- 4 tablespoons almond butter
- 2 tablespoons freshly squeezed lemon juice
- 2 tablespoons freshly squeezed lime juice
- ½ teaspoon sea salt

Directions:

1. Blanch edamame in boiling water for about 2 minutes and then drain; transfer to a serving bowl and add in salad leaves, radish, tomatoes, carrots and chicken.

2. In a bowl, whisk together fresh lemon juice, lime juice, almond butter, and sea salt until smooth; drizzle over the salad and serve.

Nutrition:

- Calories: 381, Fat: 28.5g, Total Carbs: 30.8g, Sugars: 17.4g, Protein: 6.4g

Sage Turkey Mix

Servings:3
Cooking Time:40 Minutes

Ingredients:

- 1 big turkey breast, skinless, boneless and roughly cubed
- Juice of 1 lemon
- 2 tablespoons avocado oil
- 1 red onion, chopped
- 2 tablespoons sage, chopped
- 1 garlic clove, minced
- 1 cup chicken stock

Directions:

1. Heat up a pan with the avocado oil over medium-high heat, add the turkey and brown for 3 minutes on each side.

2. Add the rest of the ingredients, bring to a simmer and cook over medium heat for 35 minutes.

3. Divide the mix between plates and serve with a side dish.

Nutrition:

- calories 382, fat 12.6, fiber 9.6, carbs 16.6, protein 33.2

Mustard Chops With Apricot-basil Relish

Servings:3
Cooking Time: 30 Minutes

Ingredients:

- ¼ cup basil, finely shredded
- ¼ cup olive oil

- ½ cup mustard
- ¾ lb. fresh apricots, stone removed, and fruit diced
- 1 shallot, diced small
- 1 tsp ground cardamom
- 3 tbsp raspberry vinegar
- 4 pork chops
- Pepper and salt

Directions:

1. Make sure that pork chops are defrosted well. Season with pepper and salt. Slather both sides of each pork chop with mustard. Preheat grill to medium-high fire.

2. In a medium bowl, mix cardamom, olive oil, vinegar, basil, shallot, and apricots. Toss to combine and season with pepper and salt, mixing once again.

3. Grill chops for 5 to 6 minutes per side. As you flip, baste with mustard.

4. Serve pork chops with the Apricot-Basil relish and enjoy.

Nutrition:

- Calories per Serving: 486.5; Carbs: 7.3g; Protein: 42.1g; Fat: 32.1g

Chicken Quinoa Pilaf

Servings:3
Cooking Time:30 Minutes

Ingredients:

- 2 (8-oz.) boneless, skinless chicken breasts, cut into 1/2-in. cubes
- 3 TB. extra-virgin olive oil
- 1 medium red onion, finely chopped
- 1 TB. minced garlic
- 1 (16-oz.) can diced tomatoes, with juice
- 2 cups water
- 2 tsp. salt
- 1 TB. dried oregano
- 1 TB. turmeric
- 1 tsp. paprika
- 1 tsp. ground black pepper
- 2 cups red or yellow quinoa
- 1/2 cup fresh parsley, chopped

Directions:

1. In a large, 3-quart pot over medium heat, heat extra-virgin olive oil. Add chicken, and cook for 5 minutes.

2. Add red onion and garlic, stir, and cook for 5 minutes.

3. Add tomatoes with juice, water, salt, oregano, turmeric, paprika, and black pepper. Stir, and simmer for 5 minutes.

4. Add red quinoa, and stir. Cover, reduce heat to low, and cook for 20 minutes. Remove from heat.

5. Fluff with a fork, cover again, and let sit for 10 minutes.

6. Serve warm.

Meatloaf

Servings:7
Cooking Time:35 Minutes

Ingredients:

- 2 lbs ground beef
- 2 eggs, lightly beaten
- 1/4 tsp dried basil
- 3 tbsp olive oil
- 1/2 tsp dried sage
- 1 1/2 tsp dried parsley
- 1 tsp oregano
- 2 tsp thyme
- 1 tsp rosemary
- Pepper
- Salt

Directions:

1. Pour 1 1/2 cups of water into the instant pot then place the trivet in the pot.

2. Spray loaf pan with cooking spray.

3. Add all ingredients into the mixing bowl and mix until well combined.

4. Transfer meat mixture into the preparation ared loaf pan and place loaf pan on top of the trivet in the pot.

5. Seal pot with lid and cook on high for 35 minutes.

6. Once done, allow to release pressure naturally for 10 minutes then release remaining using quick release. Remove lid.

7. Serve and enjoy.

Nutrition:

- Calories 365 Fat 18 g Carbohydrates 0.7 g Sugar 0.1 g Protein 47.8 g Cholesterol 190 mg

Lemon Garlic Chicken

Servings:3
Cooking Time:12 Minutes

Ingredients:

- 3 chicken breasts, cut into thin slices
- 2 lemon zest, grated
- ¼ cup olive oil
- 4 garlic cloves, minced
- Pepper
- Sa

Directions:

1. Warm-up olive oil in a pan over medium heat. Add garlic to the pan and sauté for 30 seconds. Put the chicken in the pan and sauté within 10 minutes. Add lemon zest and lemon juice and bring to boil. Remove from heat and season with pepper and salt. Serve and enjoy

Nutrition:

- Calories: 439 ,Fat: 27.8g ,Protein: 42.9g ,Carbs: 4.9g ,Sodium 306 mg

Clean Eating Lemon Grilled Tuna & Avocado Vegetable Salad

Servings:3
Cooking Time:10 Minutes

Ingredients:

- 3 (150g each) tuna fillet
- ¼ cup freshly squeezed lemon juice
- A pinch of sea salt
- A pinch of pepper
- 1 small red onion, sliced into thin rings
- 1 cup watercress, rinsed
- 1 zucchini, shaved
- 1 small broccoli head, rinsed and cut in small florets
- 1 avocado, diced
- 2 tablespoon s fresh lemon juice
- 1 tablespoon extra-virgin olive oil
- ½ teaspoon Dijon mustard
- ½ teaspoon sea salt
- ¼ cup crushed toasted almonds
- 1 tablespoon chia seeds

Directions:

1. In a bowl, mix lemon juice, salt and pepper until well combined; smear on the fish fillets until well coated and grill on a preheated charcoal grill for about 7 minutes per side or until browned and cooked to your liking.

2. In another bowl, mix together the veggies until well combined.

3. In a small bowl, whisk together lemon juice, olive oil, mustard and salt until well blended; pour over the salad

and toss until well coated. Add almonds and chia seeds and toss to combine. Set the salad aside for at least 5 minutes for flavors to combine before serving.

4. Serve the salad drizzled with the dressing and topped with the grilled tuna for a satisfying meal.

Nutrition:

- Calories: 250, Fat: 15.5g, Total Carbs: 11.5g, Sugars: 3.7g, Protein: 19.2g

Chicken Pie

Servings:3
Cooking Time:50 Minutes

Ingredients:

- ¼ cup green peas, frozen
- 1 carrot, chopped
- 1 cup ground chicken
- 5 oz puff pastry
- 1 tablespoon butter, melted
- ¼ cup cream
- 1 teaspoon ground black pepper
- 1 oz Parmesan, grated

Directions:

1. Roll up the puff pastry and cut it on 2 parts.
2. Place one puff pastry part in the non-sticky springform pan and flatten.
3. Then mix up together green peas, chopped carrot, ground chicken, and ground black pepper.
4. Place the chicken mixture in the puff pastry.
5. Pour cream over mixture and sprinkle with Parmesan.
6. Cover the mixture with second puff pastry half and secure the edges of it with the help of the fork.
7. Brush the surface of the pie with melted butter and bake it for 50 minutes at 365F.

Nutrition:

- calories 223, fat 14.3, fiber 1, carbs 13.2, protein 10.5

Lemony Lamb And Potatoes

Servings:3
Cooking Time:30 Minutes

Ingredients:

- 2 pound lamb meat, cubed
- 2 tablespoons olive oil
- 2 springs rosemary, chopped
- 2 tablespoons parsley, chopped
- 1 tablespoon lemon rind, grated

- 3 garlic cloves, minced
- 2 tablespoons lemon juice
- 2 pounds baby potatoes, scrubbed and halved
- 1 cup veggie stock

Directions:

1. In a roasting pan, combine the meat with the oil and the rest of the ingredients, introduce in the oven and bake at 400 degrees F for 2 hours and 10 minutes.
2. Divide the mix between plates and serve.

Nutrition:

- calories 302, fat 15.2, fiber 10.6, carbs 23.3, protein 15.2

Pork And Peas

Servings:3
Cooking Time:30 Minutes

Ingredients:

- 4 ounces snow peas
- 2 tablespoons avocado oil
- 1 pound pork loin, boneless and cubed
- ¾ cup beef stock
- ½ cup red onion, chopped
- Salt and white pepper to the taste

Directions:

1. Heat up a pan with the oil over medium-high heat, add the pork and brown for 5 minutes.
2. Add the peas and the rest of the ingredients, toss, bring to a simmer and cook over medium heat for 15 minutes.
3. Divide the mix between plates and serve right away.

Nutrition:

- calories 332, fat 16.5, fiber 10.3, carbs 20.7, protein 26.5

Stewed Chicken Greek Style

Servings:9
Cooking Time:60 Minutes

Ingredients:

- ½ cup red wine
- 1 ½ cups chicken stock or more if needed
- 1 cup olive oil
- 1 cup tomato sauce
- 1 pc, 4lbs whole chicken cut into pieces
- 1 pinch dried oregano or to taste
- 10 small shallots, peeled

- 2 bay leaves
- 2 cloves garlic, finely chopped
- 2 tbsp chopped fresh parsley
- 2 tsps butter
- Salt and ground black pepper to tast

Directions:

1. Bring to a boil a large pot of lightly salted water. Mix in the shallots and let boil uncovered until tender for around three minutes. Then drain the shallots and dip in cold water until no longer warm.

2. In another large pot over medium fire, heat butter and olive oil until bubbling and melted. Then sauté in the chicken and shallots for 15 minutes or until chicken is cooked and shallots are soft and translucent. Then add the chopped garlic and cook for three mins more.

3. Then add bay leaves, oregano, salt and pepper, parsley, tomato sauce and the red wine and let simmer for a minute before adding the chicken stock. Stir before covering and let cook for 50 minutes on medium-low fire or until chicken is tender.

Nutrition:

- Calories per Serving: 644.8; Carbs: 8.2g; Protein: 62.1g; Fat: 40.4g

Ginger Chicken Drumsticks

Servings:4
Cooking Time:30 Minutes
Ingredients:

- 4 chicken drumsticks
- 1 apple, grated
- 1 tablespoon curry paste
- 4 tablespoons milk
- 1 teaspoon coconut oil
- 1 teaspoon chili flakes
- ½ teaspoon minced ginger

Directions:

1. Mix up together grated apple, curry paste, milk, chili flakes, and minced garlic.

2. Put coconut oil in the skillet and melt it.

3. Add apple mixture and stir well.

4. Then add chicken drumsticks and mix up well.

5. Roast the chicken for 2 minutes from each side.

6. Then preheat oven to 360F.

7. Place the skillet with chicken drumsticks in the oven and bake for 25 minutes.

Nutrition:

- calories 150, fat 6.4, fiber 1.4, carbs 9.7, protein 13.5

Cayenne Pork

Servings:3
Cooking Time:30 Minutes
Ingredients:

- 8 oz beef sirloin
- 1 poblano pepper, grinded
- 1 teaspoon minced garlic
- ½ cup of water
- 1 tablespoon butter
- 1 teaspoon ground black pepper
- 1 teaspoon salt
- ½ teaspoon paprika
- 1 teaspoon cayenne pepper

Directions:

1. Toss the butter in the saucepan and melt it.

2. Meanwhile rub the beef sirloin with minced garlic, salt, ground black pepper, paprika, and cayenne pepper.

3. Put the meat in the hot butter and roast for 5 minutes from each side over the medium heat.

4. After this, add water and poblano pepper.

5. Cook the meat for 50 minutes over the medium heat.

6. Then transfer the beef sirloin on the cutting board and shred it with the help of the fork.

Nutrition:

- calories 97, fat 5.5, fiber 0.5, carbs 3, protein 9.5

Chicken Pilaf

Servings:4
Cooking Time:30 Minutes
Ingredients:

- 4 tablespoons avocado oil
- 2 pounds chicken breasts, skinless, boneless and cubed
- ½ cup yellow onion, chopped
- 4 garlic cloves, minced
- 8 ounces brown rice
- 4 cups chicken stock
- ½ cup kalamata olives, pitted
- ½ cup tomatoes, cubed
- 6 ounces baby spinach
- ½ cup feta cheese, crumbled
- A pinch of salt and black pepper

- 1 tablespoon marjoram, chopped
- 1 tablespoon basil, chopped
- Juice of ½ lemon
- ¼ cup pine nuts, toasted

Directions:

1. Heat up a pot with 1 tablespoon avocado oil over medium-high heat, add the chicken, some salt and pepper, brown for 5 minutes on each side and transfer to a bowl.

2. Heat up the pot again with the rest of the avocado oil over medium heat, add the onion and garlic and sauté for 3 minutes.

3. Add the rice, the rest of the ingredients except the pine nuts, also return the chicken, toss, bring to a simmer and cook over medium heat for 20 minutes.

4. Divide the mix between plates, top each serving with some pine nuts and serve

Nutrition:

- calories 283, fat 12.5, fiber 8.2, carbs 21.5, protein 13.4

Lamb And Tomato Sauce

Servings:3
Cooking Time:55 Minutes

Ingredients:

- 9 oz lamb shanks
- 1 onion, diced
- 1 carrot, diced
- 1 tablespoon olive oil
- 1 teaspoon salt
- 1 teaspoon ground black pepper
- 1 ½ cup chicken stock
- 1 tablespoon tomato paste

Directions:

1. Sprinkle the lamb shanks with salt and ground black pepper.

2. Heat up olive oil in the saucepan.

3. Add lamb shanks and roast them for 5 minutes from each side.

4. Transfer meat in the plate.

5. After this, add onion and carrot in the saucepan.

6. Roast the vegetables for 3 minutes.

7. Add tomato paste and mix up well.

8. Then add chicken stock and bring the liquid to boil.

9. Add lamb shanks, stir well, and close the lid.

10. Cook the meat for 40 minutes over the medium-low heat.

Nutrition:

- calories 232, fat 11.3, fiber 1.7, carbs 7.3, protein 25.1

Beef And Zucchini Skillet

Servings:4
Cooking Time:30 Minutes

Ingredients:

- 2 oz ground beef
- ½ onion, sliced
- ½ bell pepper, sliced
- 1 tablespoon butter
- ½ teaspoon salt
- 1 tablespoon tomato sauce
- 1 small zucchini, chopped
- ½ teaspoon dried oregano

Directions:

1. Place the ground beef in the skillet.

2. Add salt, butter, and dried oregano.

3. Mix up the meat mixture and cook it for 10 minutes.

4. After this, transfer the cooked ground beef in the bowl.

5. Place zucchini, bell pepper, and onion in the skillet (where the ground meat was cooking) and roast the vegetables for 7 minutes over the medium heat or until they are tender.

6. Then add cooked ground beef and tomato sauce. Mix up well.

7. Cook the beef toss for 2-3 minutes over the medium heat

Nutrition:

- calories 182, fat 8.7, fiber 0.1, carbs 0.3, protein 24.1

Pan-seared Tuna Salad With Snow Peas & Grapefruit

Servings:4
Cooking Time:10 Minutes

Ingredients:

- 4 (100g) skin-on tuna fillets
- 1/8 teaspoon sea salt
- 2 teaspoons extra virgin olive oil
- 4 cups arugula
- 8 leaves Boston lettuce, washed and dried

- 1 cup snow peas, cooked
- 2 avocados, diced
- For Grapefruit-Dill Dressing:
- 1/4 cup grapefruit juice
- 1/4 cup extra virgin olive oil
- 1 teaspoon raw honey
- 1 tablespoon Dijon mustard
- 1 tablespoon chopped fresh dill
- 2 garlic cloves, minced
- 1/2 teaspoon salt

Directions:

1. Sprinkle fish with about 1/8 teaspoon salt and cook in 2 teaspoons of olive oil over medium heat for about 4 minutes per side or until golden.

2. In a small bowl, whisk together al dressing ingredients and set aside. Divide arugula and lettuce among four serving plates.

3. Divide lettuce and arugula among 4 plates and add the remaining salad ingredients; top each with seared tuna and drizzle with dressing. Enjoy!

Chicken And Semolina Meatballs

Servings:3
Cooking Time:10 Minutes

Ingredients:

- 1/3 cup carrot, grated
- 1 onion, diced
- 2 cups ground chicken
- 1 tablespoon semolina
- 1 egg, beaten
- ½ teaspoon salt
- 1 teaspoon dried oregano
- 1 teaspoon dried cilantro
- 1 teaspoon chili flakes
- 1 tablespoon coconut oil

Directions:

1. In the mixing bowl combine together grated carrot, diced onion, ground chicken, semolina, egg, salt, dried oregano, cilantro, and chili flakes.

2. With the help of scooper make the meatballs.

3. Heat up the coconut oil in the skillet.

4. When it starts to shimmer, put meatballs in it.

5. Cook the meatballs for 5 minutes from each side over the medium-low heat.

Nutrition:

- calories 102, fat 4.9, fiber 0.5, carbs 2.9, protein 11.2

Chicken Fry With Peanut Sauce

Servings:4
Cooking Time:15 Minutes

Ingredients:

- Meat from 4 chicken thighs, cut into bite-size pieces
- 2 tbsp. + ¼ cup peanut oil
- ½ cup peanut butter
- 3 tbsp. toasted sesame oil
- 2 tbsp. soy sauce
- 1 tbsp. lime juice
- 1 clove garlic, minced
- 1 tsp. powdered ginger
- 1-2 tsp. hot sauce, if desired
- 2 red bell peppers, chopped
- 2 tbsp. toasted sesame seeds
- 4 green onions, thinly sliced

Directions:

1. Heat 2 tbsp. peanut oil in a large frying pan.

2. Add the chicken and cook for about 10 minutes, until no pink remains.

3. Meanwhile, mix together the peanut butter, ¼ cup peanut oil, sesame oil, soy sauce, lime juice, garlic, ginger, and hot sauce.

4. Add more water if needed to achieve a smooth consistency.

5. When the chicken is done, add the red pepper and cook for 1 minutes more.

6. Divide the chicken and peppers between four plates and top with peanut sauce, toasted sesame seeds, and green onions.

Nutrition:

- Calories: 426.9 ,Sugars: 4.8 g ,Total Carbohydrate: 16.9 g ,Protein: 38.7 g

Greek Styled Lamb Chops

Servings:3
Cooking Time:10 Minutes

Ingredients:

- ¼ tsp black pepper
- ½ tsp salt
- 1 tbsp bottled minced garlic
- 1 tbsp dried oregano
- 2 tbsp lemon juice

- 8 pcs of lamb loin chops, around 4 oz
- Cooking spray

Directions:

1. Preheat broiler.
2. In a big bowl or dish, combine the black pepper, salt, minced garlic, lemon juice and oregano. Then rub it equally on all sides of the lamb chops.
3. Then coat a broiler pan with the cooking spray before placing the lamb chops on the pan and broiling until desired doneness is reached or for four minutes.

Nutrition:

- Calories per Serving: 131.9; Carbs: 2.6g; Protein: 17.1g; Fat: 5.9g

Simple Sautéed Spinach

Servings:3
Cooking Time:30 Minutes

Ingredients:

- 1/4 teaspoon crushed red pepper
- 4 cloves garlic, thinly sliced
- 2 tablespoons extra-virgin olive oil
- 20 ounces fresh spinach
- 1/4 teaspoon low sodium salt
- 1 tablespoon lemon juice

Directions:

1. Set your oil to get hot on medium heat in a Dutch oven.
2. Add in your garlic then cook until lightly brown (about 1minutes).
3. Stir in your spinach to coat. Cover then cook until the spinach wilts1 (about 5 minutes).
4. Remove from the heat and add in salt, crushed red pepper and lemon juice.
5. Toss and serve immediately.

Shrimp Fried 'rice'

Servings:4
Cooking Time:15 Minutes

Ingredients:

- 2 + 2 tbsp. coconut oil
- 3 cups grated cauliflower
- 2 bell peppers, chopped
- 6 green onions, thinly sliced
- 1 lb. shrimp
- 4 eggs, lightly beaten

- 1 tbsp. soy sauce
- 2 tbsp. toasted sesame oil

Directions:

1. Heat 2 tbsp. of coconut oil in a large skillet over high heat. Add shrimp and cook for 2-4 minutes until opaque and pink.
2. Remove from pan and set aside.
3. Add 2 tbsp. coconut oil and add the cauliflower, peppers, and green onions.
4. Sautee for 4-5 minutes, stirring frequently.
5. Add the eggs and soy sauce to the pan and stir continuously until the eggs are firm.
6. Add the toasted sesame oil and stir, then toss with the shrimp and serve.

Nutrition:

- Calories 482 ,Carbs 44.5g .Protein 29.5g ,Fat 15g

Chicken And Butter Sauce

Servings:5
Cooking Time:30 Minutes

Ingredients:

- 1-pound chicken fillet
- 1/3 cup butter, softened
- 1 tablespoon rosemary
- ½ teaspoon thyme
- 1 teaspoon salt
- ½ lemon

Directions:

1. Churn together thyme, salt, and rosemary.
2. Chop the chicken fillet roughly and mix up with churned butter mixture.
3. Place the preparation ared chicken in the baking dish.
4. Squeeze the lemon over the chicken.
5. Chop the squeezed lemon and add in the baking dish.
6. Cover the chicken with foil and bake it for 20 minutes at 365F.
7. Then discard the foil and bake the chicken for 10 minutes more.

Nutrition:

- calories 285, fat 19.1, fiber 0.5, carbs 1, protein 26.5

Parmesan Chicken

Servings:3

Cooking Time:30 Minutes

Ingredients:

- 1-pound chicken breast, skinless, boneless
- 2 oz Parmesan, grated
- 1 teaspoon dried oregano
- ½ teaspoon dried cilantro
- 1 tablespoon Panko bread crumbs
- 1 egg, beaten
- 1 teaspoon turmeric

Directions:

1. Cut the chicken breast on 3 servings.
2. Then combine together Parmesan, oregano, cilantro, bread crumbs, and turmeric.
3. Dip the chicken servings in the beaten egg carefully.
4. Then coat every chicken piece in the cheese-bread crumbs mixture.
5. Line the baking tray with the baking paper.
6. Arrange the chicken pieces in the tray.
7. Bake the chicken for 30 minutes at 365F.

Nutrition:

- calories 267, fat 9.5, fiber 0.5, carbs 3.2, protein 40.4

Wild Rice Prawn Salad

Servings:6

Cooking Time:35 Minutes

Ingredients:

- ¾ cup wild rice
- 1¾ cups chicken stock
- 1 pound prawns
- Salt and pepper to taste
- 2 tablespoons lemon juice
- 2 tablespoons extra virgin olive oil
- 2 cups arugula

Directions:

1. Combine the rice and chicken stock in a saucepan and cook until the liquid has been absorbed entirely.
2. Transfer the rice in a salad bowl.
3. Season the prawns with salt and pepper and drizzle them with lemon juice and oil.
4. Heat a grill pan over medium flame.
5. Place the prawns on the hot pan and cook on each side for 2-3 minutes.
6. For the salad, combine the rice with arugula and prawns and mix well.
7. Serve the salad fresh.

Nutrition:

- Calories: 207 ,Fat: 4g ,Protein: 20.6g ,Carbohydrates: 17g

Toasted Sardines With Parsley

Servings:4

Cooking Time:15 Minutes

Ingredients:

- 400 g fresh sardines already cleaned
- 2 lemons zest
- Salt
- 50 g chopped parsley
- 1 teaspoon black pepper
- 1 crushed clove garlic
- 2 tbsp. white wine
- 1 tablespoon extra-virgin olive oil

Directions:

1. Preparation are the sauce by blending the parsley, pepper, garlic clove and thinly grated lemon zest. Also add the white wine, lemon juice and oil.
2. Cook the sardines in a non-stick pan (or grill) for one minute per side.
3. When serving, pour a little sauce on the plate, lay the sardines on top and season with other sauce. Complete with a pinch of salt and lemon zest cut into strips.

Nutrition:

- Calories: 300 ,Fat: 16.9g ,Protein: 20.3g ,Carbohydrate: 6.9g ,Fiber: 0.9g

Greek Chicken Stew

Servings:3

Cooking Time:60 Minutes

Ingredients:

- 10 smalls shallots, peeled
- 1 cup olive oil
- 2 teaspoons butter
- 1 (4 pound) whole chicken, cut into pieces
- 2 cloves garlic, finely chopped
- ½ cup red wine
- 1 cup tomato sauce
- 2 tablespoons chopped fresh parsley
- salt and ground black pepper to taste

- 1 pinch dried oregano, or to taste
- 2 bay leaves
- 1 ½ cups chicken stock, or more if needed

Directions:

1. In a large pot, fill half full of water and bring to a boil. Lightly salt the water and once boiling add shallots and boil uncovered for 3 minutes. Drain and quickly place on an ice bath for 5 minutes. Drain well.

2. In same pot, heat for 3 minutes and add oil and butter. Heat for 3 minutes.

3. Add chicken and shallots. Cook 15 minutes.

4. Add chopped garlic and cook for another 3 minutes or until garlic starts to turn golden.

5. Add red wine and tomato sauce. Deglaze pot.

6. Stir in bay leaves, oregano, pepper, salt, and parsley. Cook for 3 minutes.

7. Stir in chicken stock.

8. Cover and simmer for 40 minutes while occasionally stirring pot.

9. Serve and enjoy while hot with a side of rice if desired

Nutrition:

- Calories per Serving: 574; Carbs: 6.8g; Protein: 31.8g; Fats: 45.3g

Chicken And Black Beans

Servings:3

Cooking Time:20 Minutes

Ingredients:

- 12 oz chicken breast, skinless, boneless, chopped
- 1 tablespoon taco seasoning
- 1 tablespoon nut oil
- ½ teaspoon cayenne pepper
- ½ teaspoon salt
- ½ teaspoon garlic, chopped
- ½ red onion, sliced
- 1/3 cup black beans, canned, rinsed
- ½ cup Mozzarella, shredded

Directions:

1. Rub the chopped chicken breast with taco seasoning, salt, and cayenne pepper.

2. Place the chicken in the skillet, add nut oil and roast it for 10 minutes over the medium heat. Mix up the chicken pieces from time to time to avoid burning.

3. After this, transfer the chicken in the plate.

4. Add sliced onion and garlic in the skillet. Roast the vegetables for 5 minutes. Stir them constantly. Then add black beans and stir well. Cook the ingredients for 2 minute more.

5. Add the chopped chicken and mix up well. Top the meal with Mozzarella cheese.

6. Close the lid and cook the meal for 3 minutes.

Nutrition:

- calories 209, fat 6.4, fiber 2.8, carbs 13.7, 22.7

Healthy Chicken Orzo

Servings:4

Cooking Time:15 Minutes

Ingredients:

- 1 cup whole wheat orzo
- 1 lb. chicken breasts, sliced
- ½ tsp red pepper flakes
- ½ cup feta cheese, crumbled
- ½ tsp oregano
- 1 tbsp fresh parsley, chopped
- 1 tbsp fresh basil, chopped
- ¼ cup pine nuts
- 1 cup spinach, chopped
- ¼ cup white wine
- ½ cup olives, sliced
- 1 cup grape tomatoes, cut in half
- ½ tbsp garlic, minced
- 2 tbsp olive oil
- ½ tsp pepper
- ½ tsp salt

Directions:

1. Add water in a small saucepan and bring to boil. Heat 1 tablespoon of olive oil in a pan over medium heat. Season chicken with pepper and salt and cook in the pan for 5-7 minutes on each side. Remove from pan and set aside.

2. Add orzo in boiling water and cook according to the packet directions. Heat remaining olive oil in a pan on medium heat, then put garlic in the pan and sauté for a minute. Stir in white wine and cherry tomatoes and cook on high for 3 minutes.

3. Add cooked orzo, spices, spinach, pine nuts, and olives and stir until well combined. Add chicken on top of orzo and sprinkle with feta cheese. Serve and enjoy.

Nutrition:

- Calories: 518 ,Fat: 27.7g ,Protein: 40.6g ,Carbs: 26.2g ,Sodium 121mg

Hot Pork Meatballs

Servings:3

Cooking Time:10 Minutes

Ingredients:

- 4 oz pork loin, grinded
- ½ teaspoon garlic powder
- ¼ teaspoon chili powder
- ¼ teaspoon cayenne pepper
- ¼ teaspoon ground black pepper
- ¼ teaspoon white pepper
- 1 tablespoon water
- 1 teaspoon olive o

Directions:

1. Mix up together grinded meat, garlic powder, cayenne pepper, ground black pepper, white pepper, and water.
2. With the help of the fingertips make the small meatballs.
3. Heat up olive oil in the skillet.
4. Arrange the kofte in the oil and cook them for 10 minutes totally. Flip the kofte on another side from time to time.

Nutrition:

- calories 162, fat 10.3, fiber 0.3, carbs 1, protein 15.7

Yummy Turkey Meatballs

Servings:3

Cooking Time:30 Minutes

Ingredients:

- ¼ yellow onion, finely diced
- 1 14-oz can of artichoke hearts, diced
- 1 lb. ground turkey
- 1 tsp dried parsley
- 1 tsp oil
- 4 tbsp fresh basil, finely chopped
- Pepper and salt to taste

Directions:

1. Grease a cookie sheet and preheat oven to 350oF.
2. On medium fire, place a nonstick medium saucepan and sauté artichoke hearts and diced onions for 5 minutes or until onions are soft.
3. Remove from fire and let cool.

4. Meanwhile, in a big bowl, mix with hands parsley, basil and ground turkey. Season to taste.
5. Once onion mixture has cooled add into the bowl and mix thoroughly.
6. With an ice cream scooper, scoop ground turkey and form into balls, makes around 6 balls.
7. Place on preparation ped cookie sheet, pop in the oven and bake until cooked through around 15-20 minutes.
8. Remove from pan, serve and enjoy.

Nutrition:

- Calories per Serving: 328; Carbs: 11.8g; Protein: 33.5g; Fat: 16.3g

Chicken And Spinach Cakes

Servings:3

Cooking Time:15 Minutes

Ingredients:

- 8 oz ground chicken
- 1 cup fresh spinach, blended
- 1 teaspoon minced onion
- ½ teaspoon salt
- 1 red bell pepper, grinded
- 1 egg, beaten
- 1 teaspoon ground black pepper
- 4 tablespoons Panko breadcrumbs

Directions:

1. In the mixing bowl mix up together ground chicken, blended spinach, minced garlic, salt, grinded bell pepper, egg, and ground black pepper.
2. When the chicken mixture is smooth, make 4 burgers from it and coat them in Panko breadcrumbs.
3. Place the burgers in the non-sticky baking dish or line the baking tray with baking paper.
4. Bake the burgers for 15 minutes at 365F.
5. Flip the chicken burgers on another side after 7 minutes of cooking.

Nutrition:

- calories 171, fat 5.7, fiber 1.7, carbs 10.5, protein 19.4

Beef Spread

Servings:3
Cooking Time:25 Minutes

Ingredients:

- 8 oz beef liver
- ½ onion, peeled
- ½ carrot, peeled
- ½ teaspoon peppercorns
- 1 bay leaf
- ½ teaspoon salt
- 1/3 cup water
- 1 teaspoon ground black pepper

Directions:

1. Chop the beef liver and put it in the saucepan.
2. Add onion, carrot, peppercorns, bay leaf, salt, and ground black pepper.
3. Add water and close the lid.
4. Boil the beef liver for 25 minutes or until all ingredients are tender.
5. Transfer the cooked mixture in the blender and blend it until smooth.
6. Then place the cooked pate in the serving bowl and flatten the surface of it.
7. Refrigerate the pate for 20-30 minutes before serving.

Nutrition:

- calories 109, fat 2.7, fiber 0.6, carbs 5.3, protein 15.3

Coconut Chicken

Servings:3
Cooking Time:10 Minutes

Ingredients:

- 6 oz chicken fillet
- ¼ cup of sparkling water
- 1 egg
- 3 tablespoons coconut flakes
- 1 tablespoon coconut oil
- 1 teaspoon Greek Seasoning

Directions:

1. Cut the chicken fillet on small pieces (nuggets).
2. Then crack the egg in the bowl and whisk it.
3. Mix up together egg and sparkling water.
4. Add Greek seasoning and stir gently.
5. Dip the chicken nuggets in the egg mixture and then coat in the coconut flakes.

6. Melt the coconut oil in the skillet and heat it up until it is shimmering.
7. Then add preparation ared chicken nuggets.
8. Roast them for 1 minute from each or until they are light brown.
9. Dry the cooked chicken nuggets with the help of the paper towel and transfer in the serving plates.

Nutrition:

- calories 141, fat 8.9, fiber 0.3, carbs 1, protein 13.9

Spiced Chicken Meatballs

Servings:3
Cooking Time:20 Minutes

Ingredients:

- 1 pound chicken meat, ground
- 1 tablespoon pine nuts, toasted and chopped
- 1 egg, whisked
- 2 teaspoons turmeric powder
- 2 garlic cloves, minced
- Salt and black pepper to the taste
- 1 and ¼ cups heavy cream
- 2 tablespoons olive oil
- ¼ cup parsley, chopped
- 1 tablespoon chives, chopped

Directions:

1. In a bowl, combine the chicken with the pine nuts and the rest of the ingredients except the oil and the cream, stir well and shape medium meatballs out of this mix.
2. Heat up a pan with the oil over medium-high heat, add the meatballs and cook them for 4 minutes on each side.
3. Add the cream, toss gently, cook everything over medium heat for 10 minutes more, divide between plates and serve.

Nutrition:

- calories 283, fat 9.2, fiber 12.8, carbs 24.4, protein 34.5

Fragrant Asian Hotpot

Servings:2

Cooking Time:15 Minutes

Ingredients:

- 1 tsp tomato purée
- 1 star anise, squashed (or 1/4 tsp ground anise)
- Little bunch (10g) parsley, stalks finely cleaved
- Little bunch (1Og) coriander, stalks finely cleaved
- Juice of 1/2 lime
- 500ml chicken stock, new or made with 1 solid shape
- 1/2 carrot, stripped and cut into matchsticks
- 50g broccoli, cut into little florets
- 50g beansprouts
- 100 g crude tiger prawns
- 100 g firm tofu, slashed
- 50g rice noodles, cooked according to parcel directions
- 50g cooked water chestnuts, depleted
- 20g sushi ginger, slashed
- 1 tbsp. great quality miso glue

Directions:

1. Spot the tomato purée, star anise, parsley stalks, coriander stalks, lime juice and chicken stock in an enormous container and bring to a stew for 10 minutes.

2. Include the carrot, broccoli, prawns, tofu, noodles and water chestnuts and stew tenderly until the prawns are cooked through.

3. Expel from the warmth and mix in the sushi ginger and miso glue. Serve sprinkled with the parsley and coriander leaves.

Nutrition:

- Calories 434 ,Fat: 2 g ,Carbohydrates: 12 g ,Protein: 12 g ,Fiber: 0 g

Chicken & Veggies With Toasted Walnuts

Servings:3

Cooking Time:15minutes

Ingredients:

- 4 (about 250g) chicken tenderloins
- 1 teaspoon extra virgin olive oil
- 1 small zucchini, sliced
- 2 cups drained and rinsed cannellini beans
- 1 cup chopped green beans
- 1/4 cup pitted and halved green olives
- 1 tablespoon fresh lemon juice
- 2 garlic cloves, sliced
- 400g can cherry tomatoes
- 1 teaspoon harissa paste
- 1 teaspoon smoked paprika
- Fresh parsley sprigs
- 1 cup toasted walnuts, chopped

Directions:

1. In a plastic container, mix together lemon juice, garlic, harissa, and paprika until well combined; add in chicken and shake to coat well. Let sit a few minutes.

2. Heat oil in a skillet and add in the chicken along with the marinade; cook for about 2 minutes per side or until golden browned.

3. Stir in the veggies and simmer for about 10 minutes or until tender. Divide among serving plates and serve topped with fresh parsley and toasted walnuts.

Nutrition:

- Calories: 200, Fat: 6.0g, Total Carbs: 32.4g, Sugars: 15.3g, Protein: 11.7g

Turkey And Cranberry Sauce

Servings:3

Cooking Time:50 Minutes

Ingredients:

- 1 cup chicken stock
- 2 tablespoons avocado oil
- ½ cup cranberry sauce
- 1 big turkey breast, skinless, boneless and sliced
- 1 yellow onion, roughly chopped
- Salt and black pepper to the taste

Directions:

1. Heat up a pan with the avocado oil over medium-high heat, add the onion and sauté for 5 minutes.

2. Add the turkey and brown for 5 minutes more.

3. Add the rest of the ingredients, toss, introduce in the oven at 350 degrees F and cook for 40 minutes

Nutrition:

- calories 382, fat 12.6, fiber 9.6, carbs 26.6, protein 17.6

Brazilian Inspired Shrimp Stew

Servings:5

Cooking Time:20 Minutes

Ingredients:

- 1 ½ pounds jumbo shrimp, peeled and deveined
- 2 cloves garlic, minced
- ¼ cup olive oil
- 1 small yellow onion, diced
- ¼ cup fresh cilantro, chopped
- ¼ cup roasted red peppers, diced
- 1 (14 ounce) can chopped tomatoes with chilies
- 2 tablespoons Sambal Oelek – check in the Asian food section in the supermarket or food store
- 1 cup full-fat coconut milk
- Juice of 1 lime
- Freshly ground pepper and sea salt to taste

Directions:

1. Pour the olive oil in a saucepan over medium to high heat and sauté the onions until tender.

2. Stir in the roasted peppers and garlic and cook until fragrant, careful not to burn the garlic.

3. Stir in the shrimp, tomatoes and three quarter of the cilantro. Cook until the shrimp turns opaque for 5-8 minutes.

4. Stir in the Sambal Oelek and pour in the coconut milk. Reduce heat to low and cook for 5 minutes then add the lime juice and season well with pepper and salt.

5. Turn of the heat and garnish with the extra cilantro and serve hot.

Rosemary Cauliflower Rolls

Servings:3

Cooking Time:30 Minutes

Ingredients:

- 1/3 cup of almond flour
- 4 cups of riced cauliflower
- 1/3 cup of reduced-fat, shredded mozzarella or cheddar cheese
- 2 eggs
- 2 tablespoon of fresh rosemary, finely chopped
- ½ teaspoon of sal

Directions:

1. Preheat your oven to 4000F

2. Combine all the listed ingredients in a medium-sized bowl

3. Scoop cauliflower mixture into 12 evenly-sized rolls/biscuits onto a lightly-greased and foil-lined baking sheet.

4. Bake until it turns golden brown, which should be achieved in about 30 minutes.

5. Note: if you want to have the outside of the rolls/biscuits crisp, then broil for some minutes before serving.

Nutrition:

- Calories: 254 ,Protein: 24g ,Carbohydrate: 7g ,Fat: 8 g

Sautéed Cabbage

Servings:3

Cooking Time:30 Minutes

Ingredients:

- 1/2 head red cabbage, chopped
- 3 tablespoons olive oil
- 1 small red bell pepper, chopped
- 1 small yellow bell pepper, chopped
- 1/2 onion, chopped
- low sodium salt and ground black pepper to tast

Directions:

1. Set your oil on high heat in a skillet to get hot.

2. Stir in your bell peppers, cabbage, and onion. Cook, pausing to stir every 30 seconds until tender (about 7 minutes).

3. Season to taste. Enjoy!

Nutrition:

- Calories 476, Fat 40, Fiber 9, Carbs 33, Protein 6

Saffron Beef

Servings:3

Cooking Time:15 Minutes

Ingredients:

- ¾ teaspoon saffron
- ¾ teaspoon dried thyme
- ¾ teaspoon ground coriander
- ¼ teaspoon ground cinnamon
- 1 tablespoon butter
- 1/3 teaspoon salt
- 9 oz beef sirloin

Directions:

1. Rub the beef sirloin with dried thyme, ground coriander, saffron, ground cinnamon, and salt.

2. Leave the meat for at least 10 minutes to soak all the spices.

3. Then preheat the grill to 395F.

4. Place the beef sirloin in the grill and cook it for 5 minutes.

5. Then spread the meat with butter carefully and cook for 10 minutes more. Flip it on another side from time to time.

Nutrition:

- calories 291, fat 13.8, fiber 0.3, carbs 0.6, protein 38.8

Paprika And Feta Cheese On Chicken Skillet

Servings:3

Cooking Time:30 Minutes

Ingredients:

- ¼ cup black olives, sliced in circles
- ½ teaspoon coriander
- ½ teaspoon paprika
- 1 ½ cups diced tomatoes with the juice
- 1 cup yellow onion, chopped
- 1 teaspoon onion powder
- 2 garlic cloves, peeled and minced
- 2 lb. free range organic boneless skinless chicken breasts
- 2 tablespoons feta cheese
- 2 tablespoons ghee or olive oil
- Crushed red pepper to taste
- Salt and black pepper to taste

Directions:

1. Preheat oven to 400oF.

2. Place a cast-iron pan on medium high fire and heat for 5 minutes. Add oil and heat for 2 minutes more.

3. Meanwhile in a large dish, mix well pepper, salt, crushed red pepper, paprika, coriander, and onion powder. Add chicken and coat well in seasoning.

4. Add chicken to pan and brown sides for 4 minutes per side. Increase fire to high.

5. Stir in garlic and onions. Lower fire to medium and mix well.

6. Pop pan in oven and bake for 15 minutes.

7. Remove from oven, turnover chicken and let it stand for 5 minutes before serving.

Nutrition:

- Calories per Serving: 232; Carbs: 5.0g; Protein: 33.0g; Fats: 8.0g

Gingery Lemon Roasted Chicken With Steamed Greens

Servings:3

Cooking Time:30 Minutes

Ingredients:

- 1 tablespoon extra-virgin olive oil
- ½ cup fresh lemon juice
- 2 tablespoons fresh lemon zest
- 3 cloves garlic, minced
- 2-3 tablespoons minced ginger
- 3 pound whole chicken
- 1 pound chopped carrots
- handful of rosemary
- Pinch of sea salt
- Pinch of pepper
- Steamed greens for serving

Directions:

1. Preheat oven to 400°F. Place chicken in a baking dish. In a bowl, whisk together olive oil, lemon juice, lemon zest, garlic, and ginger until well combined; pour over the chicken and top with carrots and rosemary.

2. Sprinkle with salt and pepper and roast for about 1 ½ hours or until chicken is cooked through. Serve warm over a bowl of steamed greens.

Nutrition:

- Calories: 381, Fat: 28.5g, Total Carbs: 30.8g, Sugars: 17.4g, Protein: 6.4g

Tuscan Bean Stew

Servings:1

Cooking Time:40 Minutes

Ingredients:

- 1 tbsp. additional virgin olive oil
- 50g red onion, finely hacked
- 30g carrot, stripped and finely chopped
- 30g celery, cut and finely hacked
- 1 garlic clove, finely hacked
- ½ 10,000 foot bean stew, finely slashed (discretionary)
- 1 tsp herbs de Provence
- 200ml vegetable stock
- 1 x 400g tin hacked Italian tomatoes

- 1 tsp tomato purée
- 200g tinned blended beans
- 50g kale, generally hacked
- 1 tbsp. generally hacked parsley
- 40g buckwheat

Directions:

1. Spot the oil in a medium pot over a low–medium warmth and delicately fry the onion, carrot, celery, garlic, chili (if utilizing) and herbs, until the onion is delicate yet not shaded.

2. Include the stock, tomatoes and tomato purée and bring to the bubble. Include the beans and stew for 30 minutes.

3. Include the kale and cook for another 5–10 minutes, until delicate, then include the parsley. In the interim, cook the buckwheat according to the bundle Directions, deplete, and afterward present with the stew.

Nutrition:

- Calories 289 ,Fat: 2 g ,Carbohydrates: 10 g ,Protein: 12 g ,Fiber: 0 g

Chicken Meatballs With Stir-fried Greens

Servings:3
Cooking Time:30 Minutes

Ingredients:

- 500g chicken mince
- 2 green onions, chopped
- 2 garlic cloves, crushed
- 1 medium zucchini, grated
- 1/4 cup oyster sauce
- 1/2 cup frozen peas
- 2 tablespoons canola oil
- Stir-fried greens
- 1/2 cup dried gluten-free breadcrumbs

Directions:

1. Preheat your oven to 400 degrees and line a greased baking tray with baking paper.

2. In a bowl, mix together peas, oyster sauce, zucchini, garlic, red onion, gluten-free breadcrumbs, pepper and mince until well combined. Shape into meat balls.

3. Heat oil in a skillet and in batches, cook in the meat balls for about 4 minutes per side or until golden brown.

4. Transfer the balls on the preparation ared tray and bake for about 20 minutes until cooked through. Serve the meat balls with stir fried greens.

Nutrition:

- Calories: 250, Fat: 15.5g, Total Carbs: 11.5g, Sugars: 3.7g, Protein: 19.2g

Jalapeno Beef Chili

Servings:3
Cooking Time:30 Minutes

Ingredients:

- 1 lb ground beef
- 1 tsp garlic powder
- 1 jalapeno pepper, chopped
- 1 tbsp ground cumin
- 1 tbsp chili powder
- 1 lb ground pork
- 4 tomatillos, chopped
- 1/2 onion, chopped
- 5 oz tomato paste
- Pepper
- Salt

Directions:

1. Add oil into the instant pot and set the pot on sauté mode.

2. Add beef and pork and cook until brown.

3. Add remaining ingredients and stir well.

4. Seal pot with lid and cook on high for 35 minutes.

5. Once done, allow to release pressure naturally. Remove lid.

6. Stir well and serve.

Nutrition:

- Calories 217 Fat 6.1 g Carbohydrates 6.2 g Sugar 2.7 g Protein 33.4 g Cholesterol 92 mg

Tasty Beef Stew

Servings:3
Cooking Time:30 Minutes

Ingredients:

- 2 1/2 lbs beef roast, cut into chunks
- 1 cup beef broth
- 1/2 cup balsamic vinegar
- 1 tbsp honey
- 1/2 tsp red pepper flakes
- 1 tbsp garlic, minced

- Pepper
- Salt

Directions:

1. Add all ingredients into the inner pot of instant pot and stir well.

2. Seal pot with lid and cook on high for 30 minutes.

3. Once done, allow to release pressure naturally. Remove lid.

4. Stir well and serve

Nutrition:

- Calories 562 Fat 18.1 g Carbohydrates 5.7 g Sugar 4.6 g Protein 87.4 g Cholesterol 253 mg

Chicken Lettuce Wraps

Servings:3

Cooking Time:30 Minutes

Ingredients:

- 500g chicken breast, minced
- 2 teaspoons extra-virgin olive oil
- 2 cups shredded cabbage
- 1 large carrot, grated
- 1 celery stick, chopped
- 2 garlic cloves, chopped
- 1/2 red onion, chopped
- 2 spring onions, sliced
- 2 tablespoons chopped coriander
- 1 iceberg lettuce, halved, cored

Directions:

1. Heat a skillet over medium high heat; cook in chicken mince, stirring to break up the chicken with a spoon for about 5 minutes or until cooked through. Transfer to a dish.

2. Add oil to the pan and sauté red onions and garlic until fragrant and then stir in celery for about 3 minutes. return the chicken and cook for about 1 minute or until flavors blend; stir in carrots, cabbage, spring onions, and pepper and then remove the pan from the heat.

3. Divide the lettuce leaves among four serving plates and spoon the chicken mixture onto each serving. Top each with coriander and the remaining spring onions. Enjoy!

Nutrition:

- Calories: 381, Fat: 28.5g, Total Carbs: 30.8g, Sugars: 17.4g, Protein: 6.4g

Chicken And Artichokes

Servings:3

Cooking Time:20 Minutes

Ingredients:

- 2 pounds chicken breast, skinless, boneless and sliced
- A pinch of salt and black pepper
- 4 tablespoons olive oil
- 8 ounces canned roasted artichoke hearts, drained
- 6 ounces sun-dried tomatoes, chopped
- 3 tablespoons capers, drained
- 2 tablespoons lemon juice

Directions:

1. Heat up a pan with half of the oil over medium-high heat, add the artichokes and the other ingredients except the chicken, stir and sauté for 10 minutes.

2. Transfer the mix to a bowl, heat up the pan again with the rest of the oil over medium-high heat, add the meat and cook for 4 minutes on each side.

3. Return the veggie mix to the pan, toss, cook everything for 2-3 minutes more, divide between plates and serve.

Nutrition:

- calories 552, fat 28, fiber 6, carbs 33, protein 43

Vegetable Lover's Chicken Soup

Servings:3

Cooking Time:20 Minutes

Ingredients:

- 1 ½ cups baby spinach
- 2 tbsp orzo (tiny pasta)
- ¼ cup dry white wine
- 1 14oz low sodium chicken broth
- 2 plum tomatoes, chopped
- 1/8 tsp salt
- ½ tsp Italian seasoning
- 1 large shallot, chopped
- 1 small zucchini, diced
- 8-oz chicken tenders
- 1 tbsp extra virgin olive oil

Directions:

1. In a large saucepan, heat oil over medium heat and add the chicken. Stir occasionally for 8 minutes until browned. Transfer in a plate. Set aside.

2. In the same saucepan, add the zucchini, Italian seasoning, shallot and salt and stir often until the vegetables are softened, around 4 minutes.

3. Add the tomatoes, wine, broth and orzo and increase the heat to high to bring the mixture to boil. Reduce the heat and simmer.

4. Add the cooked chicken and stir in the spinach last.

5. Serve hot

Nutrition:

- Calories per Serving: 207; Carbs: 14.8g; Protein: 12.2g; Fat: 11.4g

Roasted Chicken

Servings:3

Cooking Time:1 Hour 30 Minutes

Ingredients:

- 1 (5-lb.) whole chicken
- 1 TB. extra-virgin olive oil
- 2 TB. minced garlic
- 1 tsp. salt
- 1 tsp. paprika
- 1 tsp. black pepper
- 1 tsp. ground coriander
- 1 tsp. seven spices
- 1/2 tsp. ground cinnamon
- 1/2 large lemon, cut in 1/2
- 1/2 large yellow onion, cut in 1/2
- 2 sprigs fresh rosemary
- 2 sprigs fresh thyme
- 2 sprigs fresh sage
- 2 large carrots, cut into 1-in. pieces
- 6 small red potatoes, washed and cut in 1/2
- 4 cloves garlic

Directions:

1. Preheat the oven to 450ºF. Wash chicken and pat dry with paper towels. Place chicken in a roasting pan, and drizzle and then rub chicken with extra-virgin olive oil.

2. In a small bowl, combine garlic, salt, paprika, black pepper, coriander, seven spices, and cinnamon. Sprinkle and then rub entire chicken with spice mixture to coat.

3. Place 1/4 lemon, 1/4 yellow onion, 1 sprig rosemary, 1 sprig thyme, and 1 sprig sage in chicken cavity.

4. Place remaining rosemary, thyme, sage, lemon, and onion around chicken in the roasting pan. Add carrots, red potatoes, and garlic cloves to the roasting pan.

5. Roast for 15 minutes. Reduce temperature to 375ºF, and roast for 1 more hour, basting chicken every 20 minutes.

6. Let chicken rest for 15 minutes before serving.

Nutrition:

- Calories: 200, Fat: 6.0g, Total Carbs: 32.4g, Sugars: 15.3g, Protein: 11.7g

Kefta Burgers

Servings:3

Cooking Time:10 Minutes

Ingredients:

- 1 lb. ground beef
- 1 cup fresh parsley, finely chopped
- 1 tsp. seven spices
- 11/2 tsp. salt
- 1 large yellow onion, finely sliced
- 1 TB. sumac
- 1/2 cup mayonnaise
- 3 TB. tahini paste
- 2 TB. balsamic vinegar
- 1/2 tsp. ground black pepper
- 4 (4-in.) pitas
- 1 medium tomato, sliced

Directions:

1. In a large bowl, combine beef, 1/2 cup parsley, seven spices, 1 teaspoon salt. Form mixture into 4 patties.

2. In a medium bowl, combine remaining 1/2 cup parsley, yellow onion, and sumac.

3. In a small bowl, whisk together mayonnaise, tahini paste, remaining 1/2 teaspoon salt, balsamic vinegar, and black pepper.

4. Preheat a large skillet over medium-high heat. Place patties in the skillet, and cook for 5 minutes per side.

5. To assemble burgers, open each pita into a pocket, and spread both sides with tahini mayonnaise. Add 1 burger patty, some parsley mixture, and a few tomato slices, and serve.

Nutrition:

- Calories 476, Fat 40, Fiber 9, Carbs 33, Protein 6

Paprika Chicken Wings

Servings:3

Cooking Time:10 Minutes

Ingredients:

- 4 chicken wings, boneless
- 1 tablespoon honey
- ½ teaspoon paprika

- ¼ teaspoon cayenne pepper
- ¾ teaspoon ground black pepper
- 1 tablespoon lemon juice
- ½ teaspoon sunflower oil

Directions:

1. Make the honey marinade: whisk together honey, paprika, cayenne pepper, ground black pepper, lemon juice, and sunflower oil.

2. Then brush the chicken wings with marinade carefully.

3. Preheat the grill to 385F.

4. Place the chicken wings in the grill and cook them for 4 minutes from each side.

Nutrition:

- calories 26, fat 0.8, fiber 0.3, carbs 5.1, protein 0.3

Cumin Lamb Mix

Servings:3
Cooking Time:30 Minutes

Ingredients:

- 2 lamb chops (3.5 oz each)
- 1 tablespoon olive oil
- 1 teaspoon ground cumin
- ½ teaspoon salt

Directions:

1. Rub the lamb chops with ground cumin and salt.

2. Then sprinkle them with olive oil.

3. Let the meat marinate for 10 minutes.

4. After this, preheat the skillet well.

5. Place the lamb chops in the skillet and roast them for 10 minutes. Flip the meat on another side from time to time to avoid burning.

Nutrition:

- calories 384, fat 33.2, fiber 0.1, carbs 0.5, protein 19.2

Beef Dish

Servings:3
Cooking Time:20 Minutes

Ingredients:

- 1 lb. skirt steak
- 2 TB. minced garlic
- 1/4 cup fresh lemon juice
- 2 TB. apple cider vinegar
- 3 TB. extra-virgin olive oil

- 1 tsp. salt
- 1/2 tsp. ground black pepper
- 1/4 tsp. ground cinnamon
- 1/4 tsp. ground cardamom
- 1 tsp. seven spices

Directions:

1. Using a sharp knife, cut skirt steak into thin, 1/4-inch strips. Place strips in a large bowl.

2. Add garlic, lemon juice, apple cider vinegar, extra-virgin olive oil, salt, black pepper, cinnamon, cardamom, and seven spices, and mix well.

3. Place steak in the refrigerator and marinate for at least 20 minutes and up to 24 hours.

4. Preheat a large skillet over medium heat. Add meat and marinade, and cook for 20 minutes or until meat is tender and marinade has evaporated.

5. Serve warm with pita bread and tahini sauce.

Nutrition:

- Calories 476, Fat 40, Fiber 9, Carbs 33, Protein 6

Chicken With Artichokes And Beans

Servings:3
Cooking Time:30 Minutes

Ingredients:

- 2 tablespoons olive oil
- 2 chicken breasts, skinless, boneless and halved
- Zest of 1 lemon, grated
- 3 garlic cloves, crushed
- Juice of 1 lemon
- Salt and black pepper to the taste
- 1 tablespoon thyme, chopped
- 6 ounces canned artichokes hearts, drained
- 1 cup canned fava beans, drained and rinsed
- 1 cup chicken stock
- A pinch of cayenne pepper
- Salt and black pepper to the taste

Directions:

1. Heat up a pan with the oil over medium-high heat, add chicken and brown for 5 minutes.

2. Add lemon juice, lemon zest, salt, pepper and the rest of the ingredients, bring to a simmer and cook over medium heat for 35 minutes.

3. Divide the mix between plates and serve right away.

Nutrition:

- calories 291, fat 14.9, fiber 10.5, carbs 23.8, protein 24.2

Sesame Chicken With Black Rice, Broccoli & Snap Peas

Servings:3

Cooking Time:25 Minutes

Ingredients:

- 2/3 cup black rice
- 2 (200g each) chicken breast fillets
- 2 cups chopped broccoli
- 200g snap peas, trimmed
- 1 1/2 cups picked watercress leaves
- 1 1/2 tablespoon salt-reduced tamari
- 1 tablespoon sesame seeds
- 2 tablespoons tahini
- 1/2 teaspoon raw honey

Directions:

1. Boil rice in a saucepan for about 15 minutes or until al dente; drain.

2. Coat chicken fillets with sesame seeds and cook in hot oil in a skillet set over medium high heat for about 5 minutes per side or until cooked through.

3. Let cool and slice. In the meantime, steam broccoli and peas until tender.

4. In a small bowl, whisk together tahini, tamari and raw honey until very smooth. Divide cooked black rice among serving bowls and top each with broccoli and peas. Top with chicken and watercress; drizzle each serving with tahini dressing. Enjoy!

Nutrition:

- Calories: 250, Fat: 15.5g, Total Carbs: 11.5g, Sugars: 3.7g, Protein: 19.2g

Lamb Chops

Servings:3

Cooking Time:10 Minutes

Ingredients:

- 6 (3/4-in.-thick) lamb chops
- 2 TB. fresh rosemary, finely chopped
- 3 TB. minced garlic
- 1 tsp. salt
- 1 tsp. ground black pepper
- 3 TB. extra-virgin olive oil

Directions:

1. In a large bowl, combine lamb chops, rosemary, garlic, salt, black pepper, and extra-virgin olive oil until chops are evenly coated. Let chops marinate at room temperature for at least 25 minutes.

2. Preheat a grill to medium heat.

3. Place chops on the grill, and cook for 3 minutes per side for medium well.

4. Serve warm

Chicken Breast & Zucchini Linguine

Servings:3

Cooking Time:10 Minutes

Ingredients:

- 450g chicken breast fillets, halved
- 1 tablespoon olive oil
- 2 garlic cloves, crushed
- 3 cups zucchini noodles
- 1/2 cup coconut cream
- 1/3 cup homemade chicken broth
- 1 tablespoon fresh dill leaves
- 2 tablespoons fresh chives, chopped
- 1 cup baby spinach
- ½ cup toasted chopped cashews

Directions:

1. Coat a pan with oil and set over medium high heat; season chicken with salt and pepper and cook in the pan for about 3 minutes per side or until cooked through; transfer to a plate and keep warm.

2. Add oil to the pan and sauté garlic until fragrant; stir in zucchini noodles and cook for about 2 minutes; stir in coconut cream and chicken broth and simmer for about 2 minutes or until tender.

3. Slice the chicken and add to the zucchini sauce along with chives and dill. Divide among serving bowls and top each with spinach and toasted cashews.

4. Enjoy!

Nutrition:

- Calories: 200, Fat: 6.0g, Total Carbs: 32.4g, Sugars: 15.3g, Protein: 11.7g

Pork Chops And Relish

Servings:3

Cooking Time:14 Minutes

Ingredients:

- 6 pork chops, boneless
- 7 ounces marinated artichoke hearts, chopped and their liquid reserved
- A pinch of salt and black pepper
- 1 teaspoon hot pepper sauce
- 1 and ½ cups tomatoes, cubed
- 1 jalapeno pepper, chopped
- ½ cup roasted bell peppers, chopped
- ½ cup black olives, pitted and sliced

Directions:

1. In a bowl, mix the chops with the pepper sauce, reserved liquid from the artichokes, cover and keep in the fridge for 15 minutes.

2. Heat up a grill over medium-high heat, add the pork chops and cook for 7 minutes on each side.

3. In a bowl, combine the artichokes with the peppers and the remaining ingredients, toss, divide on top of the chops and serve.

Nutrition:

- calories 215, fat 6, fiber 1, carbs 6, protein 35

Coriander And Coconut Chicken

Servings:4

Cooking Time:30 Minutes

Ingredients:

- 2 pounds chicken thighs, skinless, boneless and cubed
- 2 tablespoons olive oil
- Salt and black pepper to the taste
- 3 tablespoons coconut flesh, shredded
- 1 and ½ teaspoons orange extract
- 1 tablespoon ginger, grated
- ¼ cup orange juice
- 2 tablespoons coriander, chopped
- 1 cup chicken stock
- ¼ teaspoon red pepper flakes

Directions:

1. Heat up a pan with the oil over medium-high heat, add the chicken and brown for 4 minutes on each side.

2. Add salt, pepper and the rest of the ingredients, bring to a simmer and cook over medium heat for 20 minutes.

3. Divide the mix between plates and serve hot.

Nutrition:

- calories 297, fat 14.4, fiber 9.6, carbs 22, protein 25

Detox Salad With Grilled White Fish

Servings:3

Cooking Time:10 Minutes

Ingredients:

- For the Salad:
- 2 (150g each) pre-grilled white fish
- ½ cup snap peas, sliced
- 1 cup baby spinach
- 1 cup chopped Romaine lettuce
- ½ cup avocado, sliced
- ½ cup blueberries
- 2 green onions, sliced
- ½ cup shredded carrot
- 1 large cucumber, chopped
- 1 tablespoon chia seeds
- For the Dressing:
- ¼ teaspoon oregano
- 1 clove garlic, minced
- 1 tablespoon tahini
- 1 teaspoon honey
- 1 tablespoon rice wine vinegar
- 1 tablespoon lemon juice
- 1 teaspoon sesame oil
- 1/8 teaspoon red pepper flakes
- ¼ teaspoon black pepper

Directions:

1. In a large bowl, combine all salad ingredients, except fish.

2. Whisk together the ingredients for your dressing until well blended; pour over the salad and toss until well blended. Top each serving with the grilled white fish and enjoy

Nutrition:

- Calories: 200, Fat: 6.0g, Total Carbs: 32.4g, Sugars: 15.3g, Protein: 11.7g

Bulgur And Chicken Skillet

Servings:3
Cooking Time:40 Minutes
Ingredients:

- 4 (6-oz.) skinless, boneless chicken breasts
- 1 tablespoon olive oil, divided
- 1 cup thinly sliced red onion
- 1 tablespoon thinly sliced garlic
- 1 cup unsalted chicken stock
- 1 tablespoon coarsely chopped fresh dill
- 1/2 teaspoon freshly ground black pepper, divided
- 1/2 cup uncooked bulgur
- 2 teaspoons chopped fresh or 1/2 tsp. dried oregano
- 4 cups chopped fresh kale (about 2 1/2 oz.)
- 1/2 cup thinly sliced bottled roasted red bell peppers
- 2 ounces feta cheese, crumbled (about 1/2 cup)
- 3/4 teaspoon kosher salt, divided

Directions:

1. Place a cast iron skillet on medium high fire and heat for 5 minutes. Add oil and heat for 2 minutes.
2. Season chicken with pepper and salt to taste.
3. Brown chicken for 4 minutes per side and transfer to a plate.
4. In same skillet, sauté garlic and onion for 3 minutes. Stir in oregano and bulgur and toast for 2 minutes.
5. Stir in kale and bell pepper, cook for 2 minutes. Pour in stock and season well with pepper and salt.
6. Return chicken to skillet and turn off fire. Pop in a preheated 400oF oven and bake for 15 minutes.
7. Remove form oven, fluff bulgur and turn over chicken. Let it stand for 5 minutes.
8. Serve and enjoy with a sprinkle of feta cheese.

Nutrition:

- Calories per Serving: 369; Carbs: 21.0g; Protein: 45.0g; Fats: 11.3g

Lemon & Garlic Barbecued Ocean Trout With Green Salad

Servings:3
Cooking Time:10 Minutes
Ingredients:

- 1.5kg piece trout fillet
- 2 tablespoons lemon juice
- 4 garlic cloves, sliced
- 1 long red chilli, sliced
- 2 tablespoons chopped capers
- 1/2 cup fresh parsley
- 1/2 cup olive oil
- Lemon wedges
- Salad greens for serving

Directions:

1. Brush the trout with 2 tablespoons of oil and then place it, skin-side up on a barbecue plate.
2. Cook over the preheated barbecue on high for about 5 minutes and then turn it over. Close the hood and cook on medium heat for another 15 minutes or until cooked through. Transfer to a plate.
3. In a pan, heat the remaining oil and then sauté garlic until lightly browned. Remove from heat and stir in chili, capers and fresh lemon juice; drizzle over the fish and then sprinkle with parsley. Serve garnished with fresh lemon wedges.

Nutrition:

- Calories: 250, Fat: 15.5g, Total Carbs: 11.5g, Sugars: 3.7g, Protein: 19.2g

Bell Peppers On Chicken Breasts

Servings:6
Cooking Time:30 Minutes
Ingredients:

- ¼ tsp freshly ground black pepper
- ½ tsp salt
- 1 large red bell pepper, cut into ¼-inch strips
- 1 large yellow bell pepper, cut into ¼-inch strips
- 1 tbsp olive oil
- 1 tsp chopped fresh oregano
- 2 1/3 cups coarsely chopped tomato
- 2 tbsp finely chopped fresh flat-leaf parsley
- 20 Kalamata olives
- 3 cups onion sliced crosswise
- 6 4-oz skinless, boneless chicken breast halves, cut in half horizontally
- Cooking spray

Directions:

1. On medium high fire, place a large nonstick fry pan and heat oil. Once oil is hot, sauté onions until soft and translucent, around 6 to 8 minutes.
2. Add bell peppers and sauté for another 10 minutes or until tender.

3. Add black pepper, salt and tomato. Cook until tomato juice has evaporated, around 7 minutes.

4. Add olives, oregano and parsley, cook until heated through around 1 to 2 minutes. Transfer to a bowl and keep warm.

5. Wipe pan with paper towel and grease with cooking spray. Return to fire and place chicken breasts. Cook for three minutes per side or until desired doneness is reached. If needed, cook chicken in batches.

6. When cooking the last batch of chicken is done, add back the previous batch of chicken and the onion-bell pepper mixture and cook for a minute or two while tossing chicken to coat well in the onion-bell pepper mixture.

7. Serve and enjoy.

Nutrition:

- Calories per Serving: 261.8; Carbs: 11.0g; Protein: 36.0g; Fat: 8.2g

Turkey And Chickpeas

Servings:3
Cooking Time:10 Minutes

Ingredients:

- 2 tablespoons avocado oil
- 1 big turkey breast, skinless, boneless and roughly cubed
- Salt and black pepper to the taste
- 1 red onion, chopped
- 15 ounces canned chickpeas, drained and rinsed
- 15 ounces canned tomatoes, chopped
- 1 cup kalamata olives, pitted and halved
- 2 tablespoons lime juice
- 1 teaspoon oregano, dried

Directions:

1. Heat up a pan with the oil over medium-high heat, add the meat and the onion, brown for 5 minutes and transfer to a slow cooker.

2. Add the rest of the ingredients, put the lid on and cook on High for 5 hours.

3. Divide between plates and serve right away!

Nutrition:

- calories 352, fat 14.4, fiber 11.8, carbs 25.1, protein 26.4

Peas And Ham Thick Soup

Servings:3

Cooking Time:30 Minutes

Ingredients:

- Pepper and salt to taste
- 1 lb. ham, coarsely chopped
- 24 oz frozen sweet peas
- 4 cup ham stock
- ¼ cup white wine
- 1 carrot, chopped coarsely
- 1 onion, chopped coarsely
- 2 tbsp butter, divided

Directions:

1. On medium fireplace a medium pot and heat oil. Sauté for 6 minutes the onion or until soft and translucent.

2. Add wine and cook for 4 minutes or until nearly evaporated.

3. Add ham stock and bring to a simmer and simmer continuously while covered for 4 minutes.

4. Add peas and cook for 7 minutes or until tender.

5. Meanwhile, in a nonstick fry pan, cook to a browned crisp the ham in 1 tbsp butter, around 6 minutes. Remove from fire and set aside.

6. When peas are soft, transfer to a blender and puree. Return to pot, continue cooking while seasoning with pepper, salt and ½ of crisped ham. Once soup is to your desired taste, turn off fire.

7. Transfer to 4 serving bowls and garnish evenly with crisped ham.

Nutrition:

- Calories per Serving: 403; Carbs: 32.5g; Protein: 37.3g; Fat: 12.5g

Pepper Chicken And Lettuce Wraps

Servings:3
Cooking Time:10 Minutes

Ingredients:

- 450g lean diced chicken
- 1 tablespoon extra-virgin olive oil
- 1 teaspoon black pepper
- 1 teaspoon white pepper
- 1 teaspoon salt
- 1 cup bean sprouts, trimmed
- 16 baby cos lettuce leaves
- 1 large red onion, diced
- 12 fresh lemon wedges
- 16 large fresh mint leaves

Directions:

1. Preheat your pan over medium high heat; in a bowl, mix together oil, white pepper, salt and black pepper until well combined; add in chicken and toss to coat well. Grill for about 5 minutes per side or until cooked through. Let rest for at least 5 minutes.

2. Arrange lettuce leaves on serving plates and top each mint and bean sprouts. Serve topped with sliced beef and garnished with lemon wedges.

Nutrition:

- Calories: 381, Fat: 28.5g, Total Carbs: 30.8g, Sugars: 17.4g, Protein: 6.4g

Sautéed Cauliflower Delight

Servings:3

Cooking Time:30 Minutes

Ingredients:

- 1 head cauliflower, cut into florets
- 1/4 teaspoon red pepper flakes
- 1/4 cup olive oil
- 1 cup cherry tomatoes, halved, or more to taste
- 1 red onion, chopped
- 1 teaspoon natural sweetener as per your taste (raw honey or maple syrup are good options)
- 2 tablespoons raisins
- 1 clove garlic, minced
- 1 teaspoon dried parsley
- 1 tablespoon fresh lemon juice, or to taste (optional)

Directions:

1. Set your oil on medium heat to get hot.

2. Cook and stir onion until tender (5 to 10 minutes).

3. Add raisins, cauliflower, sweetener and cherry tomatoes; cover and cook until tender (about 5 minutes), stirring occasionally.

4. Add in your red pepper flakes, parsley and garlic. Switch to high heat and sauté until cauliflower is browned (about 2 minutes).

5. Drizzle lemon juice over cauliflower.

Nutrition:

- Calories 476, Fat 40, Fiber 9, Carbs 33, Protein 6

Basil And Shrimp Quinoa

Servings:3

Cooking Time:20 Minutes

Ingredients:

- 3 TB. extra-virgin olive oil
- 2 TB. minced garlic
- 1 cup fresh broccoli florets
- 3 stalks asparagus, chopped (1 cup)
- 4 cups chicken or vegetable broth
- 11/2 tsp. salt
- 1 tsp. ground black pepper
- 1 TB. lemon zest
- 2 cups red quinoa
- 1/2 cup fresh basil, chopped

Directions:

1. 1/2 lb. medium raw shrimp (18 to 20), shells and veins removed

2. In a 2-quart pot over low heat, heat extra-virgin olive oil. Add garlic, and cook for 3 minutes.

3. Increase heat to medium, add broccoli and asparagus, and cook for 2 minutes.

4. Add chicken broth, salt, black pepper, and lemon zest, and bring to a boil. Stir in red quinoa, cover, and cook for 15 minutes.

5. Fold in basil and shrimp, cover, and cook for 10 minutes.

6. Remove from heat, fluff with a fork, cover, and set aside for 10 minutes. Serve warm

Nutrition:

- Calories 476, Fat 40, Fiber 9, Carbs 33, Protein 6

Pan-seared Tuna With Crunchy Cabbage Slaw & Toasted

Macadamias

Servings:7

Ingredients:

- 4 x 180g tuna skin-on
- 1 1/2 tablespoons olive oil
- 4 cups thinly sliced cabbage
- 2 teaspoons raw honey
- 1/4 cup fresh lime juice
- 2 spring onions, chopped
- 1 yellow capsicum, thinly sliced
- 200g seedless white grapes, halved
- 1/2 cup fresh mint leaves
- 1/2 cup fresh coriander leaves
- 1/2 cup chopped toasted macadamias
- Lime wedges

Directions:

1. Heat half tablespoon of oil in a skillet over medium heat; place in tuna, skin side down and cook for about 5 minutes or until the skin is crisp; turn over to cook the other side for about 3 minutes or until cooked through.

2. In the meantime, whisk together raw honey, lime juice, lime zest, salt and the remaining oil until well blended; add in grapes, cabbage, spring onions, capsicum, mint and coriander.

3. Stir in salt and pepper. Divide the cabbage slaw among serving plates and to each serving with tuna.

4. Sprinkle with toasted macadamia and garnish with lime wedges. Enjoy!

Nutrition:

- Calories: 381, Fat: 28.5g, Total Carbs: 30.8g, Sugars: 17.4g, Protein: 6.4g

DRINKS RECIPES AND SMOOTHIE RECIPES

Peach And Kiwi Smoothie

Servings:2
Cooking Time:10 Minutes
Ingredients:

- 1 cup plain low fat yogurt
- ½ cup peach chunks
- 1 tablespoon protein powder
- Water as needed
- ½ cup kiwi fruit

Directions:

1. Blend powder and fruits finely in liquid, serve chilled when smooth.

Glory Smoothie

Servings:2
Cooking Time:10 Minutes
Ingredients:

- ¼ cup kale
- A handful of romaine
- A handful of broccoli stems
- A celery stalk
- 1cup juice of green apple
- 2 big cucumber slices
- ½ of a lemon juice and zest both

Directions:

1. This smoothie is preparation ared by combining all ingredients listed above with juice and shake well to form a smooth drink to serve. Use ice or chilled juice to get drink chilled.

Nutrition:

- Calories 69, Fat 6.5 g, Fiber 2.6 g, Carbs 10.6 g, Protein 9.4 g

Oatmeal Blast With Fruit

Servings:2
Cooking Time:10 Minutes
Ingredients:

- ½ cup oats (steel cut)
- A pinch of ground cinnamon
- Ice cubes as needed
- 1 cup water
- ½ cup pineapple chunks

Directions:

1. Throw oats in a blender and slightly blend with water, add the fruit and other ingredients afterwards and blend again

Nutrition:

- Calories 150, Fat 3, Fiber 2, Carbs 6, Protein 8

Lemon And Garlic Smoothie

Servings:2
Cooking Time:10 Minutes
Ingredients:

- 1 lemon juice
- 1 small clove of fresh garlic
- 1 glass water
- Few mint leaves
- 1 teaspoon brown sugar

Directions:

1. Chop, slice or crush garlic clove and add in an electric mixer with water, lemon juice, sugar and mint leaves to blend and serve immediately. It is better to serve warm.

Nutrition:

- Calories 170, Fat 3, Fiber 6, Carbs 8, Protein 5

Blue Breeze Shake

Servings:2
Cooking Time:10 Minutes
Ingredients:

- ½ cup blueberries
- 1 small banana
- 1 cup chilled unsweetened vanilla almond milk
- Water as needed
- 1 scoop unflavored protein powder

Directions:

1. Mix in a blender for 40-50 seconds and serve as ready.

Nutrition:

- Calories 476, Fat 40, Fiber 9, Carbs 33, Protein 6

Smooth Root Green Cleansing Smoothie

Servings:2
Cooking Time:10 Minutes
Ingredients:
- ½ cup fresh lettuce leaves
- ¼ green apple chunks
- A handful of cilantro
- ¼ lime juice
- Couple of cucumber slices
- 1 date without pit
- 1 cup chilled water

Directions:
1. Wash apple and leaves well before use, do not peel apple just remove seeds and inedible parts, mix all the ingredients blend and serve.

Nutrition:
- Calories 140, Fat 4, Fiber 2, Carbs 7, Protein 8

Watermelon Drink

Servings:2
Cooking Time:10 Minutes
Ingredients:
- 2 cups watermelon
- ¼ cup tomatoes
- ¼ cup apples
- ¼ cup pears

Directions:
1. In a blender place all ingredients and blend until smooth
2. Pour smoothie in a glass and serve

Nutrition:
- Calories 140, Fat 4, Fiber 2, Carbs 7, Protein 8

Blueberry Smoothie

Servings:2
Cooking Time:10 Minutes
Ingredients:
- ½ cup blueberries
- 1 cup milk
- 1 tsp honey
- 1 fresh mint
- ice cubes

Directions:

1. In a blender place all ingredients and blend until smooth
2. Pour smoothie in a glass and serve

Nutrition:
- Calories 69, Fat 6.5 g, Fiber 2.6 g, Carbs 10.6 g, Protein 9.4 g

Soothing Smoothie For Stomach

Servings:2
Cooking Time:10 Minutes
Ingredients:
- 1 teaspoon brown sugar
- 1 teaspoon lime juice
- 1 cup lite coconut milk
- ¾ cup papaya

Directions:
1. Pour a cup of the milk in an electric blender and mix in the lime juice, papaya and sugar then mix and serve, add ice if you want to in crushed form only 2-3 cubes.

Nutrition:
- Calories 191, Fat 10, Fiber 3, Carbs 13, Protein 1

Pp Cleansing Smoothie

Servings:2
Cooking Time:10 Minutes
Ingredients:
- 1 cup water
- ½ cup papaya chunks
- ¼ cup organic pineapple chunks
- 1 teaspoon anti parasitic coconut oil
- 1 teaspoon raw pumpkin seeds
- A pinch of garlic paste

Directions:
1. Mix all the ingredients in a blender and blend well till mixed well, add ice if needed and you can also add more water if consistency is thick to drink easily.

Nutrition:
- Calories 476, Fat 40, Fiber 9, Carbs 33, Protein 6

Muskmelon Juice

Servings:2

Cooking Time:10 Minutes

Ingredients:

- 2 cups muskmelon
- 2 cups pineapple
- 1 cup ice

Directions:

1. In a blender place all ingredients and blend until smooth
2. Pour smoothie in a glass and serve

Nutrition:

- Calories 191, Fat 10, Fiber 3, Carbs 13, Protein 1

Heavy Metal Cleansing Smoothie

Servings:2

Cooking Time:10 Minutes

Ingredients:

- 1 cup soy milk
- A pinch of turmeric
- A pinch of freshly crushed ginger
- 1 teaspoon cinnamon powder
- 1 tablespoon maple syrup
- A big date without pit

Directions:

1. Take a blender and combine all ingredients to mix and serve when smooth. Serve at room temperature or slightly warm as you like.

Nutrition:

- Calories 69, Fat 6.5 g, Fiber 2.6 g, Carbs 10.6 g, Protein 9.4 g

Clean Liver Green Juice

Servings:2

Cooking Time:10 Minutes

Ingredients:

- 2½ C. fresh spinach
- 2 large celery stalks
- 2 large green apples, cored and sliced
- 1 medium orange, peeled, seeded and sectioned
- 1 tbsp. fresh lime juice
- 1 tbsp. fresh lemon juice

Directions:

1. In a juicer, add all ingredients and extract the juice according to manufacturer's directions.

2. Transfer into 2 serving glasses and stir in lime and lemon juices.
3. Serve immediately.

Nutrition:

- Calories 476, Fat 40, Fiber 9, Carbs 33, Protein 6

Twin Berry Smoothie

Servings:2

Cooking Time:10 Minutes

Ingredients:

- ½ cup peach chunks
- ¾ cup almond milk
- A handful of cranberries and raspberries
- Peel of an orange
- 1 scoop protein powder (whey)
- Ice cubes as required

Directions:

1. Chop berries well, use natural orange peel, add all foods in a blender and shake to serve.

Nutrition:

- Calories 150, Fat 3, Fiber 2, Carbs 6, Protein 8

Coconut Breezy Shake Dose

Servings:3

Cooking Time:10 Minutes

Ingredients:

- 1 cup skimmed milk (chilled)
- 1 cup pineapple chunks
- 4 tablespoons shredded coconut
- Water as needed
- ½ scoop of vanilla protein powder

Directions:

1. Mix all the ingredients in a mixer and shake well for 20 seconds, serve when smooth texture is seen. Pour in a large glass, use water to make proper smoothness only.

Nutrition:

- Calories 476, Fat 40, Fiber 9, Carbs 33, Protein 6

Smoothie With A Spirit

Servings:2

Cooking Time:10 Minutes

Ingredients:

- ¼ cup greek yogurt
- ½ of a banana
- 1 teaspoon spirulina

- ¼ cup blueberries
- ½ cup chilled almond milk
- ¼ cup peach chunks

Directions:

1. Mix all the ingredients in a mixing blender and serve as soon as it becomes smooth.

Nutrition:

- Calories 69, Fat 6.5 g, Fiber 2.6 g, Carbs 10.6 g, Protein 9.4 g

Papaya Juice

Servings:2
Cooking Time:10 Minutes

Ingredients:

- ½ cup papaya cubes
- ½ cup coconut
- ½ cup coconut water
- 1 cup ice

Directions:

1. In a blender place all ingredients and blend until smooth
2. Pour smoothie in a glass and serve

Nutrition:

- Calories 191, Fat 10, Fiber 3, Carbs 13, Protein 1

Triple C Shake

Servings:2
Cooking Time:10 Minutes

Ingredients:

- ¼ cup raw spinach
- 1 tablespoon cacao nibs
- 1 cup skimmed chocolate nut milk
- ¾ cup black or blue berries
- A dash of red pepper flakes
- A scoop of chocolate whey powder
- Water as needed
- 6 crushed ice cubes
- A handful of nuts
- A pinch of cinnamon powder

Directions:

1. Put all the ingredients in a blender and shake well till smooth. Serve chilled in a large glass and enjoy.

Nutrition:

- Calories 476, Fat 40, Fiber 9, Carbs 33, Protein 6

Detox Action Super Green Smoothie

Servings:2

Cooking Time:10 Minutes

Ingredients:

- 1 cup chilled mango juice
- ¼ cup chopped flat leaf parsley
- ¼ cup chilled tangerine
- 1 Medium ribs celery
- ½ cup orange pulp without seeds

Directions:

1. Blend all the above listed ingredients in an electric blender and serve immediately. Fresh smoothie is the best to consume.

Nutrition:

- Calories 69, Fat 6.5 g, Fiber 2.6 g, Carbs 10.6 g, Protein 9.4 g

White Bean Smoothie To Burn Fats

Servings:2
Cooking Time:10 Minutes

Ingredients:

- 1 cup unsweetened rice milk (chilled)
- ¼ cup peach slices
- ¼ cup white beans cooked
- A pinch of cinnamon powder
- A pinch of nutmeg

Directions:

1. Pour milk in the blender and add other ingredients to blend till smooth enough to serve and drink.

Nutrition:

- Calories 150, Fat 3, Fiber 2, Carbs 6, Protein 8

Beetroot & Parsley Smoothie

Servings:2
Cooking Time:10 Minutes

Ingredients:

- 1 cup carrot
- 1 cup beetroot
- 1 tablespoon parsley
- 1 tablespoon celery
- 1 cup ice

Directions:

1. In a blender place all ingredients and blend until smooth
2. Pour smoothie in a glass and serve

Nutrition:

- Calories 100, Fat 1, Fiber 2, Carbs 2, Protein 6

Bb Citric Blast Smoothie

Servings:2

Cooking Time:10 Minutes

Ingredients:

- ½ cup strawberries without stems and raspberries mixed
- 1 cup chilled fresh orange juice
- 1 teaspoon honey
- A pinch of lemon zest

Directions:

1. Take a mixer and add all the ingredients, fruits and juice in it to mix for few seconds and serve chilled.

Nutrition:

- Calories 170, Fat 3, Fiber 6, Carbs 8, Protein 5

Creamy Milk Smoothie As Meal Replacement

Servings:2

Cooking Time:10 Minutes

Ingredients:

- ½ teaspoon cinnamon powder
- ½ teaspoon ground ginger
- 1 cup almond milk
- ¼ cup plain soy yogurt
- 1 tablespoon whey protein vanilla
- Spearmint to toss in

Directions:

1. Shake this creamy smoothie with a blending machine and pour in a glass to drink.

Nutrition:

- Calories 191, Fat 10, Fiber 3, Carbs 13, Protein 1

Smoothie With Ginger And Cucumber

Servings:2

Cooking Time:10 Minutes

Ingredients:

- 1 cup chilled water
- 2 slices of cucumber
- 1 tablespoon lime juice
- Couple of mint leaves
- 1 small piece of ginger fresh

Directions:

1. Add chilled cup of water in an electric mixer, grate ginger piece. Mix with cucumber slices, lime juice and mint leaves to serve.

Nutrition:

- Calories 170, Fat 3, Fiber 6, Carbs 8, Protein 5

Carrot Drink

Servings:2

Cooking Time:10 Minutes

Ingredients:

- 2 cups carrots
- 1 cup apple
- ½ tsp brown sugar

Directions:

1. In a blender place all ingredients and blend until smooth
2. Pour smoothie in a glass and serve

Nutrition:

- Calories 140, Fat 4, Fiber 2, Carbs 7, Protein 8

Grapes And Peach Smoothie

Servings:2

Cooking Time:10 Minutes

Ingredients:

- 1 cup red grapes juice
- 3 tablespoon shredded coconut
- ½ scoop protein powder
- A handful of chopped pistachios
- 1 small guava and peach chopped
- Ice as required

Directions:

1. Use natural juice to add in the smoothie, mix all the foods in a blender and shake to make it a smooth drink.

Nutrition:

- Calories 150, Fat 3, Fiber 2, Carbs 6, Protein 8

Smoothie For Detoxification

Servings:2

Cooking Time:10 Minutes

Ingredients:

- 1 cup unsweetened chilled coconut water
- 1 teaspoon cinnamon powder
- ¼ cup kale
- A handful of blackberries
- Slices of a small banana

Directions:

1. Chop kale and add in coconut water with berries and cinnamon powder to blend and serve when smooth.

Nutrition:

- Calories 69, Fat 6.5 g, Fiber 2.6 g, Carbs 10.6 g, Protein 9.4

Melon And Nuts Smoothie

Servings:2

Cooking Time:10 Minutes

Ingredients:

- 1 cup water melon chunks
- ¼ cup mixed nuts
- 1 cup soy milk
- ½ cup tofu
- Chilled water as needed
- 1 scoop of chocolate whey protein powder

Directions:

1. Blend all ingredients greatly to attain a smooth and soft drink.

Nutrition:

- Calories 191, Fat 10, Fiber 3, Carbs 13, Protein 1

Light Fiber Smoothie

Servings:2

Cooking Time:10 Minutes

Ingredients:

- 2 teaspoons nutmeg

- 1 ½ scoop vanilla protein powder mix
- 1½ cup soy milk
- ½ cup low fat egg nog
- A pinch of cinnamon
- 4-5 crushed ice cubes
- 1 lemon zest

Directions:

1. Grab the ingredients, measure and add them all in a blender to mix for a drink.

Nutrition:

- Calories 150, Fat 3, Fiber 2, Carbs 6, Protein 8

Grapefruit Smoothie With Cinnamon

Servings:2

Cooking Time:10 Minutes

Ingredients:

- 1 cup grapefruit juice, use pulp for fiber (optional)
- Ice cubes in crushed form as needed (2-3)
- 1 cinnamon stick
- 1 sliced banana
- 1 teaspoon brown sugar

Directions:

1. Mix all ingredients in a blender and mix for 30 seconds to blend well, when done, serve

Nutrition:

- Calories 170, Fat 3, Fiber 6, Carbs 8, Protein 5

CPSIA information can be obtained
at www.ICGtesting.com
Printed in the USA
LVHW061105070323
741095LV00007B/332

9 781803 679525